UBUNTU
RELATIONAL LOVE

UBUNTU
RELATIONAL LOVE

DECOLONIZING BLACK MASCULINITIES

Devi Dee Mucina

UMP

UNIVERSITY OF MANITOBA PRESS

Ubuntu Relational Love: Decolonizing Black Masculinities
© Devi Dee Mucina 2019

23   22   21   20   19   1   2   3   4   5

University of Manitoba Press
Winnipeg, Manitoba, Canada
Treaty 1 Territory
uofmpress.ca

Cataloguing data available from Library and Archives Canada
ISBN 978-0-88755-842-9 (PAPER)
ISBN 978-0-88755-588-6 (PDF)
ISBN 978-0-88755-586-2 (EPUB)

Cover image: Friday Mustapher Ahmed
Cover design by Kirk Warren
Interior design by Karen Armstrong

Printed in Canada

The University of Manitoba Press acknowledges the financial support for
its publication program provided by the Government of Canada through
the Canada Book Fund, the Canada Council for the Arts, the Manitoba
Department of Sport, Culture, and Heritage, the Manitoba Arts Council,
and the Manitoba Book Publishing Tax Credit.

Funded by the Government of Canada | Canada

Contents

GLOSSARY OF UBUNTU TERMS

Abantu Abamhlope	white people
Abantu Abansundu	literally means dark brown, but in a racially conscious political world it means Black people
Amai	mother and also can be used to honour daughters
Ambuya	maternal grandmother
Baba	father and also can be used to honour sons
Baba mukulo	Ngoni older father, uncle, or older male
Dadakazi	female father
Gogo	grandmother
Inkatha	unity and strength of nationhood
Innyathi	buffalo
Komba	our totem of galago
Kwaca	the freedom spirit of dawn, the start of a renewed Black spirit
Ma	the first being and mother of all beings
Maafa	disaster, terrible occurrence or great tragedy; e.g., the African Holocaust from the 500 years of suffering of people of African heritage through slavery, imperialism, colonialism, apartheid, rape, oppression, invasions, and exploitation
Maiguru	older mother and teacher, maternal aunt
Mama mukulo	Ngoni older mother, auntie, or older female
Ngoni	Ubuntu people who migrated from Southern Africa
Sisi	sister
Seano	totem or object of reverence
Ubuntu	to denote human beings
Umkulumqango	the Great Deviser, the Eternal Spirit, or the Creator
Unkulunkulu	the Greatest of All

GLOSSARY OF PUNJABI TERMS

Nanaa	maternal grandfather
Nani	maternal grandmother
Bibi	great-grandmother
Mama	mother's brother
Mami	mother's brother's wife
Masi	mother's sister

GLOSSARY OF PICTOGRAPHS

Sankofa, the Adinkra cultural symbol, which communicates that we can bring those useful things from our historical past and use them as we go forward into the future.

The Zulu High Priest Vusa'mazulu Credo Mutwa in *Indaba, My Children* (1964, 678) communicates that these Ubuntu pictographs serve as text among the larger Nungi collective. This particular text represents the importance of open conversations and dialogues, when our people address governance issues.

This Ubuntu pictograph text (Mutwa 1964, 673) conveys how we Ubuntu centre spiritual guidance in our work.

The sunrise pictograph text (Mutwa 1964, 672) also communicates birth, which is the start of our new future.

Mutwa (1964, 676) informs us that this pictograph text symbolizes the keeping of our ethnic oratures, secrets, and knowledges for future generations.

Mutwa (1964, 671) informs us that this Ubuntu text and pictograph symbolizes the Nguni family.

Mutwa (1964, 671) communicates that this Ubuntu text and pictograph symbolizes the Goddess Mother (Ma) who is the creative source of all things.

Mutwa (1964, 678) informs us that this Ubuntu pictograph and text symbolizes fatherhood.

Mutwa (1964, 383) informs us that this Ubuntu text and pictograph conveys the importance of education to the Ubuntu.

Mutwa (1964, 672) informs us that this Ubuntu pictograph and text symbolizes the stars, which inspire oratures of hope and divine guidance for the Ubuntu.

Mutwa (1964, 678) communicates that this Ubuntu pictograph and text symbolizes hope. In my orature, it has been my aim to inspire hopeful action through the sharing of oratures.

Acknowledgements

First, let me offer an Ubuntu greeting as a form of acknowledgement to our ancestors, our old ones, our mothers, our fathers, our brothers, our sisters, those yet unborn, and all of creation. "Sanibonani" means "We see you," but it also implies that, at a deep spiritual level, I am never alone as my ancestors are always with me. Consequently, I see you with my ancestors. The response to this is "Yebo Sanibonani" meaning "Yes, we see you too." Again, the implication is that you and your ancestors are in agreement about your observation of us. So, to our ancestors, to our old ones, to our parents, to our sisters and brothers, to those yet unborn, and to all of creation, "Sanibonani." To speak this way is to acknowledge our living relations while also honouring our ancestral spirits. We also remind ourselves to exercise caution because we know that the act of speaking can be used to deny, refuse, ignore, and silence our relatedness.

The act of centring Indigenous knowledge is itself a form of social political love and in this process I have been guided, supported, and other-mothered (community parenting beyond biological connection) by Dr. Njoki Nathani Wane. Your willingness to share and explore African systems of knowledge and African feminism has been immeasurably helpful to me. I remember how you introduced me to *The Joys of Motherhood* by Buchi Emecheta and *So Long a Letter* by Mariama Bâ. In so doing, you centred my masculinity within the Black femininity from which it emerged. To me, you are my Amai and I love you for your generous care and teachings. I also want to thank Yvonne Shorter Brown for writing *Dead Woman Pickney: A Memoir of Childhood in Jamaica,* because through her writing and through referencing other Black feminist scholars like bell hooks, an approach emerged for engaging my biological Amai's experience. Dr. Tanya Titchkosky, thank you for helping me engage with the complex multiplicities of human embodiment and interaction using a social disabilities lens. You have also helped me interact with the power of words and social political interpretation. Dr. Ardra Cole, thank you for helping me develop a structure that allowed me to use Ubuntu knowledge in a way that made it accessible to my Indigenous African communities while honouring our African ancestors. I feel privileged to have worked with such wise feminist professors, who thoughtfully challenged me and motivated me through their own research and through their willingness to encourage me to keep taking honest, bold steps when I felt tired and questioned the value of my own work. For your support and hard work, thank you.

I would also like to thank the old one Dr. George Dei, who inspired me to go to the Ontario Institute for Studies in Education (OISE), and the following professors who offered their knowledge to me when I started putting the framework for this work together as a PhD student: Dr. Carl James, Dr. Susan Don, and Dr. Celia Haig-Brown. Jo-Ann Archibald / Q'um Q'um Xiiem, as I edited my book, I found your scholarship on Indigenous orality talking to me, at times affirming me, at times reminding me about overlooked information, and at times giving me new language. Gillian McDonald, thank you for your editorial work.

I would also like to thank the many women and men who other-mothered and other-fathered me, your caring community parenting beyond biological connection has allowed me to do this work. Amai (mother), your loving bravery is beyond my understanding, so I am asking you in the realm of the dead to please be patient as I struggle to understand you and your actions. I thank you for giving me life. Baba (father), our love has been full of struggles, but I would like to start off by thanking you for giving me the hope to begin reuniting our fragmented family. Dadakazi (female father), you are the glue that holds us together. Thank you, great Komba, for helping me in the process of putting our fragmented family together. To Dr. Mandeep Kaur Mucina, I would like to thank you so much for being a dear friend, a great academic colleague, but, more importantly, for being a partner in life and in parenting. You have helped me so much through this academic process; I hope my actions reciprocate an equal measure of my love and support for you. Finally, I would like to thank my dear friends and family with special mention to all of our Komba family members, my in-laws, and the Ferguson family: I am because you are. Nandi and Khumalo, without you this book would not be. These are fragments of our whole oratures; I offer and give them to you as acts of resistance against colonialism, but, more importantly, I give them to you as acts of loving Indigenous resurgence on the territories of other Indigenous peoples.

Acknowledging and Honouring the People of Turtle Island

To enact our African Indigenous Ubuntu resurgence, while living on the territories of other Indigenous peoples, requires an acute relational awareness. By this, I mean that our actions at the very least should cause no harm and, in fact, should contribute to the positive work of the local Indigenous people. As an act of being accountable as an Ubuntu for my relational obligations on the territories of other Indigenous peoples, I respectfully acknowledge the Lekwungen-speaking peoples on whose traditional territory the university that I work stands. I live, work, and play as an uninvited guest on the lands and waters of the Songhees, Esquimalt, and WSÁNEĆ peoples whose historical relationships with the lands and waters continue to this day. Uninvited, I have lived for twenty-two years on many Indigenous territories on Turtle Island (North America) and, throughout this period of time, I can only recall four occasions where I asked for permission to be on other Indigenous peoples' territories. This means, in large part, that I have exercised disrespectful colonial actions and behaviours. I am an Ubuntu[1] who is Indigenous to Southern Africa, but the lure of colonial capitalistic life made me a willing partner of colonial settlement in Canada. This means my colonial benefits come at the expense of Indigenous peoples and nations in Canada. Confronting such colonial realities can give us a *nervous condition* (Dangarembga 1989) or it can offer us *a way of being free* (Okri 1997). With all the complications of intersecting realities and identities that the colonial empires have produced, I am currently in a position that allows me to focus my actions on Indigenous ways of being free. In this process, I am confronted with many contradictions and tensions that challenge my actions, but my relational bonds to our ancestors, the work of our current generations, and the aspirations that I hold for future generations keep me motivated in the pursuit of Indigenous ways of being free.

But we cannot be free if we do not take responsibility for our actions. To all my Indigenous relatives on Turtle Island I extend my deepest felt apology and humbly ask for your forgiveness. Such disrespectful actions and behaviours are not the Indigenous teachings of our Ubuntu traditions. These are all my mistakes and I can assure you that I am working hard to rectify the mistakes that I have made. For example, through the assistance of Professor Shanne McCaffrey, I was part of a ceremony for new Indigenous faculty and students at the University of Victoria who publicly sought permission to work, play, and live on the territories of the Lekwungen, Songhees, Esquimalt, and WSÁNEĆ peoples. It is my hope that I, and others, can keep looking for ways to demonstrate respect and reverence to the Indigenous peoples and their territories. "Sanibonani" my relations.

Yet, generously and caring, Turtle Island and its Indigenous peoples, with whom I continue to develop stronger relations, are every day teaching me how to be a good relative. It is my promise to you, brothers and sisters, that I will do my best to honour your peoples, your lands, your waters, and all the relations in-between. "Sanibonani" my relations.

As I speak from your lands and waters about our Indigenous Blackness, I mean no disrespect, but only wish to add our relational Indigenous Black voices to our common Indigenous reawakening. I extend my arms, voice, and mind to the cause of all the diverse Indigenous people and Nations of Turtle Island. As I speak, could I engage you in dialogue without making presumptions about talking for you? "Sanibonani" my relations.

I hope you see my oratures (embodied and performative ways of engaging people about teaching knowledge as shared through stories) as my effort to engage you, my relations, in a continued dialogue that our ancestors started a long time ago. I hope my oratures communicate my willingness to hear from you (all the diverse Indigenous people and Nations of Turtle Island), and I hope that my responses to your communication efforts convey my willingness to hear your teaching as your visitor. I hope you will continue to teach us how to respect all your relations in your territories. I also hope that my Ubuntu actions will communicate our respect, reverence, and love for you. Let us talk from familial bonds, because I can see that we are linked by so many oratures that make me ask: Where do I end and where do you begin? Could it be the sacred cycle of breath connecting us all as Ubuntu?

UBUNTU
RELATIONAL LOVE

WARNING: There are jarring, violent
scenes described very vividly in sections of
this book that you will confront suddenly
without forewarning.

Introduction

In this book, I use my relational Indigenous Black maleness as a position for critically engaging fathering and other-fathering, mothering and other-mothering, Indigenous masculinities, Indigenous feminism, and Ubuntuness through a letter-writing structure. My Ubuntuness is grounded in the philosophical reality of our lived experience and in that of our ancestors, but, even more importantly, my Ubuntuness derives its power from our African spiritual connection to all relational energies. This spiritually communicated Black personhood (Ubuntu) is shaped by the philosophical realities and spiritualities of being connected to all global relations and energies. Yet, in the current context, the Ubuntu way is threatened by imposed colonial masculinities, which enact power through the intersections of racialized domination, gendered violence, and exploitative governance structures that uphold imperialist white supremacy as sensible governance for Ubuntu people. The leaderships and actions of Indigenous women, queer folks, and other justice-seeking folks locally and globally are inspiring me to enact relationally and responsibly as someone who identifies as masculine. As a man who has been harmed and who has caused harm, I am working at being accountable for my actions while taking steps to centre the critical nurturing and caring Ubuntu masculinities without presenting masculinities as being binaries of femininities, because for us as Ubuntu, masculinities emerge out of femininities.

This point is supported by the Ubuntu creation orature, which teaches that the first Ubuntu being was Ma and she birthed everything into being (Mutwa 1964). This means my engagement with Indigenous Ubuntu knowledge is like planting seeds of relational love in an ever-changing world, which requires critical decolonizing oratures and actions to bring into existence new futures. I believe these Indigenous decolonizing Ubuntu oratures expose and depart from how white supremacy calls us to a compulsory submission of its power structure, which is wielded through colonial patriarchy, exploitative racism, dispossessive capitalism, and always positioning our non-white bodies in the savagery binary logics, which in the histories of colonial white supremacy have justified deadly violence against Indigenous peoples. In this colonial matrix, white supremacy is a call to participate in colonial patriarchy, exploitative racism, and dispossessive capitalism, while never thinking outside the logic of white supremacy. This book advocates and shows how we can centre our diverse Indigenous knowledges, which for us from Southern Africa is Ubuntu. To centre Ubuntu is to be critical of how our realities are political in an interconnected and interdependent world. I believe that by sharing our social oratures we build collective confidence to engage and challenge each other with respectful curiosity and, above all, with love. Love is the expression of relational care for our interconnectedness, which is the basis for researching our truths in our shared humanity. Could love create possibilities beyond fear, pain, isolation, abandonment, and hate?

How to Orient to This Writing Method

Before we can create a new world we must first unearth and destroy the myths and realities, the lies and propaganda which have been used to oppress, enslave, incinerate, gas, torture and starve the human beings of this planet. Facing the lies of history is a basic human responsibility. It is unpleasant to do, but liberating to accomplish. It liberates all of us.

—Ben Okri, *A Way of Being Free*

In *Representation: Cultural Representations and Signifying Practices,* Stuart Hall (1997) conveys that the continual process of knowledge making, philosophizing, and encoding into memory is one of the important acts of living as a human being. This continual process of knowledge making, philosophizing, and encoding into memory that Hall references is what we Ubuntu call orature. The Ubuntu oratures that I share are grounded in lived experience and passed-down memories of our existence as communicated by our spoken words in our Ubuntu languages (Imbo 2002; Okihiro 1996; Ong 2002; p'Bitek 1984). Yet, by taking these Ubuntu oratures and putting them into text using the colonizers' language of English, am I aiding the colonial project, while voicing Indigenous resurgence? But how else will I speak to diverse Indigenous Ubuntu when I cannot write in any of our Indigenous languages because of my learning disabilities, which require me to use assistive technology when the pen fails me? These technologies are only in English and not Ubuntu languages, so how will I speak across so many Ubuntu languages? I hope our ancestors and my relatives will forgive my failing. I hope in the written text using the colonizer's language the Ubuntu spirit will find us all and guide us all home. Mama mukulo (Ngoni older female) would remind me by saying: "The words that we share are from our ancestors. They spoke these words to connect us to our past and I share these words with you to connect the present to the future. In breathing my breath, you meet the past and when you exhale your breath, you give it so that our future may be. Remember we should always know who we are" (Personal communication, 1981 and 1982). This teaching was given to me in Chewa, yet I am struggling to retain it and all the other Indigenous languages that I was born into. Ancestors, can you still hear me, can you help me get my family back home to you and to our ways?

It is important that I am clear that these oratures are an open invitation to a social dialogue because even our individual[1] oratures are being fragmented. The individual Ubuntu memory, which is the basic unit of the collective memory, is still under attack from the colonial imperialist reality that bell hooks (2000) defined as white supremacy in *Feminist Theory: From Margin to Center*. hooks succinctly defines white supremacy as the intersection of racial superiority and domination concepts, within a structure of patriarchy, classism, and capitalism. I therefore find the term *white supremacy* to be a political discursive term in relation to engaging colonial domination and the intersectional impacts that it produces in the context of race, gender, class, and ability. Knowing these facts, I actively privilege Indigenous Ubuntu knowledge as a way of expressing the importance of communal orality in drawing our attention to the power and wisdom of Blackness (Hall 1997). My privileging of Ubuntu knowledge as the guiding framework for Black dialogue can be read as trying to impose a single Black solution on others. If such a question is worrying you, let me address it by turning to Samuel Oluoch Imbo (2002), who, in *Oral Traditions as Philosophy: Okot p'Bitek's Legacy for African Philosophy*, reminds us that the interpretation of Blackness should always be placed in a historical cultural context. In his own words: "At stake is an authentic understanding of the social, religious, and intellectual developments taking place among the various peoples of Africa. A Western mind-set that partitions the world into just two groups—the civilized and the primitive— effectively prevents the 'civilized' from truly experiencing Africa and results in anthropologists setting out to prove a nonexistent preconceived model of society" (3).

Imbo (2002) seems to suggest that dichotomies grow from and support pre-established systems of thought as opposed to seeking understanding. In no way or form does Ubuntuness impose conformity. I have taken this to mean that the reading of the diverse forms of Black embodiment should be done in relation to individual and collective understanding of social place, geographical location, history, and cultural knowledge production so that we do not collapse the diversity of Blackness into an imposed singularity. What Ubuntuness brings to our individual and collective awareness is the knowledge of our relational interconnectedness. This means that my Blackness allows me to connect with other people, while honouring the intersectional diversity that materializes through our social relational interdependence. My own personal experience has taught me that Blackness is a marker of oppression and resistance. So, when I see other Black people during my daily activities, I greet them or give them a downward head nod. I would like to focus on this head nod and expose it as being a complex greeting, which is embedded in a history of survival and resistance. The downward head nod, for me, is a way of saying "Sanibonani," I see your Blackness; it is my way of letting you know that I am in solidarity with you against the oppression of Blackness and I stand with all the ancestors projecting power toward you.

The upward head nod for me is a question that I direct to my sister or brother. It inquires about how she or he is holding up against the perils posed by neo-colonialism. In our contemporary society, the upward head nod has taken on an aggressive challenging quality because our youth are losing the historical memory of Black oppression, which gave rise to global Black codified communication. In order to survive, our ancestors learned to communicate using few gestures. Molefi Kete Asante (1996), in *Afrocentricity: The Theory of Social Change,* calls Black codified communication our "fraternal reactions to assaults on our humanity" (26). This means that I need to teach my son and daughter that when I give another Black person the downward head nod, I am giving that person strength and love. The opposite is also true because when I receive the downward head nod, I take strength and love from that person, as their gesture has been codified to mean, "I see your Blackness and I feel your power." The upward head nod can also be a question about what dangers surround the present environment. For example, in my early child-hood in Zimbabwe, hunger drove us to steal corn from white farmers' fields while trying to avoid the ruthless beating we would get if we were caught by white farmers' guards. This meant, if I saw another child coming from the direction of a cornfield, I would inquire about the dangers in that direction through an upward head nod, as speaking would draw attention to our location. A downward head nod by the other child meant it was safe and a shake of the head meant danger awaited me in the direction I was heading. I am sure other Black people could share their oratures about their experiences of these common themes.

The corn-stealing orature exemplifies how white supremacy and its colonizing settler economic society made us hypervisible in the materiality of crime and poverty and invisible in the power structure of governance. Blackness is indeed a site of conflict. It allows Rinaldo Walcott (1997), through the title of his book, to pose the question to folks like me: *Black Like Who?* To this question, I sometimes contradictorily reply in anger, "Too white to be Black," "Too Western to be Black," "Too Christian to be Black," "Too Muslim to be Black," and, at times I say, "Too African to be Black." Yet most of this conflict is created from an approximation to whiteness about our/my Blackness. So what is whiteness? According to Njoki Wane (2009), Robert McRuer (2006), and bell hooks (2000), whiteness is an ideological value about attaining a compulsory white able-bodied maleness, which is unattainable. No one is at the centre of this compulsory whiteness, and yet everyone is measured by her/his approximation to this compulsory white able-bodied maleness. This being said, this idealized whiteness has its greatest appeal to those who see themselves as having a greater approximation to this whiteness than others have. For example, the Anglo-Saxon male, who perceives himself as being able-bodied and having capital influence, will most vigorously defend whiteness as compared to someone who feels a greater distance to the approximation of whiteness based on race, gender, sexuality, ableism, class, and so on. Enrique Salmón (2012), in *Eating the Landscape: American Indian Stories of Food, Identity, and Resilience,* states that the "communal orature has a way of correcting itself. The corrections are not seeking absolute truth, but communal truth" (21). The point that I draw from Enrique's quote is that there is not a single absolute definition of what constitutes Blackness, but there are some communal truths and experiences that convey a Black philosophical reality that is relationally connected to other beings and other energy forms as expressed through Ubuntuness.

Without losing sight of all our relational learnings, we need to start moving toward Ubuntuness by reclaiming and regenerating our Ubuntu spirituality through our music, our dances, our languages, our ceremonies, and our gendered politics because in these actions we reassert communal Ubuntu love by accepting accountability and responsibility for our Ubuntu governance. Taking these Ubuntu actions is our healing medicine against the structural oppression created by colonialism, which calls us to embody an identity of compulsory whiteness through racist patriarchal domination (hooks 2000). This is the work of imperialist white supremacy, which endeavours to distort Blackness through violence, co-optation, seductive trickery, and attempted Black mental genocide (Fanon [1952] 1967). Even in the midst of such colonial distraction and fragmentation, we can still find each other and learn from each other's oratures. This is the wondrous complexity of our relational oratures: they help us see our communal sameness and our individuation, which in turn gives rise to Ubuntu worldsense.[2] Ubuntu worldsense is our everyday struggle to convey and give meaning through our oratures, as articulated through our educational relational engagement. It is this relational element in our Ubuntu worldsense that allows us to reach across cultural boundaries. The astonishing nature of this phenomenon can be seen in the movement of oratures and music across the globe. This means that, as I tell you about my orature, it may start talking to you about your orature and at this point, my orature becomes your orature. In other words, oratures have their own ways of entering many terrains in the service of making us matter to each other. Ben Okri (1997) captures this point in *A Way of Being Free* when he states:

> Storytelling is always, quietly, subversive. It is a double-headed axe. You think it faces only one way, but it also faces you. You think it cuts only in one direction, but it also cuts you. You think it applies to others only, when it applies mainly to you. When you think it is harmless, that is when it springs its hidden truths, its uncomfortable truths, on you. It startles your complacency. And when you no longer listen, it lies silently in your brain, waiting. Stories are very patient things. They drift about quietly in your soul. They never shout their most dangerous warnings. They sometimes lend amplification to the promptings of conscience, but their effect is more pervasive. They infect your dreams. (43)

In *Methodology of the Oppressed*, Paula Gunn Allen conveys that an orature about you does not need to talk to you directly to fragment and dispossess you: "The only home/is each other/they've occupied all/the rest/colonised it; an/idea about ourselves is all/we own" (as cited in Sandoval 2000, 67). If compulsory able-bodied whiteness has colonized everything else and all we own about ourselves is an idea, we should ask, what is this idea? How complete is this idea? I would argue from my social location that the idea we have of ourselves is fragmented. We, the descendants of the old Ubuntu nations, call our fragmented knowledge Ubuntu, which is shared and lived Black experience that only comes to life when we share it. Without structures for sharing our oratures, our Ubuntu knowledges remain scattered fragments. As I shout and fight about the importance of orature, let me also acknowledge that silence has served as a protective force against the annihilation of our ancestral beings. In the face of colonial genocide, our ancestors' silence was an action of survival, and their survival now gives me voice. Roumen Dimitrow (2010) in *Strategic Silence: Public Relations and Indirect Communication,* states that "communicative silence is a carrier of meaning. Structurally, it makes communication possible. Strategically, it makes indirect communication efficient. Strategic silence is the extreme form of direct communication" (1). Sankofa, Sankofa, Sankofa, I am going back to reclaim my past so I can go forward.

Thoughtfully, the Nigerian African scholar and orator Chimamanda Ngozi Adichie cautions me against relying on one orature to understand a person, a family, a community, a nation, and, for that matter, an entire race of people. In her lecture titled "The Danger of a Single Story" on TEDGlobal (July 2009), she states, "When we reject the single story, when we realize there is never a single story about any place, we regain a kind of paradise." This is why my orature should be read as one voice among many voices, which all have oratures to add to our collective power, remembering that no one orature can speak for all of us. I return to Samuel Oluoch Imbo (2002) in *Oral Traditions as Philosophy* to support my position, where he states: "The real Africa has been distorted by Western scholars beyond recognition. Either because of a failure of memory or because of the wickedness of the storytellers, the stories of the traditional gods and ancient civilizations of Egypt and medieval kingdoms of Africa that began four million years ago in East Africa ceased to be an African story. European narratives rendered these African stories primitive and barbaric" (2).

Such racism has power over us only when we acquiesce to its demand for us to remain silent and pretend we are happy. How can we be happy fragmented by colonialism? How can we be happy dispossessed of our lands through colonial governmental structures and colonial state boundaries? How can we be happy when colonial tactics of divide and conquer have led to us abandoning each other in fear of colonial consequences? We are not happy but we are silent, and we marginalize the Black brave ones that speak out on our behalf. Such fear we must rupture. Let us use our oratures to challenge the external colonizer and the internal colonizer who invade our minds. Let us rupture the colonially created racism, fear, abandonment, and fragmentation. Let our oratures expose the shame of colonialism while illuminating our Ubuntu path of love. Each of us must fight the racist fear that invades our minds and then share the learning so that we regenerate Ubuntu knowledge and create collective new knowledge beyond oppositional challenge to colonialism. Brothers and sisters, do not allow colonialism to undermine your sharing of your social actions of Ubuntu regeneration through and beyond colonialism. To succumb to colonial trickery is to accept colonial social isolation while believing the colonial lie that the white knight will come and rescue you from your misery. This is the greatest colonial trick because no one is coming to save you; we are our own heroes and each other's. You are the Black knight in shining armour, there is no greater living mortal that can save you; the source of power is you, and realizing this is the beginning of your socially informed Ubuntu actions of regeneration beyond colonialism.

By now it should be clear to you that the oratures I share on these pages do not belong to me alone, because my oratures are nested in my family, which is nested in our communities, which are nested in our Maseko Ngoni Inkatha (unity of nationhood), which is nested in Southern Africa among the Nguni[3] and Chewa, which is one micro-orature among larger macro-oratures about Ubuntu families that have been stolen from Africa, fractured and exiled across the globe by colonialism (Asante 1996). This is why each social Black orature is important to the diversity of our collective Black memory and education. I am hopeful that, in our rivalled interpretations about what constitutes Ubuntu, we will see beyond our own imposed limitations by entering the larger Black dialogues of Ubuntu. Charles E. Reagan and David Stewart (1978), in their edited work entitled *The Philosophy of Paul Ricoeur: An Anthology of His Work*, remind me that "to speak is to say something about something" (137). Now that I am saying something about Ubuntu, I am sure you and the rest of our Black communities will also have something to say about Ubuntu. In our collective dialogue, we must use Ubuntu values to guide the kinds of regenerated social interpretations of Ubuntu meaning that we will live by. This being said, I also hope to be critical of the shortcomings and misuses of Ubuntu in addressing some of our contemporary Black realities. If Ubuntu is Black knowledge, then it is our responsibility to ensure that it serves us to live better-informed Black lives in our interconnected global world.

Since time immemorial, the storying of our Ubuntu lives has been philosophized using Ubuntu meaning-making tools and symbols like cave paintings, hieroglyphics, poetry, songs, proverbs, folk tales, fables, the hum of the drum, the cry of the horns, and a host of other social acts (D.D. Mucina 2006). These processes of philosophizing Ubuntu oratures were developed to review and strengthen our approaches of passing on knowledge from older generations to newer generations in an ever-changing world. Our ancestors, knowing that change was the inevitable phenomenon that it is, prepared our Ubuntu philosophizing approaches to address change while drawing on past lessons. In 2008, at the age of thirty-five, I went home for the first time, and I knew I was home because I was communally claimed in our ancestral villages. In meeting my relatives, I also met my communal responsibility to all our relational ancestors through a welcoming ceremony that was performed in our ancestral burial grounds. Yet, just from my contextual location, it is clear that my familial knowledge is limited, so I will not speak for my family; I will not speak for the Maseko Ngoni; I will not speak for the Nguni; I will not speak for the Chewa; I will not speak for the Ubuntu; I will not speak for Africans; and I will not speak for humanity. I will speak for myself as one who is nested and interlocked into all these identities. This point was so aptly captured by Molefi Kete Asante (1996) in *Afrocentricity*, where he tells us: "You must always begin from where you are, that is, if you are Yoruba begin with Yoruba history and mythology; if you are Kikuyu, begin with Kikuyu history and mythology; if you are African-American, begin with African-American history and mythology" (7).

Where I am reflects the relational knowledge given to me by Baba mukulo (Ngoni older father), Mama mukulo (Ngoni older mother), Ambuya (maternal grandmother), Sekuru (maternal grandfather), Baba (father), Amai (mother), Maiguru (my older mother, maternal aunt), the Shona communities, the Chewa and Ngoni communities of Southern Africa, and the Indigenous peoples of Turtle Island. All of these relations have inspired me to reach out to my family, our people, and our lands using our Ubuntu languages, to sing our songs, practise our sacred communal ceremonial rituals, and to communicate with our spiritual ancestors. These Ubuntu ways we have used since time immemorial to transmit our sacred traditions to future generations. To practise these Ubuntu research methods is to reclaim and centre Indigenous Ubuntu knowledge in our decolonizing efforts. These Ubuntu oratures embody what could be termed in Western scholarship as qualitative research approaches, because they share methods found in therapeutic narratives, grounded theory, ethnography, and phenomenology. To this body of qualitative scholarship, I add what I term as Ubuntu sensitivitism in text, which I see as expressions of all our social relations, inclusive of all elements, using our Indigenous worldsenses as expressed by our Ubuntu relational orature. In this Indigenous relational structure, these oratures keep connecting with each other; for example, the end of each orature could be the beginning of another orature, and so on. Yet all these oratures are relationally related and such Indigenous interconnectedness requires our text to embody a new kind of relational sensitivitism that centres Ubuntuness even as we impose a beginning and an ending to oratures that are meant to be cyclical. Accepting my failure to make a cyclical Ubuntu book, I have divided these educational Indigenous Ubuntu knowledges into nine oral Millet Granaries,[4] while hoping that you see and read each Millet Granary in a cyclical manner. Millet Granaries reflect Indigenous technological ingenuities in response to the cyclical teaching nature of seasons. The filling and emptying of Ubuntu granaries are done with an awareness that ensures food security and sovereignty for future generations. Millet Granaries also act as measurements of cyclical time. For example, the birthday of a child can be determined by how many Millet Granaries ago they were born.

Each Millet Granary starts with some methodological questions, which may be of interest to you as a reader, as they are designed to contemplate geo-politics, social justice, impact of colonialism on individuals and communities, individual resistance, collective resistance, and how Ubuntu philosophy is shaping change in and across African and global contexts. Each Millet Granary also concludes with some reflective questions about what you have learned from the Ubuntu oratures that I have shared with you. These methodological questions and reflections are not meant to be a structure imposed on you but rather an act of exposing my motivation for sharing these oratures with you, while concluding with an invitation to hear about what stood out for you as being educational.

Millet Granary 1 introduces my children, Nandi and Khumalo, to the structure of the Ubuntu orature as a teaching tool. The second Millet Granary communicates to Khumalo and Nandi how Ubuntu philosophy and theory are tools for engaging our changing political world. Millet Granary 3 situates my children, Nandi and Khumalo, in the global human community. In this section, it is my aim to pass on intergenerational Ubuntu knowledge to my children. In the fourth Millet Granary, I teach Khumalo and Nandi about how Ubuntu oratures are guided and set within a relationally accountable governance structure of Ubuntu.

Millet Granary 5 holds a letter that I write to my Amai (mother). In this letter, I engage Amai through my fragmented memories, which I use to give an analysis of our experience. As I am aware that I cannot adequately speak for Amai, regardless of all the African feminism that I engage, I leave some room at the end of this letter in honour and respect of her analysis. Millet Granary 6 holds a letter that I write to my Baba (father). In this letter, I present to Baba my experience and perceptions of living with him under colonial governance in Zimbabwe. I confront the struggles we faced together and the struggles we faced against each other as a way to give context to how we separated and how I ended up in the orphanage as a ward of the state. I also share my experience of being in the orphanage, followed by my experience beyond the orphanage. The seventh Millet Granary is another letter to Baba about my journey to him with my new family. It is also about Baba taking us home, which becomes the biggest rallying point for healing actions against colonial fragmentation. In respect of Baba, I leave room for him to speak beyond the grave.

The eighth Millet Granary is another letter to Nandi and Khumalo about how their mother and I came to know each other and how we came to create our interracial family against many challenges from the wider Canadian society and from within their mother's family. Millet Granary 9 holds the teaching of social actions of Ubuntu regeneration beyond colonialism, and Millet Granary 10 concludes this work by highlighting some key points from my learning position.

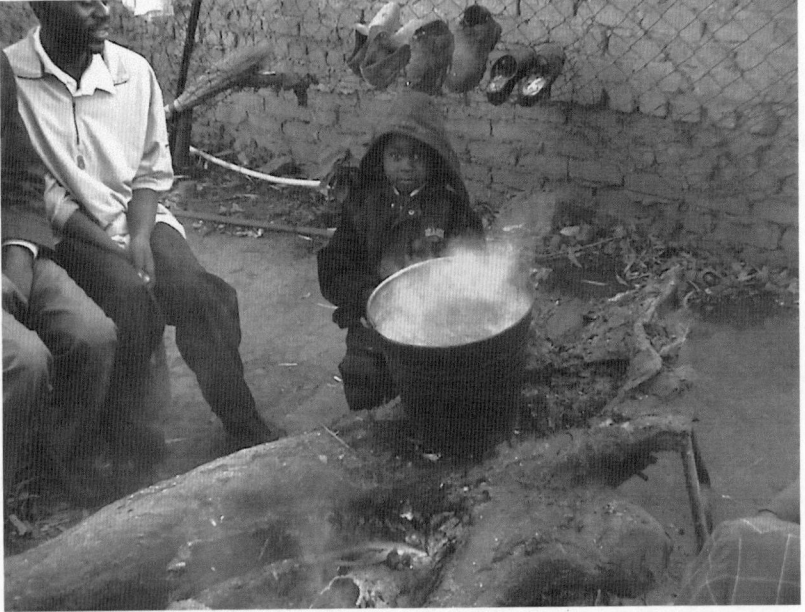

Figure 1. Most of the teaching oratures that I have were given to me around this fireplace. While warming myself by the fire, I heard about olden times, colonial times, and now I must create a new fireplace in a new place like my Baba did before me. From this new fireplace, I will teach my children to draw from the past on their way forward.

Kwakukhona as a Methodology

As stated earlier, each Millet Granary starts with some methodological questions, which I use to guide my writing because these questions help me contemplate the geopolitics of my orature from an Indigenous Ubuntu philosophy, which is shaped by change across Africa and across the global context. This said, I would like to foreground these methodological questions by stating that they guided me in creating a coherent written structure, but they should not be seen as guiding impositions on the readers. In fact, some readers with limited understanding of Ubuntu may find these questions to be irrelevant. Each Millet Granary also concludes with some philosophical questions as a way of reflecting what stood out for me as educational, but this may not be true for you as the reader. It is my hope that you will get what you require based on your own context.

Methodological questions that guided my writing of this Millet Granary:

1. *How does the Ubuntu orature work structurally as a knowledge disseminator?*
2. *What are the responsibilities of the orator in Ubuntu education?*
3. *How does the Ubuntu orature regenerate Indigenous knowledges?*

Sanibonani Khumalo and Nandi,[1]

There is so much to share with you, but before I go on, I must give you the context of why I am sharing and how this sharing will help you understand your Ubuntu heritage. Colonialism has and continues every day to silence us from sharing our Ubuntu truths by over-conflating the limitations and problems of

Ubuntu governance. This is not to say that I wish to shield Ubuntu governance from honest criticism. On the contrary, I welcome honest critical engagement as a tool of betterment and not as a tool of silencing and shaming in order to dispose us of our Ubuntu governance. Let me be the first to inform you that the current brand of Indigenous Ubuntu governance has oppressive and marginalizing practices. However, as these Ubuntu institutions are a reflection of us, we have a duty to make sure that they also reflect our reality and, where they fail to do so, we should come together and create a solution. This is how you create responsible democratic participation. No other people can give another people democracy and freedom. These things are achieved through a process of self-driven action and self-reflection about our future aspirations. Let us not allow colonialism and neo-colonialism to fragment us any further. To live an informed Ubuntu life is to create a consciousness struggle, as Ben Okri (1997) states, "Our lives have become narrow enough. Our dreams strain to widen them, to bring to our waking consciousness the awareness of greater discoveries that lie just beyond the limits of our sights" (4). The narrowing of Blackness inevitably narrows what humanity is and this is the opposite of my aim. Yet modern-day trends of academic discourse have labelled the work of individual historical remembering as navel-gazing and, in so doing, the experience of the individual, especially the colonized individual, has been rendered unreliable (Okri 1997). In other words, the individual memory is not worth listening to because there is too much mystery in it. So whom do we listen to?

The politics of state society have determined who we need to listen to. Again, I will take us back to Ben Okri (1997), who conveys to us who has been sanctioned to speak when he states: "The acknowledged legislators of the world take the world as given. They dislike mysteries, for mysteries cannot be coded, or legislated, and wonder cannot be made into law. And so these legislators police the accepted frontiers of things. Politicians, heads of state, kings, religious leaders, soldiers, the rich, the powerful [the scholars in high academics]—they all fancy themselves the masters of this earthly kingdom. They speak to us of facts, policies, statistics, programmes, abstract and severe moralities. But the dreams of the people are beyond them, and would trouble them" (4).

I do not legislate to anyone how to live. I only share my experiences and my remembered fragmented knowledge in hopes of educating our children to love their Blackness, because it is a source of great power. The oratures that I will share using the Ubuntu philosophy show that the power of our Black knowledge has been the cause of our being silenced, being dislocated, being disconnected, and being erased from our own history. In an effort to dispossess us of our Black knowledge, compulsory able-bodied whiteness with its structures of sexism, classism, and racism has endeavoured to make our own Black minds turn against themselves by creating doubt about the existence of Blackness as a powerful force of life (hooks 2000; Okri 1997).

I want you for a minute to consider the implication of Jared Diamond's (1997) Pulitzer Prize–winning book *Guns, Germs, and Steel: The Fate of Human Societies*. In his prologue, Diamond writes: "Authors are regularly asked by journalists to summarize a long book in one sentence. For this book, here is such a sentence: 'History followed different courses for different peoples because of differences among peoples' environments, not because of biological differences among peoples themselves'" (25). Yet he abandons this position when he cannot ignore the continual Black knowledge that contradicts his theory presented in *Guns, Germs, and Steel*. So what does he do? He becomes the racist that he claims he is not. He starts to play the biology game. The same biology game that, he states in his prologue, is not a viable explanation for the difference among people. In the case of Black Africa, he makes it his foundational position for explaining Blackness. Chapter 19 of Diamond's book is entitled "How Africa Became Black" (376). In this chapter, as communicated by his title, we encounter his racist scholarship, which he tries to use to discredit Black knowledge, while at the same time he appropriates it as anything but Black knowledge.

To survive such a constant attack on Blackness, Malidoma Patrice Somâe (1994), in *Of Water and the Spirit*, reminds us that due to slavery, colonialism, neo-colonialism, and the marking of our bodies as inferior beings, some of us have had to forget the power of our Blackness as a way to survive while, on the other hand, some of us have had to remember our Blackness and our spiritual past as a way to survive. To those Black people who have remembered our African ways, I hope the oratures that I share will encourage you to keep educating us, the segments of our Black communities that have forgotten our Blackness as a means of survival. To those Black people who have had to forget, suppress, and hide their Blackness in order to survive, I hope my primer (an Ubuntu cultural introduction that informs the knowing Ubuntu that cultural teachings are about to be shared) of "Many Millet Granaries ago" conveys to you that we are still here, we are still strong, and we still remember who we are, even if it is only in fragments. If we share our fragmented oratures, we get a fuller and richer picture of our Black knowledges, which helps us understand who we are. The Ubuntu have always used the orature to extol the power of experience as a teaching tool. I can use no other research tool, as this landmass called Africa is the first orature, and Ben Okri (1997) assures us that "Africa breathes stories. In Africa everything is a story, everything is a repository of stories. Spiders, the wind, a leaf, a tree, the moon, silence, a glance, a mysterious old man, an owl at midnight, a sign, a white stone on a branch, a single yellow bird of omen, an inexplicable death, an unprompted laughter, an egg by the river, are all impregnated with stories. In Africa things are stories, they store stories, and they yield stories at the right moment of dreaming, when we are open to the secret side of objects and moods" (115).

Here I quote Ben Okri's narration of oratures in an effort to explicate that oratures enable the encoding of my embodied forms of knowing and learning, as expressed by Stuart Hall (1997). To me, an Ubuntu, orature is a functional and viable (re-)search approach that one ignores at one's own peril. History reminds us that the orature is done with the purpose of maintaining cultural continuity while, at other times, the orature allows for cultural directional change. The orature honours our memory (sacred history) while at the same time validating our Ubuntu spirit of change because the only constant in our lives is change. Put simply, our oratures are our efforts to create shared interpretation structures about experience so that change has shared meaning.

Nandi and Khumalo, it is my hope that by illustrating to you the teaching power of the Ubuntu orature, you will each have a starting point for educating your children as I am educating you. So, listen well, if an old one were to utter the following introductory words—in Shona "Paivapo," in Ndebele "Kwakukhona," or in Zulu "Kwesukasukela"—the meaning is always the same: "There was this happening" or "Many, many Millet Granaries ago." Upon hearing these words draw yourselves nearer to the person that has uttered them, because these phrases let you know that the orator is offering you an Ubuntu cultural teaching from olden times. In response to the oratorical prompting of "Paivapo," in Shona the audience responds by saying "Dzepfunde," which is to say, "I am ready to learn from your pedagogical orature," or "I am ready to receive your teaching." Each time the old one introduces a new setting in the orature, a different character, or conveys the objectives of the characters in the orature, she draws in the audience by saying "Paivapo." Another point communicated by "Dzepfunde," as prompted by "Paivapo," is that, through their response, they, the audience, are actively acknowledging their consent to participate in the Ubuntu orature. Their response of "Dzepfunde" also acknowledges their familiarity with Ubuntu orature as a relational pedagogy in their social acquisition of holistic Ubuntu knowledge, which is grounded in supporting the well-being of all Ubuntu. This prompting goes on until the old one is convinced that she and her audience are synchronized in their orientation toward the teaching methods of that particular orature. Mthikazi Roselina Masubelele (2008), in her dissertation titled "The Role of Bible Translation in the Development of Written Zulu: A Corpus-Based Study," conveys how the Ubuntu Shona structure of call and response is also exemplified among the amaZulu by quoting Noverino N. Canonici's *Zulu Oral Traditions* (1996, 55):

> Zulu storytelling follows a specific pattern. It has an opening formula which the storyteller usually uses which begins thus: Kwesukasukela! (Once upon a time, it happened) to which the audience's response is Cosi (small quantity). During the storytelling the audience will be active participants, joining in song and using various facial expressions and gestures that correspond with what is happening in the story. At the end of the story the storyteller will wind up her tale using a concluding formula, which will vary from one storyteller to the other, the most popular being Cosi cosi iyaphela (This is the end of our story), and the audience will respond by saying Siyabonga! Yaze yamnandi indaba yakho (We thank you! What a nice tale it was!). (Masubelele 2008, 59–60)

Embedded within this reciprocal relational structure of communication is the balance between giving and taking. This point is well researched and communicated by the respected Indigenous scholar of the Sto:lo and Xaxli'p First Nations, Jo-Ann Archibald / Q'um Q'um Xiiem (2008), in *Indigenous Storywork: Educating the Heart, Mind, Body and Spirit*. Archibald reminds us that Indigenous oratures engage through interactive performance, meaning that both the orator and listener are actively engaged by the fact that they have very specific functions to perform in the making of the orature. The performance of the orature makes it whole in the Ubuntu structure. The repetitive qualities of an orature help facilitate the listeners in holding what they deem to be important lessons within an orature. Achiller Isaiah, may he find his way to the ancestors, was fond of saying, "The markers of an Indigenous African orature are many, but the lessons are few."

Since the dawn of human societies, and as Nobel Laureate Toni Morrison has poignantly stated, there are no other universal words that pay such noble homage to human memory than "Once upon a time…." In Morrison's own words, "This opening phrase of what must be the oldest sentence in the world, and the earliest one we remember from childhood, is the foundation stone of things memory—one of the principal ways in which we absorb knowledge" (as cited in Goss and Goss 1995, 15). Unquestionably, for Toni Morrison and most chroniclers of societal unfolding events, the orature is an important faculty of engaging critical regeneration and honest self-criticism while offering a collective vision for a community's manifest destiny. By engaging with Ubuntu orature, I hope to make our African oratures talk to other people in complex, challenging, and sometimes contradictory ways. I want us to be comfortable and uncomfortable with each other's oratures because this keeps us questioning how we matter to each other from a position of respectful curiosity. As we come to understand and know each other through relational respectful curiosity, it is my hope that we will seek to be transformed intellectually and spiritually, so that we see each other and matter to each other. Baba always reminded me that it was our ability to inquire about the aspects of an orature that moved us from comfort to discomfort, which made the orature a good teaching tool. Yet as the queer feminist scholar Roewan Crowe (2004) states in her essay "Crafting Tales of Trauma": "My inquiry is a deliberation on telling and an actual telling. Throughout the text, I am a reluctant storyteller in process, carefully considering the questions: Why tell? How to tell? What is it like to tell?" (124).

The tensions expressed by Crowe (2004) are also my tensions. I have found myself questioning why I was telling our stories, especially when speaking from my own location, as it only seemed to highlight my own contextual experience. Self-doubt and questioning were at times great. At such times of questioning, I was tempted to change my work but, somehow, the following Maseko Ngoni proverb made me believe that I was on firm ground for speaking to our people. The Maseko Ngoni proverb states: "The orature of one cannot be told without unfolding the oarture of many," and, to further diversify our many Ubuntu voices, I am also using written sources as a guide for establishing and introducing a wider understanding of Ubuntu. Yet most of the oratures that I have of Ubuntu teaching were given to me using oratures. I am aware that I share these oratures using colonially imposed structures of textual objectivism, which our Indigenous oratures do not fit. In the arts, these colonial approaches of textual objectivism are offset to some extent by textual subjectivism, but these methodologies do not centre Indigenous Ubuntu consciousness as represented by our oratures. To centre Indigenous Ubuntu consciousness, we must embody a new methodology in our using of English textual engagement. I call this new Ubuntu method of engaging Indigenous oratures in textual form "Indigenous relational sensitivitism," which I hope creates an emotive textual encounter and response to Ubuntu teaching. I also want to point out that the use of the term "Indigenous relational sensitivitism" is new only when it refers to its usage in English textual engagement because, within Ubuntu orature, relational sensitivitism has been passed down through many generations. It is a way for us to talk about how our past is in our present through our blood memory, through our relational bodies, through our relational ceremonies and rituals, through our relational connections with all elements, and through our connections to the spiritual world, which connects the present to the future.

Using Indigenous relational sensitivitism to engage relational Ubuntu oratures is the change that keeps me somewhat hopeful about moving away from the active live performative function of orature to a static textual form of writing. I am hopeful that we shall do unforetold things to textual static forms as we attempt to make them dance. In our globally connected world, the written qualitative approaches have gained more currency over the live performative approaches of orature, even in most of Africa. The advantage of these written forms is that they can be transported across the globe and can be read by a wider audience. So, through my usage of written orature, I have lost the live performative engagement of orature, but on the positive side I can talk to broader, diverse human communities. This is the reality of writing. It can never take the place of a live performative oral engagement. The dynamic relational engagement of lived oral engagement is so powerful that it can never be surpassed by any other form of social communication. This being said, the isolating qualities of capitalistic accumulation, which have flung us across the globe, still keep us disconnected. Michael White (2007), in *Maps of Narrative Practice*, informs us that writing and social media have become functional ways for us to remain socially connected. In this writing, I am working through the tensions of speaking to you, my children, and the global Black Indigenous communities, while working, playing, and living on the territories of the Lekwungen, Songhees, Esquimalt, and WSÁNEĆ peoples. It is my hope that I am not unwittingly adding to the colonial project of white supremacy through exercising colonial patriarchy, exploitative racism, and dispossessive capitalism by never thinking outside the logics of white supremacy (hooks 2000). This book advocates and shows how we can centre our diverse Indigenous knowledges to disrupt colonial toxic masculinities through relational social love and respectful caring curiosity.

As a way of orienting my Ubuntu methods, I need to point out that in traditional Ubuntu orality the orator does not give an analysis of the orature that he/she is telling. The orator leaves the analyzing of the orature to each individual listener because the orator knows that each individual will gain something different from the orature. Each listener will bring his/her experience to the analyzing of the orature, which will reflect his/her own contextual position based on age, gender, values, sexuality, political knowledge, and social position. Let me illuminate the structure of Ubuntu orature through the blending of a dream that I had and the adding of creative fictional components to create a better story flow of the disjointed dream.

To you, Khumalo and Nandi, I say, "*Paivapo.*"

And you respond to this prompting by saying, "*Dzepfunde.*"

Now let me start the orature in the following manner. On one of my many travels, I found myself in a village far away from home. Being a stranger in this village, I began to find my way toward the Chief's home so that I could introduce myself and seek refuge. Seeing a group of young girls coming from the river with balanced clay pots of water on their heads, I felt confident that they would know how to direct me to the whereabouts of the Chief's home. Respectfully, I enquired from the girls the whereabouts of the Chief's home and, to my surprise, they immediately stopped conversing among themselves. I could sense that they were afraid of talking to me. Fearing that I was transgressing some unknown cultural interaction established between the different age ranges and possibly genders, I started to look for a male who appeared to be in my age range. As I was doing this, I heard from the direction of the sunrise a voice that said, "Come this way, son." As I walked toward the voice, I could clearly see an old hut. At the entrance of the hut, the door was open and I hesitated to enter. Sensing my fear, an old woman emerged from within and, while standing aside from her hut entrance, invited me in. She offered me water to wash off my dust and then a large bowl of cool fresh water to drink. Before I could fully adjust to the light in the hut, steaming hot food was placed before me.

"Above you, Mother," I said, as a way of honouring our ancestors and this older mother for feeding me. She responded by saying, "What is there to thank." From the same pots that my food had come from, the older mother served herself a small amount of food to demonstrate that she meant me no ill intent.

I ate until I could eat no more and, to wash my food down, the older mother offered me what she called her best beer. Indeed, it was good; it was the best beer I had ever tasted. As I enjoyed the beer, the older one and I talked about my travels. At some point, our conversation ended and the older one offered to show me around the village, but, before we set off, she told me that if anyone asked who I was, we were to say I was her grandson from her first daughter who lived in Southern Africa. Seeing as this was the direction I had come from, I saw no great harm with the older one's orature.

With the older mother narrating the orature of where I came from to the village, most people were welcoming and friendly toward me. Yet, wherever we went in the village, I heard people singing this same song:

Someone would start the song thus: *"My kinfolk I die."*

Other people near the song starter would respond thus: *"If I am going, let me go."*

And the song starter would conclude thus: *"My kinfolk come and see how I die."*

And, to this singing invitation, the other people near the song starter would conclude: *"If I am going, let me go."*

Let me interrupt the orature here. As an orator this is a good time in the orature to engage you both, Nandi and Khumalo, in performative participation. Hence, I will sing the same song that I have just narrated to you both using the African musical call and response to create an invitation for you both to participate. To do this I sing in a strong voice: *"My kinfolk I die,"* and to this invitation you both are invited to respond by singing: *"If I am going, let me go."* I then conclude my call part of the song by singing: *"My kinfolk come and see how I die,"* and you both conclude your answering part by singing: *"If I am going, let me go."* To ensure we are synchronized in this call-and-answer song, we may repeat the full song about four or five times.[2] When we are done this exchange, I may ask where in the orature we stopped. At this point, it is now your responsibilities as my audience to take an active role in orientating me toward the orature so that I can continue from where I left off. Can you now see the performative participation that makes this orature a dynamic collective heritage, which demands that we continue to create new contextual meanings?

Let us assume that you, as the audience, have orientated me so that I can resume this orature. After hearing this same song so many times, I asked the older mother what the people were trying to communicate. To this inquiry, the older mother responded by saying: "In this matter we dare not speak out; however, because you are leaving early tomorrow morning I will give you this mango to eat, just before you lay your head down to dream, and in your dream this mango will tell you everything. This mango will tell you everything because it was there when it all started." Of this matter we speak no more until I am about to go to sleep. The older mother reminds me to only eat the mango when I am about to fall asleep.

Just when I cannot keep my eyes open because sleep invites me to enter the dream world, I eat the mango. My waking world and my dream world seem as one. I am aware that I am in a minibus and a soldier is asking each passenger to whisper in his ear which political party he/she supports. We are all aware that those who are giving the wrong answer are being killed; women are being raped, and even young children are being mutilated outside the minibus. The bodies of the dead are piling up high outside the minibus. Fearfully, I ask no one in particular why this is happening to Ubuntu by the hands of Ubuntu, and a woman with a child on her lap whispers: "Please, shhh brother, or he will think we are trying to fool him and then for sure he will kill us all without giving us a chance to guess the right party. So please, shhh."

I look to the other side of the minibus and I see the older mother outside the minibus. She is lying in her own blood. She stands up and I recognize that this is the mango tree in front of the older mother's hut. Slowly and painfully, her lifeblood is oozing out through her ears and mouth. I want to tell her to hang in and wait for me because I know where she is, but I am afraid to speak. She looks at me with understanding for my situation and then I hear her voice in my ear. Like a whisper, she says: "Ask the mango, boy child. It will tell you everything."

I wake up and look around for the older mother but I can find no sign of her. I go outside and see the mango tree; it is full of green mangos, except for one small, beautifully ripe, yellow mango. The contrast of its yellowness and its touch of red blush makes it irresistible to me. Standing on tiptoes, I pick the mango from its hanging branch. I am aware of the spiritual presents of the older mother and I wonder about what to do with the gift that she has given me? Why has she given it to me? As I take this violent story as a gift, which has transformed me, I still question why she gave it to me. What can I do about such Ubuntu violence in all of our communities? What can I give back in return? The burden of Ubuntu relational reciprocity, to this day, still makes me wonder if I have given meaningfully for what I have so generously received. Now that I have shared this orature with you, I wonder how this orature has transformed you? I stop my orature here, but I hope you keep growing while my orature remains stunted.[3]

I now invite you, Khumalo and Nandi, to give your analysis and interpretation of this orature. Starting in early childhood, Ubuntu children learn the art of analyzing an orature by observing how older siblings or relatives demonstrate diverse analyses of a given orature. As the young children hear the diverse and sometimes contradictory analyses of the same orature, they learn that responsible self-expression is welcome among the Ubuntu. In most situations, when everyone has shared their opinion and analysis of the orature, the orator will even go as far as asking the analysis of a young infant. Younger siblings will demonstrate and exercise empathy by speaking on behalf of infants, but even infants soon figure out that democratic participation among the Indigenous Ubuntu is an encouraged virtue and will try to express their opinions even before they have mastered the language. The excitement everyone shows about the infant trying to acquire language encourages the infant to try and express its opinions. The point being, the skill of analyzing an orature or teaching begins at a very young age, and the benefits of doing this is that children learn analytical skills and oral skills at a very young age.

So, Nandi and Khumalo, what have you learned from this orature?

What makes this orature Ubuntu?

How does this Ubuntu orature represent decolonizing actions?

What would you add or remove from this Ubuntu orature?

At this point, I want to offer some critical reflections about Ubuntu oratures as an example of my thinking after writing this section. Again, by no means am I trying to impose a meaning-making structure on you. I am just sharing the remembering that has emerged for me after learning from other Ubuntu oratures. I do not intend to repeat this process after each Millet Granary and I only do it here in an effort to encourage you to connect your learning to your remembered fragments of knowledge because, like me, you were born into Ubuntu oratures; like me, you are gaining from Ubuntu oratures, and like me, you shall add to Ubuntu oratures. I am sharing this orature with you and I am giving you this orature, which was given to me, because I will leave the orature, but this orature will go on with you. This is the reciprocal nature of Indigenous Ubuntu oratures (Archibald/Q'um Q'um Xiiem 2008). This is our orature: we co-author it. It is an orature with no beginning and it is an orature with no end. It is just, simply, our orature. This is why, when I speak about my orature, I am speaking about the period in which I am active in our orature. In honour of Ubuntu oratures, I will share my oratures from the traditional orator position and will assume the position of orator, if I may be so bold. As the orator, I assume the role of educator, which, I have been told by our old ones, is not dependent on age as it is determined by the knowledge and wisdom that one has to share. As I still have a lot to learn from the oratures that I share, I will analyze them with the aim to educate myself while sharing this process.

How I analyze these oratures as a learner and listener is not meant to reflect a specific way in which to analyze the oratures. I only offer my analysis as a way of reflecting my learning in this specific context at this specific time in my life. An even more important analysis will be the one that you make as the reader, because it will reflect your learning in your specific context. In this work, I acknowledge that I am both researcher and subject, which makes this work very hard. As committed as I am to truth, in some instances, its emotional impact may limit me, in that there are some things I will not talk about because it hurts too much to remember and I would rather forget. There are also some things I cannot talk about because processes of colonialism have taken them away from me and I cannot remember them. But I will share what little remembering I have and that stands out in my mind as educational.

By writing about our Indigenous orature, could I be creating a discourse that challenges other Ubuntus to remember their Indigenous knowledge? Could this research have implications for the African diaspora in Canada and elsewhere globally? For me, the answer to these questions is an unequivocal yes, as I believe Ubuntuness is an expression of loving humanity, but let me not create an illusionary binary between orature and writing because our ancestors utilized these two forms interchangeably. This point is articulated well in Alain Ricard's essay (2007), "Africa and Writing," published in Tejumola Olaniyan and Ato Quayson's *African Literature: An Anthology of Criticism and Theory*. Ricard has this to say about the history of writing in Africa: "Africa is everywhere inscribed. From rocks to masks, sculptures, pyramids, and manuscripts one needs but a stubborn and narrow-minded commitment to alphabetic writing to deny that the continent has left graphic marks of its history everywhere. Graphic representation is indeed present. . . . Africa is the continent with the largest number of recorded rock art paintings: from the Drakensberg and the Matopos in Southern Africa to the Air in the Sahara, the continent seems to have been populated by crowds of painters eager to record, to pray, or to celebrate" (7).

Ricard's (2007) work reminds me that Africa has been writing for a long time. This means that, when scholars say that they cannot find evidence of writing in certain parts of Africa, they are only telling us that they cannot find evidence of their own cultural understanding of writing. Africa has many diverse forms of writing that it has been practising since time immemorial. We have to be careful that we do not narrow what writing is because we want to impose our form of writing as the absolute standard of symbolic expression. To impose a single form of writing is to lose some forms of knowledge, which could be important for the advancement of humanity as a whole.

However, in Western global academic institutions, Indigenous Ubuntu ways do not enjoy the recognition of being useful scholarship. Our Ubuntu languages are not taught and, when they are taught, it is never on a full-time basis because they are always vulnerable to economic pressures. Our Black languages, our Black histories, our Black politics are forever being considered because they are on the margins and are always being defined as non-essential work. Therefore, in the little spaces allotted to Indigenous scholarship, we battle each other to talk about how the Ubuntu cave paintings are sacred knowledges or how, in the Ubuntu worldview, the intelligence of nature is recognized because we believe that nature holds bodies of knowledges. Yet, in trying to talk in the little spaces allotted to us, another problem arises for the African writer. Chinua Achebe (1988), in *Hopes and Impediments: Selected Essays*, addresses this problem in the following manner:

> One of the most critical consequences of the transition from oral traditions to written forms of literature is the emergence of individual authorship. The story told by the fireside does not belong to the storyteller once he has let it out of his mouth. But the story composed by his spiritual descendant, the writer in his study, 'belongs' to its composer. This shift is facilitated by the simple fact that, whereas a story that is told has no physical form or solidity, a book has; it is a commodity and can be handled and moved about. But I want to suggest that the physical form of a book cannot by itself adequately account for the emergent notion of proprietorship. At best it facilitates the will to ownership which is already present. This will is rooted in the praxis of individualism in its social and economic dimensions. Part of my artistic and intellectual inheritance is derived from a cultural tradition in which it was possible for artists to create objects of art which were solid enough and yet make no attempt to claim, and sometimes even go to great lengths to deny, personal ownership of what they have created. (32)

Let me remind you again, the story was here before me; I was born into the story, I have gained from the story, I have added to the story, I am sharing this story with you, and I am giving you this story, which was given to me, because I will leave the story but this story will go on. This is our story; we co-author it. It is a story with no beginning and it is a story with no end. It is just, simply, our story. This is why, when I speak about my story, I am speaking about the period I am active in our story. This idea is also found in *The Truth About Stories: A Native Narrative*, by the Cherokee Indigenous scholar and storyteller Thomas King (2003), who challenges the Western notions of property ownership. King says about the story he has shared with his readers: "It's yours. Do with it what you will. Tell it to friends. Turn it into a television movie. Forget it. But don't say in the years to come that you would have lived your life differently if only you had heard this story. You've heard it now" (29). I too say this is your story; do with it as you will.

But, as I tell you this orature, I want you to remember that white supremacy calls to me through the power of colonial patriarchy, exploitative racism, and dispossessive capitalism, by never supporting me to think outside the logics of white supremacy (hooks 2000). Yet white supremacy is always reminding me of my position through racism, which is to say I will never be fully admitted. Yet, on its racist margins, I have been trained from birth to answer its call. bell hooks (2004) conveys its call: "Today it should be obvious to any thinker and writer speaking about black males that the primary genocidal threat, the force that endangers black male life, is patriarchal masculinity . . . [because it] continues to push the notion that all black men need to do to survive is to become better patriarchs" (13). Yet, Baba mukulo (Ngoni older male) taught me that if I wanted to help our community, I needed to first heal and help myself (to be internally focused) before all else. At the time that Baba mukulo shared this wisdom with me, I could not understand his words or what they meant with reference to developing my Indigenous masculinities, which Ty P. Kawika Tengan (2008), in *Native Men Remade: Gender and Nation in Contemporary Hawai'i*, refers to as notions and actions that capture what it means to be a man within the context of relational Indigeneity. Yet, years later here in Canada, I am reflecting on Baba mukulo's words and I see the connection between what he said and the Ubuntu masculine rituals of coming of age as expressed by Tengan (2008).

For example, among Ubuntu in Southern Africa, there are coming-of-age rituals that train girls and boys about masculinities and femininities as part of a larger project about Indigenous governance (Boucher 2012). The training of Indigenous governance among the Chewa is led by a secret society known as Nyau, which is famous for the Gulu Wamkulu (the Great Dance of Life). Nyau initiates its members through the coming-of-age rituals, to know the labour of relational community health—the development and nurturing of Indigenous political governance, relational gender health, communal spiritual health, disease prevention, and community parenting (nurturing beyond biology) as adult female and male leaders of the communities (Boucher 2012). The revival and regeneration of these rituals is helping ground the soon-to-be men in the labour of relational community health, especially as colonial educational systems train our Ubuntu youth to enter the colonial capitalistic system, which fragments them from Ubuntu education and communities (D.D. Mucina 2006; Mutwa 1969). In Southern Africa, research demonstrates that men are more likely to be fragmented from their families of origin due to their pursuit of colonial capitalistic power, which physically disconnects them from their Indigenous Nations (World Health Organization [WHO] 2014; Richter and Morrell 2006; Massey 1978).

In reference to Ubuntu masculinities, all our Ubuntu coming-of-age rituals are marked times of social self-discovery. Social self-discovery is the process of understanding the meaning of the social self in relation to our philosophical ideas about Indigenous Black masculinities and Indigenous Black feminisms, notions and actions that capture what it means to be a woman (hooks 2000; Crenshaw 1991). For me, Indigenous masculinities and Indigenous feminisms reflect the Ubuntu social identities in relation to theoretical paradigms about politically gendered selves within the context of community accountability and responsibility (Kuokkanen 2015; Tengan 2008; hooks 2004). I will speak more succinctly about these philosophical ideas in later Millet Granaries, especially in the letters to Baba and Amai.

The Ubuntu coming-of-age ritual ceremonies are held away from the larger communities as a way of encouraging the social individual to reflect on his/ her positionality in relation to the collective and to potential intimate partners (Boucher 2012). During the alone time of the masculine ceremonial rituals, Baba reported posing the following questions to himself: "What makes these relationships important to me? What do I give and what do I take?" For me it is clear that these sacred masculine ceremonial rituals are about understanding the interconnectedness of all Ubuntu relationships. To give emphasis to the interconnectedness of all Ubuntu relationships, the coming-of-age masculine ritual ceremonies are conducted in sacred natural places with the aid of spiritually wise selected old ones. These particular old ones have been through the process of a masculine ritual ceremony and have been taught the skills of how to help each individual's *chi* (spirit) commune with the self of other spirits in the life flux as known by Ubuntu. Ubuntu philosophy communicates this communion as "I am because you are." Yet, as I share this Ubuntu teaching with you, a critical and more pragmatic question arises for me about the roles and positionalities of women's teachings in the masculine ceremonies and rituals of boys' transitions into manhood. This is especially true in our current context, where females and males only participate in gender-specific ritual ceremonies instead of being initiated in both the masculine and feminine rituals, as was the traditional way. The lack of time in a capitalistic-driven economy that requires greater colonial educational commitment and resources limits Indigenous people's time commitment to fully perform ritual ceremonies (Boucher 2012). This means boys only focus on masculine rituals at the exclusion of feminine rituals. This leaves me with the questions, who teaches boys about how to be in healthy relationships with women and girls? What assurance do these boys have that their learning is congruent with the expectations and the reality of women and girls? More serious academic interrogation is required for such questions, which I raised after being initiated in both the feminine and the masculine rituals as a fully grown man in 2018.

Baba reported that his sacred masculine ceremonial ritual helped him experience the relational oneness of all living things. This oneness is the formless energy we call spirit. To see the spirit in air, water, earth, fire, trees, and other elements in the web of life is to see relational sacred power. This is to be spiritually Ubuntu because you see that "you are through others," which can also be expressed as "I am because you are." This is the Ubuntu ceremonial ritual experience that my Baba experienced but that was taken from me by the imposition of colonial white supremacy and its governance structures with the aid of colonial religious institutions (Césaire 1972). This is why I treat my academic work on Ubuntuness as a regenerated ceremonial ritual, which is directing me toward our social Black Indigenous selves performed away from my African home and community. Sisters and Brothers, it is known in the Indigenous Ubuntu worldsense that the acquisition of my relational Black Indigenous history is a prerequisite for my self-examination, which is itself a requirement for seeing my relational bond with the world communities (people, lands, plants, animals, waters, and the air). Could these Indigenous Ubuntu actions be decolonizing relational Indigenous masculinities and could they be renewing Indigenous Ubuntu traditions? Could they be a roadmap for how to get back to your roots? All I can do is share the path that has led me back to Indigenous governance, rituals, ceremonies, and spirituality, which is to say I have found what equates to love for me, Ubuntu.

My Ubuntu heart remembers all that is important, like the oratures of Baba mukulo and Mama mukulo that have helped me deal with the challenges of colonialism by giving me Ubuntu teachings as reference points for engaging my world differently. Ubuntu oratures have helped me stay grounded in my

Ubuntu roots. Yet I cannot help but struggle with the following questions: Does it matter that I cannot dream or write in any Ubuntu language? I wonder, if we were telling this orature in ChiChewa, ChiShona, or ChiNgoni, would it be the same? What would be different? What has been lost in translation? Is this orature in the right context? Am I philosophizing about it in a respectful way? When did I start dreaming this colonized dream? Fragmented memories take me home to that place where my spirit comes from. Where the problems are all ours and the finger-pointing is only directed at us. But, can I ever have this Ubuntu dream back? Do I accept change while learning from the lessons of the past, and what is the Ubuntu future we are moving toward? Are we moving toward an Ubuntu future that we are co-creating or are we moving toward a colonial future imagined for us by others? I see questions like this at the centre of Ubuntu self-determination.

Ben Okri (1997) calls this the metamorphosis of exile, a process he explains in the following way: "Exile is a fleeing from one dream to another one. In the process we change, we metamorphose, and our new shapes are never settled" (54). In this metamorphosis, I am realizing that compulsory[4] white supremacy and its patriarchal capitalistic structures are continually bombarding me with the belief that the African Indigenous dream has been destroyed (hooks 2004). They told me that there was nothing left of Indigenous Africa, so I fled our African dream for their white dream. However, their dream was a nightmare of destruction aimed at all our Indigenous relations. I found no enjoyment in their nightmare, but because I entered their dream, I am changed, I have metamorphosed, and, in my new self, I am never settled. So, I wonder, what can my unsettled oratures teach you? It is my hope that my unsettled oratures will teach you to love yourself, to love your memories, to love your spiritual ancestors because they can guide you, and I want you to love humanity while being wary of the abusers and the usurpers. Whether I like it or not, all our actions are connected by the web of life. What compulsory white supremacy has done through its positioning of colonial toxic masculinities as a tool of power has affected me, and what I am doing will affect compulsory white supremacy, but I cannot determine in what ways compulsory white supremacy will change. Instead, I endeavour to enact the change that I want and, in large part, I have been inspired by Black feminist scholars like bell hooks. When I encounter the work of hooks, it always feels like she is speaking directly to me. I therefore have committed myself to speaking directly to my children and the African global community, first and foremost. Now that we are linked by this orature, where do I end and where do you begin? Could the sacred spiritual cycle of breath connect us into one Ubuntu? In the next Millet Granary, I will convey how Ubuntu constitutes functional theories, which have deep philosophical wisdom from the past. Yet Ubuntu is not stuck in the past because it is a dynamic relational way of being in the world, and this means that it is constantly emerging in the present, while educating future generations about relational responsibility for a sustainable future for all beings.

Ubuntu Philosophies Emerge from Relational Living Theories

Methodological questions that guided my writing of this Millet Granary:

1. *How do Ubuntu philosophies and theories define who is Ubuntu?*
2. *What are the important functions of Ubuntu philosophies and theories?*
3. *How do Ubuntu philosophies and theories engage the social political reality of equity and social justice?*

> *The starting point for orientation is the point from which the world unfolds.... Orientations are about how we begin; how we proceed from "here," which affects how what is "there" appears, how it represents itself.... So what is "East" is actually what is east of the prime meridian, the zero point of longitude. The East as well as the left is thus oriented; it requires its direction only by taking a certain point of view as given.... The direction we take excludes things for us, before we even get there.*
>
> —Sara Ahmed, *Queer Phenomenology*

Sanibonani Nandi and Khumalo,

If orientations are about how we begin, then I want to point out to you both that in my decolonizing process I purposefully take Ubuntu theory as the given starting point that shapes how my oratures give us a more culturally situated picture about the Ubuntu worldview. As part of centring Ubuntu, I use a discursive theoretical framework because it allows me to engage my many political arenas. A good example of this is highlighted in the way that I use the anti-colonial theory of Aimé Césaire (1972) to highlight what colonialism is in the Ubuntu context, which then allows me to enter the Ubuntu worldview in a more meaningful way. The key concepts that I use to address the Ubuntu worldview are Ubuntu as a people; Ubuntu as a theory; Ubuntu epistemology; Ubuntu honouring theory; and Africana phenomenology theory.

Aimé Césaire's (1972) anti-colonial theoretical work, entitled *Discourse on Colonialism*, serves to illustrate how the colonial institutions were justified and how this justification continues to be perpetuated. The most important function of his work is that it serves to deconstruct the false memory that colonialism is still trying to impose on me. Césaire reminds me what colonialism is with this poem:

> My turn to state an equation: colonization = "thingification." I hear the storm. They talk to me about progress, about "achievements," diseases cured, improved standards of living. I am talking about societies drained of their essence, cultures trampled underfoot, institutions undermined, lands confiscated, religions smashed, magnificent artistic creations destroyed, extraordinary possibilities wiped out. They throw facts at my head, statistics, mileages of roads, canals, and railroad tracks. I am talking about thousands of men sacrificed to the Congo-Ocean. I am talking about those who, as I write this, are digging the harbor of Abidjan by hand. I am talking about millions of men torn from their gods, their land, their habits, their life—from life, from the dance, from wisdom. I am talking about millions of men in whom fear has been cunningly instilled, who have been taught to have an inferiority complex, to tremble, kneel, despair, and behave like flunkeys. They dazzle me with the tonnage of cotton or cocoa that has been exported, the acreage that has been planted with olive trees or grapevines. I am talking about natural economies that have been disrupted—harmonious and viable economies adapted to the indigenous population—about food crops destroyed, malnutrition permanently introduced, agricultural development oriented solely toward the benefit of the metropolitan countries; about the looting of products, the looting of raw materials. They pride themselves on abuses eliminated. I too talk about abuses, but what I say is that on the old ones—very real—they have superimposed others—very detestable. They talk to me about local tyrants brought to reason; but I note that in general the old tyrants get on very well with the new ones, and that there

has been established between them, to the detriment of the people, a circuit of mutual services and complicity. (42–3)

In this short, accessible, clear poem, Césaire (1972) makes plain what so many theories and academics have failed to communicate in clear accessible language. In the Black context, Césaire communicates to all that colonialism is the gaining of power through Black dispossession. Black dispossession was hidden and silenced by white concepts of discovery, as is illustrated in the case of Cecil John Rhodes who, in colonial society, "created" Rhodesia after "discovering" the territory. How did Cecil John Rhodes accomplish such a feat? How did he make so many nations and people disappear so that he could claim discovery of a country using the concept of "terra nullius"? How could Cecil John Rhodes claim terra nullius when he had to contend with the resistance of our ancestors? To get African lands he had to use trickery, bribery, outright theft, and murder of our ancestors without fear of consequence because he and his countrymen had convinced themselves that they were dealing with primitive people. Curtis Cook and Juan D. Lindau (2000), in *Aboriginal Rights and Self-Government: The Canadian and Mexican Experience in North American Perspective*, convey how the principle of primitiveness was conceptualized in Rhodesia as a colonial tool of dispossession that used vague and arbitrary standards: "By the second decade of the twentieth century, British colonial law had come to rely on a presumptive division of the world into 'civilized' and 'primitive' in order to justify unilateral assertions of sovereignty by colonists. Seminal for this version was the 1919 decision in *Re: Southern Rhodesia of the Law Lords of the Privy Council of Great Britain*, the highest judicial authority in the Empire" (151).

Cook and Lindau (2000) show that the white colonizers developed their tools of colonialism and conquest among a specific Indigenous people in a specific geographic location and then transported those colonial techniques to other geopolitical locations. The white colonizing techniques were always being refined before being passed on to their colonizing kith and kin. Césaire (1972) reports how white colonialists eased their conscience about the evil things they did to Black people by saying that our "good backward nature" was somehow responsible for encouraging them to colonize us. Césaire captures this point when he makes the following reference: "Since, the Rev. Tempels notes with obvious satisfaction, 'from their first contact with the white men, the Bantu considered us from the only point of view that was possible to them, the point of view of their Bantu philosophy' and 'integrated us into their hierarchy of life forces at a very high level'" (59). Rev. Tempels generated his racist remarks by distorting Ubuntu philosophy and making it seem like Black people could not distinguish between white people and gods. To adequately address the racist distortion created by the Rev. Tempels, let me use Ubuntu theory. The Ubuntu philosophy teaches us that we should treat a stranger like a god because we will never know when we may find ourselves in their territory. It is hoped that by treating a stranger like a god, one will receive the same treatment when away from home. So Ubuntu courtesy and hospitality became the marker of Ubuntu ignorance in the eyes of the colonizers and today this legacy still haunts us. Fearing being labelled as backward and primitive, we have abandoned our Ubuntu ways, but, if we are to know ourselves as Ubuntu, we must take our power (Ubuntu) and use it to determine who we are and where we are going. All Ubuntu life is connected by the cycle of reciprocal relationships (Archibald/Q'um Q'um Xiiem 2008); no relationship is greater than the other. I value my relationship with my family in the same manner I value the trees, waters, rocks, and other animals. Each relationship I have sustains my life in a balance that is beyond my creation. So let us engage with who the Ubuntu are as a people.

Ubuntu as a People

The term Ubuntu has a linguistic history among Black people in Africa. Yet not all Black people identify as being Ubuntu. This I believe shows that Ubuntuness is a reflection of one contextual expression of Blackness and does not undermine other expressions of Blackness. The amaZulu of South Africa refer to a person as Muntu and people as Ubuntu. The maShona people of Zimbabwe call a person Munhu and they refer to people as Vanhu. The Chichewa people of Malawi refer to a person as Munthu and people as Watu. I highlight these three examples as a way of showing that Black people have been self-identifying as Ubuntu since time immemorial. The Zulu high priest Vusa'mazulu Credo Mutwa (1969), in *My People, My Africa*, tells us: "The Black people of Africa called themselves, and any other people on earth, the Bantu, Watu or Abantu. This loosely means 'people' or 'human beings.' People of Europe and parts of Asia are called Abantu Abamhlope, meaning literally 'human beings who are white,' while we ourselves are Abantu Abansundu, or 'human beings who are dark brown'" (18). Mutwa also informs us that the contraction *ntu* in Ubuntu or Muntu has its roots in the word "ntu-tu-ut, which is an onomatopoeic word to describe the steps of a creature walking on two legs instead of four legs" (19). In my 2006 MA thesis, "Revitalizing Memory in Honour of Maseko Ngoni's Indigenous Bantu Governance," I address our roots in a chapter titled "Origins of Our Ancestors." In an effort to clearly show how Ubuntu history is Black history, I will revisit some of the points that I made in the thesis as well as adding new information.

Stories of sacred memories and modern scholarship are in agreement on the point that the Ubuntu people migrated from a northern direction toward Southern Africa. Donald R. Morris (1965), in *The Washing of the Spears*, accepts that the Ubuntu were in Egypt and other parts of north and west Africa but has concluded thus: "No one knows from whence the Bantu came, and by the time modern man turned scientific scrutiny on the problem a century ago, the layers of evidence were irrevocably tangled" (27). On the question of the Ubuntu origin, Morris makes the following point: "The origin of the Negroes has been the greatest enigma. The variation within the Cushites, or a combination of Cushites with either Bushmen or Pygmies, has been considered"[1] (12). Hence, the white powers have rendered us invisible by the usage of the term "Negroid." A Negro is homeless, languageless, and cultureless (Malcolm X 1967). Robert O. Collins, in *Problems in African History* (1968), makes the following claims: "The term Bantu was first coined by Dr. Wilhelm Bleek in a book published in 1862 entitled *A Comparative Grammar of South African Languages*. Bleek observed that nearly every language spoken on the southern third of the African continent used prefixes, which could be attributed to a set of what he called 'proto-prefixes,' presuming a generic relationship and implying an aboriginal source" (57).

I state very forcefully that Bleek did not make a new discovery, he simply reported the knowledge that our ancestors had shared with him. White settler society, with its kith and kin, has made claims of discovery since first contact and they continue to do so at our expense. They have taken up our knowledge as their own and they have been so effective that I even found myself trying to censor my own Baba's teaching because I feared that if his teaching contradicted their writings I would be considered a revisionist. They have created the illusion that it is impossible for us to talk to each other without first talking to them. This is why, Sisters and Brothers, I am saying Sankofa, Sankofa, Sankofa, I am going back to reclaim my past before the great Maafa.

Cheikh Anta Diop (1974), in *The African Origin of Civilization: Myth or Reality*, accurately summed up the truth when he stated that the ancient Egyptians were in fact Black people and these Black people are the ancestors of the Black Southerners. The images that Diop offers are more than compelling. They are proof that the Ubuntu have had a presence in all of Africa since time immemorial. Sanusi (high priest), philosopher, and historian Vusa'mazulu Credo Mutwa has knowledge that is only available to a few chosen healers and spiritualists. Wisely, he sheds light on the origin of the Ubuntu using the intergenerational knowledge given to him as a custodian of sacred Ubuntu knowledge. Mutwa (1969) adds to Diop's (1974) scholarship when he states:

> Now the common stock, the ancestral tribe from which all Negroid tribes of Africa sprang, was known as the Ba-Tu, or the Ba-Ntu. Legends say that the stock lived in the 'Old Land.' This was far back in the bone and stone ages. Where was this 'Old Land'? It is where the 'Old Tribes' are still found today—all the tribes of the land of the Bu-Kongo right up to the southern parts of the land of the Ibo and Oyo (Nigeria). These are the tribes who identify themselves with the prefix Ba. They are Ba-Mileke, Ba-Mbara, Ba-Kongo, Ba-Ganda, Ba-Hatu, Ba-Luba, Ba-Tonka, Ba-Saka, Ba-Tswana, Ba-Kgalaka, Ba-Venda, Ba-Pedi, Ba-Sutu and Ba-Chopi. The southern offshoot of the great—Ba-Pedi, Ba-Venda, Ba-Kgalaka and Ba-Tswana—are the oldest Bantu tribes south of the level of the Limpopo and their histories within these regions go back to a thousand years B.C. All these tribes are direct offshoots of the great Ba-Ntu nations that lived in the 'Old Land,' as a properly organised tribe, a full 4500 years ago, reckoned according to the genealogies. (19)

Oral traditions tell us that we have old roots in North Africa as we have been living in these lands since time immemorial. Mutwa's (1969) knowledge about the olden Ubuntu has been supported by the scientific work of George Peter Murdock (1959) in his book entitled *Africa: Its Peoples and Their Culture History*. Murdock identifies most of the olden ethnic groups as having a linguistic foundation to what has been identified as Bantu languages and, to prove this point, he uses high- and low-density geographical mapping techniques to show how the olden ethnic groups are more densely populated according to geographic population figures and anthropological evidence. Meaning, the Ubuntu migrated from high-density population areas to areas of low-density population. The major areas that Murdock identifies as the oldest Ubuntu civilizations are located in the central great lakes areas, which are arguably the oldest Ubuntu civilizations. The next major move was to Northwestern Africa, followed by North Africa, while small groups went to Southern Africa. There are many other scholarly works that support these theories, but to highlight those theories here would be unnecessarily labouring over a point well accepted within scholarly circles. Let us now engage with the theory of Ubuntu.

Ubuntu Theory

In Western society, Ubuntuness was unknown and, in most African academic institutions, which function from a Western Eurocentric scholarly worldview, Ubuntuness was dismissed as simple African thinking. But the world became interested for a moment when Bill Clinton spoke at the British Labour Party conference in 2006 and BBC reporter Sean Coughlan (2006) quoted him as saying, "Society is important because of Ubuntu." Coughlan then plays on the ignorance of his audience by showing that "nobody" knows what this Ubuntu is or cares to know. He states: "But what is it? Left-leaning sudoku? U2's latest album? Fish-friendly sushi?" In between his mockery of Ubuntu he tells his audience, "Mr. Tutu's identification with ubuntu has given rise to the idea of 'ubuntu theology'—where ethical responsibility comes with a shared identity. If someone is hungry, the ubuntu response is that we are all collectively responsible." Coughlan (2006) then makes it clear that even this small idea of Black Africa has been co-opted:

> Ubuntu has also entered the language of development and fair trade—with campaigners using the word in aid projects for Africa in ways that suggest this will be an African solution for African problems. Ironically, says Rob Cunningham, Christian Aid's programme manager for South Africa, just as the word is taking off in Western society the values it embodies are in decline in the land of its origin. 'In my conversations with partner organisations and the communities they work with, and among older people, there's a deep sense of loss of ubuntu,' says Mr Cunningham. 'To me, it means sitting down in a Zulu hut in KwaZulu-Natal sharing scarce food and a brew and a few stories.' There are ubuntu education funds, ubuntu tents at development conferences, ubuntu villages, an ubuntu university—and it's now the name of an open-source operating system. Expect to hear more from ubuntu in the future. (n.p.)

Coughlan communicates to us that compulsory able-bodied whiteness is giving legitimacy to a simple Black idea, while also laughing at the fact that compulsory able-bodied whiteness is making a big deal out of nothing. So what is Ubuntu from an African context?

Ubuntu is a philosophical theory that guides our actions in order to maintain all our relational bonds within an Ubuntu worldview. We need to remember that ideas and philosophies created in one language cannot always be translated adequately into another language without losing some meaning because each language speaks to a specific contextual symbolic encoding (Hall 1997). Keeping these language translational limitations in mind, here are some Ubuntu philosophical principles taught to me by my family and community:

- I am a reflection of the existence of my ancestors—I exist because they exist, or as we say, "Umuntu ngumuntu ngubuntu"—A person is a person through other people, or we could also say, "A thing is a thing through other things." Meaning all things know each other in relationship to each other.
- We come from the energy flux and are the energy flux. This is why the circle is important to the Ubuntu spirituality. The circle shows that we are one.
- We respect and give thanks for all of our relations because all elements are part of the energy flux that makes up life.
- We try to live an Ubuntu life with the aim of finding integrity and wholeness in the balance of nature, which is to see the energy flux in everything.
- To each person, place, animal, or object we ask for permission before taking and give thanks for that which we have received. These prayers are directed to the spirit of the desired object. These prayers explain our actions and give justification for our actions because we respect the spirit of all things.
- Birth and death reflect the life cycle in all things and in all places.
- We honour the spirit of the land and the spirit of the water in special ways. In fact, it is said that the experience we have with specific elements helps us to develop language and knowledge as an effort to respect the space we occupy.
- Our traditional governance institutions are inclusive of nature as a decision-making relational member of Ubuntu. We honour the intelligibility of nature.
- We honour the dead because they live in a parallel world to that of the living.

Now that we have some shared meaning of what Ubuntu theory is, let us go deeper and engage with Ubuntu epistemology.

Ubuntu Epistemology

I have learned from my Ubuntu old ones to see the spirit of the creator in everything. Paradoxically, I have also been taught to understand that "the creator is distant, unconcerned with the affairs of mankind, except indirectly via animal and spirit emissaries" (Burnham 2000, 2). I am of the creator, yet I cannot fully understand my own nature, and the rock is of the creator, but I cannot speak for it as I do not understand it. In Ubuntu epistemology, a force that may be perceived as evil in one context may be good in another context, and vice versa. This is why we say that we are in a relational cycle with everything on this earth. Our job is to figure out how to nurture that relationship in a specific way and at a specific time. This is why the memory of our ancestors is important to keep alive. To know an ancestor is to invite his/her spirit to guide you when you need help. We do not need to keep inventing knowledge that was already invented by our ancestors. If we work with our ancestors, we can perfect this knowledge and move forward.

How do we know our ancestors exist? How do we know their spirits are with us? To answer this question, my Baba mukulu (Ngoni older male) once said to me:

> I know I exist because you exist. I can see you, I can feel you and
> I know my mother exists because I am here. I am of her and my
> father. Both my parents are of their parents. You can see how this
> relationship connects me with the living dead. Dreaming becomes
> at times another way to communicate with the dead. Now, would
> you believe me, if I told you as old as I am that my grandparents
> visit me in my dreams? Other relatives that I have never met come
> to me in my dreams and advise me. All dreams are communica-
> tions. You have to work out the message. (Baba mukulo, personal
> communication, 1981–2)

Baba mukulo's oratures have helped me make sense of the African epigram, "We exist because they exist," as he has demonstrated our relational link to our ancestors and how they are central to our practice of spirituality. Our ancestors are still with us in spirit but are a step closer to Umkulumqango (The Great Deviser or the Great Spirit) or we could say Unkulunkulu (The Greatest of All) who we don't know but experience in all creation. Others have defined the Great Spirit or Eternal Spirit as the known energy in all things, and it has also been perceived as the greater source of all energy. Arguably, our inability to comprehend Umkulumqango has led some of our Ubuntu to represent the Greatest of All in many forms, including "as bi-sexual, with two heads, one growing out of the top of the other, facing in opposite directions, which again symbolizes that God is all things in all time. In the old days figures of this type were carved at the top of long poles, which were then erected in the centre of the village clearing, to be used to measure the time of day from the shadow they cast" (Mutwa 1969, 133).

The ancestral spirits that we know by name, we pray to them because they can help us. For example, they can inform us about the wishes of Unkulunkulu. Spirits can also be more than just people; the spirits of animals, plants, sacred places, and sacred waters can speak to us and advise us. Owen Burnham (2000), in *African Wisdom,* reports that the African world "is a world in which wisdom and knowledge are the keys to survival in the multi-dimensional spiritual universe where we are never far from the past, present and the future as represented by the ancestral spirits that are all around us" (12). Our ancestors are motivated in their actions by their love for us. We are a continuation of their legacy or, put another way, we are a reflection of their existence. Our well-being is their well-being. To pray to them is to communicate with loving parents who know and understand us very well. In the spirit world, they are in a better place to understand Unkulunkulu and because they have been here on earth, they can understand us.

As we are in a different time dimension from that of our spiritual ancestors, we cannot see them unless they choose to make contact with us (Burnham 2000). At times, we can communicate with our ancestors and not be aware of it; for example, when we feel the world is as it should be, or when we have a premonition about a dangerous situation that is about to happen, or when we feel compelled to communicate with a total stranger. All these unexplained interactions are the result of our ancestors intervening or, at times, not intervening. The Ubuntu world is a mystery, and we are taught to respect death without fear because it is a homecoming to our true natural form, which is spirit. In the world of the living, we learn lessons and teach lessons, but our time in the living world is not determined by us, it is determined by Unkulunkulu (the energy in all things).

In order to honour our spiritual connections and relationships, we offer libations. Before killing for food, we ask through prayer for the animal or plant spirit to give us its flesh. What we receive we are thankful for and, to show our gratitude, we make sacrifices to the ancestral spirits in hope that they will communicate our thankfulness to the spirits of the animals and plants who give up their lives to feed us. We hope that by showing our gratitude our ancestral spirits will ensure that all the things that share our world and nurture us will come back and continue to share the world with us again. I do not believe we should be buried in cement because, when we die, we too should feed the earth and the creatures of the earth in the same manner that they feed us. This is the cycle of life. It is important that I state very clearly that I have never been told or taught that we make offerings or sacrifices of any kind to Unkulunkulu. To make any kind of offering to Unkulunkulu would be unacceptable to the teachings that I have been given because Unkulunkulu is of everything, and everything is of Unkulunkulu. As Mutwa (1986) conveys to us, there is nothing that we can give Unkulunkulu for he/she is ever-present in the world.

Another guiding Ubuntu principle that I remember from the stories of Baba mukulo conveys that our ancestors struggled with the idea of living with difference among each other. So, you can imagine how difficult this concept of living with differences is when we start to speak across cultures, across religious beliefs, and across racial lines. Yet we have to try to live with differences because our humanity depends upon it. The most obvious of these contradictions is that my ancestors moved away from Southern Africa in an effort to avoid war with their relatives, the amaZulu, but they in turn brought war and devastation to other ethnics as far up as central Africa. Baba affirms this view when he states: "We are the product of aggression in defense, they [non-Ngunis] know of our fury, for we were wounded innyath [buffaloes]" (Personal communication, between 27 June and 10 July, 2003). Baba's point is supported in *Witchcraft, Violence, and Democracy in South Africa* by Adam Ashforth (2005), who, in reference to "negative ubuntu," makes the following point: "To the adage 'A person is a person through other people,' the negative corollary of ubuntu adds: 'because they can destroy you.' That is, a person can survive only to the extent that others in the community choose not to destroy him or her. How they might do so is less important than the fact that they can. And when they do, whether by physical or by occult violence, the demand for justice inevitably arises" (86). Ashforth's point is that our ancestors, like some of us still do, were committing crimes against Ubuntu because they could. Military might became the ultimate power. It is at such times when Ubuntu is being misused that we need to take action because no worldsense system is infallible. We should never allow ourselves to misuse our power.

Even in the extreme cases when we can justify killing in self-defence, Baba says, "we should never take life lightly and we should always remember, no matter the circumstance, killing is and should always be a very regrettable act because the warrior that kills has one less relative" (Personal communication, 1982). In present-day society, old conflict-resolution strategies like moving away in an effort to preserve life cannot be accomplished easily. The idea of living with difference has become even more crucial. I share these facts for no other reason than to help unite our Ubuntu communities. It would seem Karl Deutsch (1969) has hit a nerve when he, in *Nationalism and Its Alternatives*, states: "A nation is a group of persons united by a common error about their ancestry and a common dislike of their neighbors" (3). Brothers and Sisters, let us not hold on too tightly to our unique Black identities because the Ubuntu (African people) known as Nguni, who are ancestors of the Maseko Ngoni, are a result of Ubuntu legendary leaders and battles; of migrations and geographical displacement; of bloody ethnic feuds and kin-group formations.

Yes, the Ngoni have been created from the ashes of war but our languages, our spirituality, and our memories connect us to our other Ubuntu relatives from North Africa to South Africa and from East Africa to West Africa. We are one people; we are Ubuntu. All of this the Ngoni know and have shared with us, their children, because memory is history and history is memory. Oratures from our history tell us that there is great diversity that makes up what is Ngoni, like the fact that almost all Maseko Ngoni are biologically and linguistically tied to the Chewa people through marriages (Kishindo 2002). Let us embrace the multiplicity as the diversity that will ensure our survival in an ever-changing world. Those who would try to create a singularity of the Ngoni identity will only neglect our other identities and undermine other valuable Ubuntu knowledges. Baba captures this problem when he states:

> The problem for us as Maseko is that we have different memories from different parts of Africa and some of us have tried to impose our single inkatha [nation/kingdom] memory as the Ubuntu blue print for Maseko Ubuntu governance. However, we know this cannot be Ubuntu as Ubuntu philosophy states, "We exist because you exist." Thus, the idea of a single inkatha dominating a region does not make sense because inkatha is how the people unite and make sense of themselves without dominating each other or the land. The land dominates us and it cannot be any other way for us. (Personal communication, 1981–2)

Baba's point about the centrality of land to knowledge production in the Indigenous context was also demonstrated by the work of Keith H. Basso

(1996), who conveyed the power of land through the title of his work, *Wisdom Sits in Places: Landscape and Language Among the Western Apache.* Yet Ubuntu wars have been waged over land as a resource (Mutwa 1969). These Ubuntu failings create paradoxes and contradictions about what it means to be Ubuntu among other relational beings. We speak of Ubuntu unity, yet we identify ourselves as Maseko Ngoni and, in so doing, we create outsiders. But who are the people silenced by our inkatha? Who are the outsiders of our inkatha and how did they come to be outsiders while we are insiders? If our experiences and knowledges give us our diversity, then let us support all our knowledges without creating a hierarchy of importance and power. Let us be proud and remember our other relatives. Let us remember that we were and are one family; let us remember the love of Ubuntu and let this love guide us to unity. We know the truth of what is being spoken here because we can recognize it, which is to say we remember it. In this section, we have engaged with Ubuntu epistemology and the political struggles we have to watch for when trying to live an informed Ubuntu life. Now let us engage with how we use Ubuntu as an honouring theory.

Ubuntu Honouring Theory

> When we arrived at new places to which we had travelled to visit relations, Grandpa would gather the soil of the land, letting it rest on his palm. Squatting froglike in the characteristic pose of ancestral address, he would mix the soil and the water. Of these muddy waters he would have us drink. It was an initiation and a rite that united us with our new spaces and released the spirit. Locked in childhood innocence, we felt safe, we felt happy, as the soft scent of decaying vegetation tickled our nostrils.
>
> —Yvonne Vera, *Why Don't You*
> *Carve Other Animals*

This orature by Vera communicates to me that the Ubuntu people of Africa understand and know that the land is intelligible. We understand that the land has knowledge, which is important for maintaining the balance of all life. As a child, when I was about to go out and play in the forest with other children, Baba would say to me, "Remember, there are sacred places in the great forest, always be respectful while you're in there." From this, I understood that the forest was a sacred place with power and that I was at its mercy when I entered its domain. The first time I entered a truly large forest, I was with some friends.

At the edge of the forest, before we entered, the other children automatically began to ask the great forest for permission to enter and for safe passage within her boundaries. I followed suit because, from Baba's teachings, I understood that nature was intelligible.

As we walked into the forest, one of the older children reminded us all that it was forbidden to kill anything without asking permission from the spirits of the forest and, once we had killed, we had to also thank the spirit of the animal that had delivered itself to us. However, on this occasion we were only interested in having fun. We found the perfect swimming pool and played in it for some time, and then we went to find some wild fruit to eat. While eating a monkey orange, I noticed that part of it was rotten and that it was riddled with worms. I threw the monkey orange down and yelled, "Yuk, that's disgusting!" Everyone came to a stop. I looked around and saw the fear on the other kids' faces. One of my friends informed me that I needed to pick up the monkey orange and place it down more respectfully. I did this without questioning but, when I was asked to apologize for being rude, I refused.

My thinking at the time was that these kids had gone overboard and my own sense of power and self-importance stopped me from apologizing. The other kids pleaded with me to apologize for my behaviour but I refused again. As we were leaving for home, none of the other kids wanted to walk behind me, as they believed that the forest spirits would not show me the way out because of my behaviour. They begged me one last time to apologize before we started for home and I told them that I did not believe anything was going to happen to me. After walking for about an hour, we realized that we were lost because it had taken us less than half an hour to get to the pool.

We spent another hour and a half trying to find the path out of the forest. When we realized that our efforts were not paying off, we all climbed some trees to see if we could identify where our end destination was. From the tops of the trees, we could all clearly see that we needed to go southwards for twenty minutes at the most. After walking for about another half an hour, we all realized that the only way we would get out was by praying to the spirits of the forest and asking for help. I started the prayer by apologizing for my errant behaviour and then we all joined hands and asked for help to get back home. After this prayer, we found our way to the edge of the forest within fifteen minutes and, when we got home, everybody knew what had happened to us. In response to this happening, Baba simply said, "I hope you have learned to be careful when you are out in sacred places," and we never talked about it again.

It is only now that I am learning that other Indigenous people across the globe hold other equally important Indigenous knowledges or have the same ones that we have (Mutwa 1964). For example, the Western Apache also know the intelligibility of nature (Basso 1996). Our old ones in our respective communities have taught our people that we are dependent on the land for our survival. This is why we have learned to honour our lands through our ceremonies and rituals. Let us use Ubuntu to move forward in our relationships with all. Now let us use Black meaning-making theory, Africana phenomenology, as a point of global engagement with the diverse Black people of the world.

Africana Phenomenology Theory

Paget Henry (2006), in *Africana Phenomenology: Its Philosophical Implications*, informs us that Africana phenomenology is not well known because it is not a Western philosophy and, more to the point, it is not Western phenomenology and it speaks to the African experience. Consequently, Henry leads us to question what Africana phenomenology is, and his response to this question is as follows: "By phenomenology, I mean the discursive practice through which self-reflective descriptions of the constituting activities of consciousness are produced after the 'natural attitude' of everyday life has been bracketed by some ego-displacing technique. An Africana phenomenology would thus be the self-reflective descriptions of the constituting activities of the consciousness of Africana peoples, after the natural attitudes of Africana egos have been displaced by de-centering techniques practiced in these cultures" (1).

The Ubuntu philosophy starts with the Africana phenomenological position of, I am because you are. This position communicates that self-reflection and meaning making occur in a social relational world. It is important for us as social beings to understand that we make social meaning of our world through older meaning created by our ancestors. On the old meanings, we construct new meanings and, with parallel meanings of the new and old, we construct more meanings. My opinion is affirmed in *I Write What I Like*, by Steve Biko (1996), which conveys Black consciousness as an "inward-looking process" that allows one to honour one's identity in relation to the other. The benefits of an "inward-looking process" as a starting point for understanding Ubuntu is that the self begins to understand its political centrality to communal African politics.

In order to understand the Ubuntu organization of meaning, Africana phenomenology investigates the interweaving arenas of embodiment, time, space, and action. These socially created phenomena help ground our interpretive relation to experience. The act of philosophizing the experience we gain through our body is conceived of as embodiment; meaning, how we experience space and occupy it. The process of change created by newness and dying, between day and night or winter and summer, can be understood in relation to the concept of time. Place gives rise to the concept of occupation, which is reflective of our geopolitics in relationship to space. We do things in order to create change or, I could say, our doing creates change. Hence, action is connected to purposeful change. Yet purposeful change is such a contested interpretation that making it measurable becomes subjective and controversial. This is why in the Ubuntu worldview the main theoretical occupation is interpreting relational bonds and trying to understand how change, the constant fact, impacts everything. Yet, of such Ubuntu phenomenology we hear little, because Black people are preoccupied with addressing racism. Henry (2006) illuminates this point in the following manner: "Rather, the occasion for reflection has been the racist negating of the humanity of Africans and the caricature of 'the negro' that it has produced. Unlike European phenomenology, these Africana reflections have been interested in clarifying the systemic error producing foundations of the European humanities and social sciences that have had to legitimate and make appear as correct this racist reduction of African humanity" (4).

The colonial thinking of compulsory whiteness, which we have been fighting since contact, is reflective of the thinking used by Robert Horwitz when he reflects on Thomas Aquinas's (1966) *Summa Theologiae* in which he includes reference to John Locke's *Questions Concerning the Law of Nature* and states from a Western educational perspective: "A rational creature therefore possesses a share of the eternal reason, whereby it has a natural inclination to its proper act and end, and this participation of the eternal law in the rational creature is called the natural law" (as cited in Locke, Horwitz, Clay, and Clay 1990, 13). Here we encounter a problem of interpretation, in that, we should ask how we determine embodiment, time, space, and action without being limited by Western arguments of rational, reasonable, and purposeful action. I am aware that, at the inception of these arguments of rational, reasonable, and purposeful action, specific persons are being excluded from the imaginable persons who were rational and reasonable. An American physician by the name of Samuel A. Cartwright claimed, in his 1851 article "Diseases and Peculiarities of the Negro Race," that the fleeing of Black slaves from captivity was not reasonable or rational. According to Cartwright, this behaviour was, in fact, reflective of a Black person's mental illness, and he defined this so-called mental illness as a medical condition, which he named "drapetomania" or the disease causing

Negroes to run away. Emmanuel Chukwudi Eze (1997), in his edited work *Race and the Enlightenment: A Reader*, reminds us that great Western thinkers were not willing to imagine Black people as rational or reasonable beings and, in fact, used our Blackness as the grounds for labelling us as primitive. David Hume in 1776 argued, "I am apt to suspect the Negroes and in general all the other species of man (for there are four or five different kinds) to be naturally inferior to the whites" (as cited in Eze 1997, 35). Immanuel Kant in 1724 used the racial category as the absolute marker of oppression when he stated, "This fellow was quite black...a clear proof that what he said was stupid" (as cited in Eze 1997, 35). In my review of my engagement with compulsory white supremacy, I have learned an important lesson that was put in the following way by Rod Michalko and Tanya Titchkosky (2001) in "Putting Disability in Its Place":

> The question of "where we speak from" is thus fundamental to the question of self-identification. . . . The sighted person does not indicate that the door is open. A sighted person, "knowing" that the blind person will have "trouble" opening the door, opens it. The sighted person does not indicate that the door is open. The blind person "should see" that the door is open. But not seeing this, the blind person tries to open it. The sighted person is surprised. Both stand groping. The door to the building remains open, but the door to any interactional development of what it means to be blind remains closed tighter than ever. (205, 215)

Here is what I find fascinating from an Africana phenomenological perspective. The orientation of the discussion by Michalko and Titchkosky is set in the field of disability, but its implication for equality, the intersections and interlockingness of oppression, marginality, racism, and sexism are larger than disability only. It is about people who are in diverse forms of relationships with each other. Yet from our diverse social relationships with each other, we try to impose our single interpretive meaning on others even if our own interpretive meaning contradicts our own experiences. This is especially true in the white context where they know that Blackness and disability are the markers of unwantedness but can never answer the question, unwanted from what? On the other hand, disability has used the experience of Blackness in the same manner it has used feminism, to draw skills and strength in addressing issues of disability as a marker of inequity. I would like to follow this tradition of borrowing between disability and Blackness and set Michalko and Titchkosky's words within a race discourse. Let me replace blind person with Black person and sighted person with white person and review the new context of interpretive meaning that arises: "The Black person 'should see' that the door is open. But not seeing this, the Black person tries to open it. The white person is surprised. Both stand groping. The door to the building remains open, but the door to any interactional development of what it means to be Black remains closed tighter than ever." I have read many writers that highlight the problem of Africa and give us their solution as to why Africa is the problem. They seldom utter a word about Blackness. Yet we all know that from the position of compulsory whiteness, Blackness is their problem.

Africana phenomenology helps me question what is sayable and doable about Blackness within the nexus of social interpretation and meaning making. Africana phenomenology challenges me to think about who is missing in our reasoning, who is being labelled as unwanted, and what does unwanted come to mean? Africana phenomenology allows me to think about the fact that if interpretation is the creation of meaning, then meaning should also lead me to the question of interpretation. In other words, if all Ubuntu are affected by the interpretation of meaning, can we explore how certain Ubuntu voices are empowered and authenticated while certain voices are disempowered? What would it mean in our social interpretation of meaning to have certain voices that have been disempowered into silence speak from an empowered position? Africana phenomenology does not just help me question, it also helps me think about how I might validate the social interpretation of other Black people. For example, I can talk about my orature of disability as a way of engaging Blackness in relation to disability. Let me be honest, I am uncomfortable with putting Blackness and disability together because there is a history of viewing Blackness as a disability. Yet I cannot be silent about disability within Black communities. These are the tensions that I must navigate when I make Blackness and disability rub up against each other in our neo-colonial global state society. Now that we are linked by this orature, where do I end and where do you begin? Could the sacred spiritual cycle of breath connect us into one, Ubuntu? I hope we have grounded each other in our Ubuntu meaning making and Ubuntu interpretation of meaning because the stories that I will now share may challenge and decentre us. In which case, having our Ubuntu orientation becomes important for grounding us in Black power. As a way of preparing myself for talking to Amai (mother), let me engage with African feminism as a way of opening myself to her reality.

African Feminist Theory

They are all slaves, including us. If their masters treat them badly, they take it out on us. The only difference is that they are given some pay for their work, instead of having been bought.

—Buchi Emecheta,
The Joys of Motherhood

Bought like meat, my Amai (mother); it is not a thought that I have ever seriously considered, but this could be because of my African male privilege. Being a male, with access to Western education, the thought of being married off is laughable and the thought of being forced into marriage because of monetary gain is inconceivable to me. However, if you speak about marrying someone in order to escape poverty, my Black male ears hear you very well. So in Amai's silence, the quote from Buchi Emecheta's (1979) orature has left me questioning, was my Amai bought against her will? Like Baba, other African fathers were absent from family life because the colonial white system had forced, lied, and cajoled them into neo-slave jobs. All the knowledge that I gained from my formative early years was heavily influenced by my Baba's male-dominated perspective. I, therefore, knew my Amai through the memories of my Baba. I would not be exaggerating if I stated that from Baba's stories my Amai was the calculating money-stealing bitch who abandoned her child and her husband with the aid of her parents when the money was gone. My Baba always said, "What kind of woman would leave my two beautiful children—Misheck and Mary—to die alone while she tried to satisfy her sweet tongue? To think her own family helped her turn into a prostitute. So they as a whole family could enjoy the things money bought them. The white man's ways and money had taught them that materialism was more important than people."

In the orphanage, I was raised primarily by males. Hence, my motherlust, my sense of abandonment, and my sense of disconnection all became associated with my perception of my Amai's inability to fulfill her role as a woman and as a mother. But, could African feminist thought challenge my male position and perspectives? Could African feminist thought help me meet my Amai from a Black feminist position and perspective? Could I understand my Amai's orature if I reflected on her experiences using a discourse that is not familiar and comfortable to my Black maleness? Could I listen to her when she comes to me from the spirit world to communicate her unique contextual location? Could I know my Amai anew?

Could African feminist theories allow me to honour all the wonderful women who have other-mothered me, even the white ones? Njoki Wane (2000), in her work titled "Reflections on the Mutuality of Mothering: Women, Children, and Other-mothering," talks about how other women (and men in some situations) care for children in our communities. She makes it clear that mothering is more than the biological act of creating a child and that it is more than the gender roles society prescribes. Wane informs us, "Our mothers, aunties, sisters and community mothers carried us on their backs" (108) and this community-mothering she calls other-mothering. Meaning, we are all responsible to mother beyond our own biological children. Wane has put it thus: "Within African communities, mothering is not necessarily based on biological ties. Established African philosophy suggests that children do not solely belong to their biological parents, but to the community at large. This philosophy and tradition inform what we refer to as 'other-mothering' and 'community mothering.' Significantly, even in the face of Western conceptions of mothering, which often view community-mothering practice as deviant and negligent, African understandings of mothering continue to thrive. Throughout the African Diaspora, Black women care for one another and one another's children regardless of their cultural backgrounds" (112).

Highlighting my experience of being at times other-mothered across racial lines again exemplifies the contradictions that exist in our racist contemporary Canadian society. Just when I am comfortable seeing the racism of compulsory able-bodied whiteness, very small and at times large individual acts challenge me to have hope. Albeit slowly, the racist white world is changing; my Baba reminds me that his experience of compulsory able-bodied whiteness is not the same as mine. Baba's point has implications for mothering in the Canadian African diaspora. Again, I return us to Wane's (2000) work on other-mothering. Drawing on her own experience in the Canadian context, she informs us that, "although I focus on Black women who mother children and one another, such practices exist beyond gender and racial boundaries. It is not unusual to find young boys mothering their younger siblings and uncles and fathers mothering their nieces and/or nephews. My mothering experiences in Toronto have also shown that women from different racial backgrounds may step in as other-mothers or community other-mothers" (12). So to all the Black and white women who have other-mothered me, I say thank you for other-mothering me. What you have taught me, I will perform for my children and our community children.

This being said, for me, no one can fill my Amai's role. When I cry out for Amai, I know who I am calling, and it is this Amai that I want to meet. It is this Amai, the thinking and feeling person who is an African Black woman. A fallible human being who makes mistakes, who has dreams, whose desires motivate her and whose fears can freeze her or make her fight. I want to meet the real contradictory Amai whom I cannot shape into my idealized African personification of perfect Amaihood. African feminist theories help me move from my privileged maleness to a place of uncertainty. African feminist oratures (presented as novels) such as *The Joys of Motherhood* by Buchi Emecheta (1979), *Nervous Conditions* by Tsitsi Dangarembga (1988), and *Why Don't You Carve Other Animals* by Yvonne Vera (1992) are helping me feel uncomfortable and challenged so that I may learn to listen and hear about Amai with an African feminist sensibility.

How can I be whole if I never interpret the world from my other half, which is the feminine African self? Maleness is half of my feminine self, which I am connecting with by making myself available to learning from and by hearing the diverse oratures of our Black women. Amai, from the realm of the dead, may you help me reflect you so that your truth may be heard. I need your orature, Amai, because it is an important orature in our healing. Your orature is our orature, and our orature is my orature, because are you not in me as I once was in you (Cixous 1998)? This means our oratures can be each other's medicines to fight white supremacy's induced hate, pain, isolation, and desire for revenge. This is why Shauna Singh Baldwin (2000) says in *What the Body Remembers*: "Stories are not told for the telling, stories are told for the teaching" (50).

What Ubuntu philosophies and theories should temper
our liberation action?

What barriers do you see to applying Ubuntu philosophies and
theories in our current context?

Are you convinced that the Ubuntu philosophies and theories of
relational love could lead us out of oppression?

Figure 2. Nandi and Khumalo in South Africa.

Passing Ubuntu Knowledge to the Future

Methodological questions that guided my writing of this Millet Granary:

1. *How do I embody healthy Indigenous masculinities as a father and as a community parent?*
2. *How do I teach my children the meaning of Ubuntu?*
3. *How does relational Ubuntu function as an Indigenous philosophy?*

Sanibonani Khumalo and Nandi,

Both your arrivals into this world have changed me because each day I think of you. Each day I love you and each day (OK, most days) I plan which educational orature to give you. I give you the fragments of the little Ubuntu education that I know because they are the only valuable things I have to leave you before I go to the spirit world of my ancestors. Therefore, before I go I want to educate you on how to live healthy Ubuntu lives. The experience of doing this loving work has led me to start thinking about other ways that we can share our Ubuntu knowledge with our younger generations, and the result of that work is this book. In writing this book, I have learned that we, the Ubuntu, have been and are in relation with other cultures and their knowledges (inclusive of human and non-human relations). Our shared social knowledge is gained through dialogue but is informed by our experience in set geographical locations (Wane 2000). Through our relational contact, we share with each other our unique oratures, in hope of having our own contextual meaning valued in a shared humanity. In my engagement with other cultures, I have learned that Ubuntu knowledge is not exclusively known to the Ubuntu; it has common dimensions found in other cultures, like the pursuit of relational social justice, the practice of relational spirituality, and the search for relational knowledge (D.D. Mucina 2018). Ubuntuness is a complex worldsense (Oyěwùmí 2001) that holds in tension the contradictions of trying to highlight our uniqueness as human beings among other human beings. Yet, in our racialized social and political world, I find myself simplifying Ubuntu knowledge and making it a specific Black[1] Indigenous knowledge, which has contextual reference from Africa but connects us to the entirety of humanity through the teaching of our relational bonds.

This being said, there is nothing static about Ubuntu knowledge, as it is constantly changing. My knowledge of my Ubuntuness is not identical to that of your grandparents and the knowledge of your grandparents is not the same as that of our ancestors. Ubuntu knowledge always changes in response to our lived experience while having a continuous philosophical dimension, which allows us to use the lessons from our past to produce a renewed specific Black Indigenous knowledge for our use in decolonizing our present political society (Mutwa 1964). This is why your arrival, Khumalo and Nandi, challenges me as an Ubuntu father and leads me to the question, What am I doing to ensure that my children know their Ubuntuness, which is our specific contextual production of Black Indigenous knowledge? This letter, Khumalo and Nandi, is my effort to give you and other Black children the lessons I have learned about our Ubuntuness, which is to say our Blackness.

Blackness, the spirit of eternalness,

Differentiation the illusion that creates self-awareness,

Yet self-awareness is Ubuntu,

Ubuntu is the paradox of being human,

Yet, we do transcend the paradoxical conflict of Ubuntuness through SPIRIT,[2]

Spirit is I am Blackness,

I am boundless, limitless because I am the source,

Yet to know free will, individuation, and uniqueness I must enter Ubuntu,

Time, Form and Space become the limits of my Ubuntu,

This is the paradox of Ubuntu, to try to make boundless and limitless into form.

Nandi and Khumalo, I want to tell you an orature about how colonialism tried to impose its memory upon my Ubuntu memories. I know my orature is set in days gone by, but I am sure, from the low educational attainment of Black children (reported to be at 40 percent in the Toronto District School Board, for example [Brown 2008]), that colonialism is still at work. I know that colonialism has reinvented itself again, but I hope that you will see some of its strategies in my orature. I was born in Zimbabwe because my Baba had been forced to immigrate to Zimbabwe from Malawi in search of work, but because he was underpaid and underemployed, he could not take his family back to his home in Malawi. To create cheap labour, white settler society ushered in hut taxes against the "natives" as a way of offsetting the costs of administering colonial governance in Southern Africa (Crush et al. 2005; Massey 1978; Mutwa 1969). The need to pay these colonial hut taxes disproportionately forced many Indigenous men to migrate as part of the cheap labour movement in Southern Africa. Disconnected by distance from the everyday labour of community parenting while being underpaid meant that most men could not return home or were too ashamed to face their communities due to their perceived failures of accumulating capitalistic colonial power (D.D. Mucina 2013; Mathabane 1986; Mutwa 1969). This left Indigenous African women disproportionately attending to familial survival and communal parenting, with very limited support from their male folks (Hill Collins 2002; Vera 1999). Indigenous feminist scholars have critically highlighted this phenomenon as the imposed intersections of sexism, racism, and capitalistic classism that colonialism uses to conquer, exploit, and oppress us as Indigenous peoples (Kuokkanen 2015; hooks 2004; Hill Collins 2002). Yet I should clearly state that, unlike most children in Zimbabwe, I was in the full care of my Baba (father) and I have very limited memories of my Amai (mother). I will say more about this reality in the letters to Amai and Baba.

Being in the care of Baba, who through forced colonial circumstances (having to pay the hut taxes) sold his labour as a neo-slave male (domestic worker), meant I rarely saw any Africans challenge compulsory white supremacy because their immigration status and employment opportunities were firmly controlled by white settlers (Vera 1992). All that I saw, for the most part, was the fear that led Blacks to be subservient to their powerful white masters. As a young Black Indigenous boy, it seemed to me there were only two choices: I could be like the emasculated Africans who appeared from my observation to be inferior to their white masters, or I could be like the whites who appeared from my observation to be superior to the Africans. For me it was straightforward, I chose the latter because I wanted the power of colonial masculinity, so that I could be as close as one could be to the cultural power of what bell hooks (2000) calls "white supremacist capitalist patriarchy" while embodying the binary opposite of whiteness. However, I soon learned from the school of colonialism that there was no choice for Africans; there was only the privileging of whiteness, which was protected by the colonial governance structure rooted in white supremacy, which in its services allowed a limited number of Africans to marginally enjoy some of the gains of capitalism within the patriarchal hierarchy of whiteness first, while expecting everyone to participate in patriarchy, but always regulating everyone through race and gender. Yet, strangely, their colonial power still enticed me even though I knew I would never be admitted as an equal into white settler colonial society. You see, colonialism had me believe that their second-best position, which I could aspire toward as long as I worked hard to reflect compulsory "white supremacist capitalist patriarchy," was better than anything Black society could offer me. I only became aware that what I was chasing was a bogus colonial illusion when I heard the white family that was going to take over my guardianship from the orphanage say to their white friends in their white club in Zimbabwe: "The poor bugger is like a white boy born into the worst misery of Blackness." Their white settler arrogance was reflective of the points being made by Frantz Fanon ([1952] 1967) in *Black Skin White Masks*.

The fact that they could have this discussion within earshot of me confirmed that they viewed their whiteness as a desired commodity, which they were sure I wanted. As it was, I was only allowed to stay with this white family on weekends and holidays because my social service worker had not completed the paperwork to put me legally in their care. The end of that first weekend saw me back in the orphanage but, because I was unsettled by their denigration of my Blackness, I ran away to my stepmother's colonially created reserve of Nyamapanda, which is located at the northeastern border of Zimbabwe and Mozambique. This reserve, like many other reserves in Southern Africa, was modelled after the First Nations reserves in Canada (Cook and Lindau 2000). Reserves were a way for white settler society to possess our lands by dispossessing us (Harvey 2005). As for their question on how to placate the threat that the dispossessed "natives" posed, their kith and kin had developed a white workable solution in Canada. The Canadian solution for dispossessing and disconnecting the "natives" of their lands was workable because white settler society could identify the "natives" through their colour, which differentiated them as non-white. This is why the solution was to put the "natives" on reserves. The immediate benefit of this solution was that it made it easier to control the "natives" while giving the illusion that white settlers were helping the "natives" become civilized (Cook and Lindau 2000).

In retrospect, I ran away to the reserve of Nyamapanda because I needed to have my Indigenous social Black identity nurtured and renewed. It was among these African relatives where we engaged in a process of communally renewing our Black spirit through ceremony and, from this social engagement, I knew what it was to have my Black Indigenous spirit restored. It was among these African relatives where we engaged in the process of communally speaking with our ancestors and, from this social engagement, I felt connected to the energy flux of Blackness (Mutwa 1964). It was among these African relatives where we engaged in the process of communally respecting our Black knowledge and, from this social engagement, I felt that I had power with Blackness instead of power over or against it. It was among these African relatives where we engaged in communal Black love instead of the sporadic individualistic love of white people, who for the most part, directed a sea of hate toward Blackness from their position of compulsory "white supremacist capitalist patriarchy." Now, let me honestly say that this social experience of Indigenous Ubuntu engagement has shaped and continues to shape my interactions with other people, because it is my strongest lived Ubuntu reference point and because it is grounded in love.

I am not saying that everyone in the Black Indigenous community loved me. However, I am pointing out that my Blackness among the Africans was a point of inclusion rather than a point of exclusion, as it is in white society. When I was ready to confront white society, I went back to the orphanage and contacted my social worker. I told her that I did not want the white family to become my legal guardians. As much as I was afraid of being alone and poor, I was not willing to allow my Blackness to be denigrated any further by my own internalizations or impositions of a compulsory "white supremacist capitalist patriarchy." This is not to say I never faltered again, but it was the start of my change process and, to this day, I am working toward making better everyday acts of resurgence by centring my energies on decolonizing all my relations through critical social justice love. This means I put the care of our people first while insuring that I mediate that care from a feminist critical social justice perspective.

Sanibonani Khumalo and Nandi, I tell you all this so that you do not fall for the same insidious trickery of colonialism. In my case, I chased the illusion of compulsory "white supremacist capitalist patriarchy," which used my Blackness to put me in a subordinate position. With no one to inform me that this was the greatest trick of dispossessing me of my Indigenous identity and cultural knowledge, I fell headlong into this trap. So I will ask you: Are you aware of the token illusions that colonialism is using to seduce you? Is it money, power, drugs, the knowledge of compulsory "white supremacist capitalist patriarchy,"[3] which is stolen from other people? Has anyone told you that the longest lasting universities were built in Africa? Check the *Guinness World Records 2018* (Guinness Publishing 2017), any encyclopaedia, or any credible source. Yet how many Black Indigenous people know this? Interestingly, all that we know of Africa are the images of misery and poverty. They tell you that Africa cannot support itself, but they neglect to let you know why. They do not talk about the scramble for Africa, both past and present. Who points out that the same corporate players who arrived so long ago are still searching for raw materials today? This does not exclude religious corporations, for they want to steal our souls and bodies. They gladly point out that we are killing each other by the millions, but nobody questions where the weapons come from. As so many are dying, how is it that the extraction of gold, diamonds, and oil has increased? How is it that, regardless of how severe the wars are in parts of Africa, companies that produce junk food, cigarettes, and drugs are still able to get their products to the African markets? From our misery, they make their profit. Know your whole history and you will find your whole truth, and let that guide your actions.

Sanibonani Khumalo and Nandi, do you see how the colonial system has tried to make you and me believe that Blackness is worthless? Do you see how white supremacy has tried to close us off to what is powerful about Blackness, while at the same time claiming our knowledges through its distortions and overemphasizing and overpublicizing what is weak about Blackness so you become embarrassed of identifying with your Blackness? Yet this distortion can only occur on the surface because you cannot have world history without Blackness. You cannot have humanity without Blackness. Do you see the contradictions? Do you see the insidious trickery? It is all designed to stop you from looking at the richness of Blackness. All designed to make you fear your Blackness. Do not let anyone (including me) give you a limited, false category of what Blackness is because Blackness embodies much more than I am considering in this short academic work.

Yes, my Ubuntu spirit has been weathered by colonialism, but I am still fighting the governance structures that legitimize white supremacy. As Indigenous resurgence picks up momentum globally, I am encouraged to continue regenerating our Ubuntu ways. My questions to you, Nandi and Khumalo, are, What stands out for you in this orature? What does this orature communicate? What does this orature teach you about fathering? Where do you see power and where do you see weakness? How are you ensuring that colonialism is not tricking you into slavery? Yes, Khumalo and Nandi, I am ready as your father to help you engage your Black Indigenous power, but let us ensure that we cross-reference what I teach you so that you get a fuller picture of our communal Ubuntu knowledge, while transcending my colonially imposed limitations. Learn from our successes as well as from our failures. Take all these experiences of Blackness from past and present and use them as a blueprint to regenerate yourself, to renew yourself and create a better future for you and the next generation. But, most importantly, remember that each experience of Blackness comes with social relational responsibilities to all things Ubuntu. Take this Black Indigenous knowledge respectfully and use it respectfully because it is sacred and because it connects you to your Black Indigenous ancestors. Do not fear to regenerate this knowledge because you are Kwaca (the freedom spirit of dawn, the start of a renewed Black spirit). You are the source. You are Blackness. The cycle of Ubuntu continues.

Your loving Baba,
Dr. Devi Dee Mucina Komba
(Komba is our totem, which is a galago)

Khumalo and Nandi, I beg your pardon as I now other-father (which is to care and nurture beyond biology) more inclusively our global Indigenous children. To you, the stars of our future: The colonial power structure of compulsory white supremacy has power over us if we accept its illusionary total power. The fragmenting and co-opting of our knowledge as its own is its total insidious power. This truth that I give to you will become a revolutionary force that you will feel and understand after you have analyzed your own oratures repeatedly in relation to the colonial facts and the experiences of other colonized bodies, using Ubuntu philosophy. In this revolutionary Ubuntu process, do not be surprised to meet the colonizer that dwells within you. The internal colonizer within you has a homegrown orientation (by this I mean, not all colonizing tendencies are external or foreign), which has been nurtured by a white supremacy foreign orientation. This means that to destroy this internal colonizer within us will require consistent conscious actions of decolonizing and social caring love as spiritual work (Okri 1997; Somâe 1994; p'Bitek 1984).

I know that decolonizing and social caring love as spiritual work can sound intangible. I know that when I started on this Ubuntu journey of relational physical and spiritual self-discovery, I too had become disconnected from my Ubuntu spiritual social self. As I studied how to remember our Ubuntu ways, I started to develop strategies for applying Ubuntu philosophical teachings to my everyday actions. Please note that the strategies that I share are only examples of what I did within my context and are by no means an imposition on you in any way. Before I started to commit myself to any important actions, I would question if my actions were motivated by social caring love and, if the answer was yes, I would seek out the evidence to prove this point. I would also question what the consequences of my actions were for all our people, including non-humans. Here are some questions I found helpful: Can I keep using these actions to sustain our total relational liberation? Would others perceive my actions as relationally caring? Could I conceive any of my actions as oppressive toward others?

As I said earlier, let me not mislead you, the actions of change are only achieved through the social self, which means performing relational actions grounded in respectful curiosity and social caring love. Each of us must attend to our own change while drawing strengths from the achievement of others and learning from the pitfalls of others. The social path that we must walk with courage awaits us. If you should fall down on this path as I have, please get up and continue the journey because your actions inspire my actions. In this letter, I have tried to highlight the power of Indigenous Blackness from a relational responsible position while also highlighting the complexity of the external colonizer and the internal colonizer (Fanon [1952] 1967). The sharing of my analysis is not meant, by any means, to reflect the correct way to analyze this orature; I only give one of many possible analyses. The more important analysis is the one you make, because it will reflect your contextual position and learning. What you take and do not take from this orature speaks to your needs as reflected by your political social context.

As your caring and loving other-father, brother, grandfather, and possible son, I challenge you from a position of respectful curiosity to reflect on the political social structure that gives you the base of interpreting meaning. Whose political social structure of interpreting shared meaning are you using? How does the historical foundation of this contextual political social interpretation of meaning impact your power to create shared philosophical engagements of meaning? The answers you generate from this section are important for motivating you to create social actions of love. Later, we will discuss more succinctly Ubuntu social actions of emancipation, but for now let us proceed to provide an orientation for understanding the overall structure of how to think about accountability and responsibility for the Ubuntu oratures that we share. Each Ubuntu teaching, like each drum, sets its own tone but, like a drum, each teaching must communicate with other teachings.

Why do you think I am sharing this Ubuntu orature with you?

What makes this Ubuntu engagement decolonizing?

What makes Ubuntu orature life-affirming actions?

Figure 3. After harvest, the food-processing period begins, and it is during this period that the older generation while working with the younger generations begins sharing and transmitting ancestral knowledge. In this photograph, my Dadakazi (female father) is shelling peanuts with her grandson while Baba relaxes. Both Dadakazi and Baba are transmitting Ubuntu ancestral knowledge through orature. At the end of the peanut shelling, Dadakazi says: "It feels good to have the young interested in us once more."

Ubuntu Oratures and Relational Accountability

Methodological questions that guided my writing of this Millet Granary:

1. *Who am I responsible and accountable to?*
2. *Why do Ubuntu oratures matter in a world dominated by colonial structures?*
3. *Can I speak about relational accountability when my familial and communal structures are fragmented and broken?*

Sanibonani Nandi and Khumalo,

In this Millet Granary, my major goal is to highlight how Ubuntu orature is guided by relational responsibility and accountability. My orature is nested in my family, which is nested in our community, which is nested in our Maseko Ngoni Inkatha (unity of nationhood), which is nested in Southern Africa among the Nguni[1] and is one micro-orature of a larger macro-orature about Ubuntu families that have been stolen from Africa, fractured into fragmentation and exiled across the globe by colonialism. As I analyze my (our) oratures I engage you, the reader, in a conflict of interpretation about Ubuntu identity, belonging, ethnic boundaries versus colonial borders, and knowledges. I am hopeful that in our rivalled interpretations about what constitutes Ubuntu we will see beyond our own imposed limitations by entering the larger dialogues of Ubuntu. This being said, I also hope to be critical of the shortcomings and misuses of Ubuntu in addressing some of our contemporary realities. If Ubuntu is Indigenous African knowledge, then it is our responsibility to be accountable to how we take up Ubuntu. This means in my usage of Ubuntu as a philosophic worldview, which helps me to live a better-informed life, I am responsible and accountable to the Ubuntu structures through my relational responsibilities to my families, our communities, our nations, and our global relations.

My Location Represents My Relational Responsibilities

When I was in Swaziland trying to acquire information about our history as Ngoni, using my family name, an older one made me share my family history for over an hour before he would acknowledge being a Masina. The older one told me that, before he could share any information with me, he needed to know the familial and communal structure to hold me accountable for any information that I misused. Being that most of my family is in Zimbabwe, Malawi, and Mozambique, the older one had no way of confirming my accountability structure at that moment. He therefore decided to disclose only

Figure 4. Meeting some of my paternal family members in Mozambique. We did not know of each other's existence until this meeting. This family reunion is a first step in healing and changing beyond the actions of colonial fragmentation. The next step for us is to break the silence that keeps us separated as a family.

a certain amount of information while at the same time agreeing to accept me as a part of his family. This older one agreed that as our family bonds grew, he would disclose, at some point in the future, his Swazi names and other ancestral knowledges. Unfortunately, before this older one could share any more information with me, he crossed over to the ancestral spiritual world, but his family and I have remained close. This example illustrates how Ubuntu hold each other accountable in the ways that we use traditional Ubuntu information. Through what I make public, I am first accountable to my family, and my family and I are accountable to our communities. This Indigenous Ubuntu structure holds me accountable and responsible through my relational connections. This means that these relationships have power over my actions, but, again, I do not want to create a binary and give the impression that I would act unethically in order to maintain a relationship. All Ubuntu relationships are bound by reciprocal responsible accountability (Archibald/Q'um Q'um Xiiem 2008). Thus, to be Ubuntu is to be open to honest and respectful criticism.

I also locate myself in my writing as a way of respecting other African knowledges that are different from the ones that I have acquired from our communities. My contextual knowledge reflects my nested multiple identities and lived experiences as an Ubuntu, of Maseko Ngoni and Chewa, with Shona maternal familial lineage and having an animal totem of Komba (galago), which intersect and interlock to give me voice here (Canada) while talking about there (Southern Africa). My Indigenous insider voice embodies a lived intersectional identity (Hill Collins and Bilge 2016; Crenshaw 1991), which has been expanded through my living and engaging with other Indigenous peoples of Turtle Island. I was raised within Ngoni/Chewa and Shona culture, have parentage from these ethnic communities, which share a oneness through their common ancestral Ubuntu roots. I have also lived in these Ubuntu communities and travelled to other Ubuntu places as a way of connecting with some of our lands. Yet I am also limited by the fact that I did not grow up in my traditional paternal family under the inkatha (strength of working in unity or, arguably, nationhood) of the Maseko Ngoni in Lizwe la Lizulu (the Land of the Zulu, located on the border between Malawi and Mozambique and within the territory of the Chewa people).

I was raised in Zimbabwe under my Mashona maternal family, but when I was between three and four years old, the strategies of white supremacy as embodied by the structures of colonial capitalism had induced unimaginable poverty in Southern Africa through land theft, forced resettlement programs using the native reserve system, and the impositions of the hut tax. All of these colonial tactics of dispossession were meant to undermine native resistance while creating a cheap labour force for their industrial development (D.D. Mucina 2013; Richter and Morrell 2006; Mathabane 1986). From about four years on, I remember living with Baba on the streets of Harare at times. I can also remember living in poor Black townships with families that were kind enough to take me in. When Baba did secure employment, I had to be hidden in the servants' quarters as African families were not allowed in white neighbourhoods. This was my reality until I was found living on the streets of Harare by social services and placed into an orphanage at nine years old. Hence, my formative years were spent on the streets of Harare as a beggar, and my teen years were spent in an orphanage. These experiences at times made me feel like a cultural outsider to familial and communal life in Zimbabwe while my experience of homelessness and poverty made me a cultural insider to the experience of colonial fragmentation and dispossession.

As silent as Baba was about many aspects of his past, he did share important information about Lizwe la Lizulu, which helped me feel and know that I belonged to the Maseko Ngoni who had intermarried with the Chewa. However, when I arrived in Lizwe la Lizulu, commonly referred to as Lizulu, a certain amount of my outsiderness was exposed because I lacked the knowledge of certain common cultural practices. It would therefore seem that my insider voice was limited by my contextual experience. Even Baba made it clear that my experience in Canada would affect how I would be seen in relation to my family members in Lizulu. For starters, everyone was a little more understanding of my poor Chewa language skills, as I integrated very poorly three Indigenous languages into a single conversation. There were many cultural practices that I struggled to remember then and still struggle with today. I share this information with you so that you understand that making mistakes is common for me. For example, when I went to the burial site where Baba's remains are, I did not know how to begin the process of acknowledging and putting to rest my dead Baba, as I had never experienced this among our family because I was born away from my community and family. This is why you must not be fooled by my writing, because I am no expert, I am part of the fragmented body of people trying to reconnect using fragmented bits of knowledges.

In trying to understand the meanings of my names, I have come to appreciate the power of naming people, things, actions, and the unknown as a structure for conveying relational responsibility and accountability among and between the Ngoni and Chewa. The act of naming is a powerful sacred endeavour for us as Ubuntu. This means that the renaming and changing of our Ubuntu

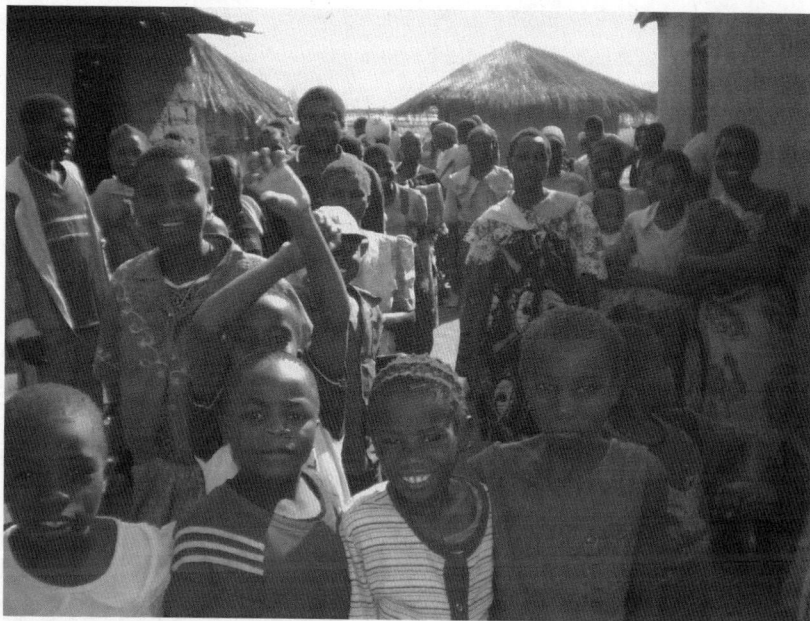

Figure 5. All of these people are my paternal family members living in Mozambique, and every single one of them is connected to me by blood and by the totem name, Komba. Until this meeting, none of these family members existed for me. All I had was the name Komba from Baba's oratures.

worldsense by colonizers was a tactical colonial strategy for dispossessing and fragmenting us from our relational knowledge production. Interestingly, Tengan, in *Native Men Remade: Gender and Nation in Contemporary Hawai'i*, speaks to the point of how we were forced to abandon our naming of sacred power. Yet we can still see the resistance of our ancestors to colonial naming by the survival of our clan names, totem names, and inkatha names (unity and strength of nationhood), which they adapted into surnames and first names within the colonial structures (Vera 1992). These survival strategies highlight the political nature of naming the sacred outside the traditional dialoguing ceremonies, which brought families and communities together. An example of this is reflected in the surname that I use. At our family reunion, my surname sparked conflict. Baba's sister, whom I address as Dadakazi, which means female father and implies that masculinity among the Ngoni in specific contextual settings goes beyond biological categories of sex, said to me: "The name you are using is not our family name. Ask your Baba where this name comes from." I do not think I would be wrong if I stated that Dadakazi's statement showed a high level of antagonistic challenge toward Baba, because when a child has a maternal name, it is a sign of relational breakdown between the maternal family and the paternal family. This could be because no relationship exists between the families or it could be a form of protest by the maternal family because the paternal family has not paid the bridal price.

Dadakazi can carry her paternal name but can never pass it on to her children and grandchildren, as they are the gifts to their paternal family by their maternal family and therefore must carry their paternal names. I think this was because of a traditional patriarchal practice, which prescribed that Dadakazi's family name be carried forward by me. Yet, here I was, with a maternal name of Mucina, which had no connection to Dadakazi. From this perspective, I can understand Dadakazi's sense of erasure, for here we were, post-independence, and still the legacy of colonial contact continued to fragment us (Hill Collins and Bilge 2016; Vera 1992). However, I was taken off guard by the tone of her resentful and scornful questioning of Baba, when she asked: "Do we change our names like clothes?" To this challenging question, Baba remained uncomfortably quiet. Baba's lack of response made me remember the tactical silence that he employed with his white masters to ensure the conflict ended without him losing his job. Why was Baba not justifying his break from tradition, why was he not reminding her that his own father had abandoned him to her mother's care when his mother died, while he was still an infant? Why was he not reminding her that her mother had mistreated him because he was the heir to his father's fortune and he had not come from her womb? Why did he not point out that the people who possess this name had tried to kill him?

As I reflect on this moment now, I am aware of how little I knew my Baba. All my memories of him and reference points are embedded in him fighting to survive in a colonial compulsory white supremacy governance structure, which did not value his humanity beyond the usefulness of his easily disposable cheap labour. I should also mention that my reference points coincide with the time he had custody of me between 1976 and 1981. So, in a flash, I was questioning myself: Was Baba using his old tactics in this familial conflict? I felt uncomfortable because I did not know how to react in this familial situation. Seeing that Baba had been cornered into giving a response, I started to talk about something else so that Baba would not have to be forced to explain himself. So much was left unsaid in that conflict, and to this day I am left with many questions. I am sure Dadakazi knew what I was doing because she followed my lead and started to engage me in the new conversation I had started. This naming conflict highlights the importance of names in my family, but I would argue that naming is a challenging endeavour for all humans.

Shakespeare's *Romeo and Juliet* echoes this human desire of naming as a way of giving meaning, but a challenge is raised when Juliet questions Romeo: "What's in a name?" (Shakespeare, Craig, and Dowden 1912, 325). To this question I would answer—nothing and everything. Nothing because without the name I still am, but on the other hand, I am everything because it is a social marker that connects me to a relational familial social network. Ubuntu names are sacred because they tell a story about something. To honour the meaning of a name, we engage in a dialectical dialogue before giving the name because this ensures a common shared meaning. This means among my people, the Maseko Ngoni and Chewa, the appearance of my names shows how I am first and foremost accountable to my family members and ancestral spirits, which also include all of our lands. Second, I am accountable to our communities (going beyond humans to include all other beings in the web of life) as what I say is a reflection of our relational ties, which are born of our social interaction. Third, I am accountable to Kanjedza Inkosi ya Maskosi Gomani IV, who is the Paramount King of all Maseko Ngoni from Lizwe la Zulu. In an izibongo (praise) by Enoch Timpunza Mvula and Chikumbutso Mkwamba Ngozo (2008), we see how Kanjedza Inkosi ya Makosi Gomani IV's name connects him to his history and to his ancestors:

> Hail! Inkosi ya Makosi Gomani IV.... You are the son of Willard Bvalani Nkhwende Kwacha Phillip Gomani, The defender of independence and freedom, Conqueror of the Federation of Rhodesia and Nyasaland; Willard Gomani, the son of Zitonga Phillip Gomani, Zitonga Phillip Gomani chaser of British colonialists With his spears and knobkerries. Zitonga Phillip Gomani, the son of Gomani Chikuse. Chikuse, the collector of men and cattle, When the victims cried war, he thundered on them, The cattle he had already taken, The people he had already taken. Chikuse the son of Mputa, Mputa, he who appeared to the waters of the Zambezi, Then crossed the Zambezi and settled at Domwe. Mputa, the aggressor and the lightning, The lightning that struck on all tribes along its path to Songea, Songea land of the Matengo, the Ambo, and the Mtumba. He who took away their spears and shields, He whose ashes were thrown into a river in Songea. Kanjedza Gomani, our lion and king, You are indeed the descendant of Mputa, Mputa, the son of Ngcamane Maseko; Ngcamane Maseko, the son of Nsele Maseko, Nsele Maseko, the son of Luhleko Maseko I, Luhleko Maseko I, the

son of Ntshangase Maseko, Ntshangase Maseko, the son of Mafu
Maseko, Mafu Maseko, the son of Sidwabasiluthuli Maseko,
Sidwabasiluthuli Maseko, the son of Maseko Khubonye Ndlovu,
Maseko Khubonye Ndhlovu, the son of Ndlovu Ntu, Ndlovu Ntu,
founder of the Ngunis....Maseko, when the white ones killed our
Inkosi ya Makosi, The colonialists thought the sun had set for us
at Chiole, But Maseko, God in heaven, the creator of all things,
the great spirit, Made the sun rise at Lizulu, Lizulu, land of the
Zulus. Let us go, Maseko, let us go! Let us go home! They asked
him, "Ngcamane, where are we off to?" He said, "We are going
where people never die, There people are killed with age, There
people eat meat and drink milk, There people do not grow thin,
There beautiful and polite women are abundant." Let us go to
Lizulu. Hail! Your Majesty! Hail! Our lion! Hail! Our hero and
Chief of chiefs! (9–10)

This izibongo highlights how an Ubuntu name communicates to us a person's
rights and responsibilities. Even with the fragmentation of my names and
the adoptions of new ones, all my names hold me accountable to communal
responsibilities to my Shona, Ngoni, and Chewa families. My names also
convey my Baba's colonially induced disconnection from his paternal family
through colonially imposed hut taxes, in order to create labour migration to
settler industrial centres within Southern Africa (Crush et al. 2005; Massey
1978; Mutwa 1969). In Zimbabwe, white supremacy and its governing structures fragmented my connections to my maternal family by creating poverty
because of colonial land theft (Meredith 1979). Regardless of all this colonial
interruption and fragmentation, my familial responsibilities are reflected in
my names, which are Devi David Peter Dee Mucina Komba. In my naming
orature, there are gaps of silence that have been given to me by my Baba and
by my maternal family. So here I give you the fragments as they have come to
my awareness from my memory and from my familial sources.

When I was about three or four years old, my maternal family asked my
Baba to come and take me because they could not care for me on the reserve of
Chendambuya in the district of Makoni. It is under these circumstances that
I hold my first memory of being aware of my Baba and the name Devi that he
used to hold me accountable for my actions. David is the intended name my
Baba wanted me to have, but it seemed no one in our community was willing
to call me by this name. Instead, they Africanized it to Devi but, when I was
young, I maintained the use of David when engaging with white settler society.

Peter is the name given to me by my maternal family in Zimbabwe where I was born. My maternal family named me Peter because my paternal family, who were meant to organize my naming ceremony as dictated by Ubuntu tradition, were not a part of this orature. As to why my paternal family was not a part of this important ritual, there is colonially created silence, which causes us pain, but as we lovingly work through this pain, we can name it and begin to let it go as we have given witness to how it has affected us.

It is only by learning history and researching it that I have come to understand that colonially imposed hut taxes and land dispossession were the two major factors responsible for Ubuntu family disintegration all because white settler society wanted to create cheap labour forces in settler industrial centres within Southern Africa (Crush et al. 2005; Massey 1978; Mutwa 1969). To give witness to this experience is to acknowledge that we have learned something from this horrific colonial experience.

My Ambuya (maternal grandmother) once told me that, in the absence of my Baba, I was the only reflective shadow left that still reminded them that he had ever been present among them. After my Ambuya shared these words with me, she was silent; her silence was heavy because on her tongue sat heavy words that she was not willing to share with a child. As an adult, I have interpreted Ambuya's silence as an effort to protect me from the harsh realities of colonialism. What I find interesting is that, as I reflect on my Ambuya's words and tone, I sense that she viewed herself and her family as victims of colonialism while viewing Baba as an associate of colonialism. My maternal family believed that Baba was being rewarded by colonialism in the white spaces that he worked in while they starved and suffered. Baba, on the other hand, believed the colonial lies that the white settlers' media propagated about how well they took care of Africans on reserves. Such colonial trickery induced silence about how colonialism fragmented our Indigenous institutions. Our Ubuntu families are the foundations of all Indigenous Ubuntu institutions. Colonial forces past and current continue their efforts to break or fragment our families, yet we still resist and struggle to find our voices, because we know that we must speak our truths as blueprints for inspiring future Ubuntu social actions of liberation beyond colonial mimicry.

The exploitive power of colonialism is that it keeps trying to break our Ubuntu families, while simultaneously on the margins it allows us to reflect on our social actions within the framework of its own memory. This means, we never question how colonialism triggered our total silence even though now and again we remember how colonialism used its insidious power to silence us. Baba demonstrated this when he conveyed to me that in Zimbabwe the demand of maintaining a neo-slave job in a white community not only kept him away from his young family but also did not pay him enough to survive comfortably. Afraid of losing his job, Baba missed my naming ceremony and, not knowing what to do after the naming period had lapsed, my maternal family started calling me by Baba's name, Peter, as a way of naming the unnamed one. Interestingly, when I lived with my Baba in the absence of my maternal family, he too would tell me (especially when he was angry at my behaviours) that I was the embodied visual representation of my maternal family. In this family fragmentation, created by colonially induced silence, the name Peter connects me to my maternal family, whose family totem is Mojuru, which means termite. I also want to acknowledge that as much as I engaged directly with maternal family members who are implicated directly in these oratures, I am also still aware that what I write and say here will affect some of those maternal relatives, whom I have not had direct contact with. I have tried to tell the truth from my contextual position, but this is not your orature and therefore not your whole truths. It is my hope that my contextual truths convey to you some form of your fragmented historical truths, even if they are uncomfortable to deal with, I also hope that you see these oratures as a call to relational loving dialogue, I am because you are.

Baba's name of Mucina marked him as a visitor to Zimbabwe, which meant he did not feel entitled to establish a home in Zimbabwe. Yet Baba also did not even attempt to invest in building a home in Lizulu, because after the death of his mother, Falacon,[2] in 1938, he was threatened with death by members of his extended family. Dadakazi (female father) is the first to break the silence about this family tragedy in support of the orature Baba shared with me about why he left his family. Dadakazi conveys that Baba rightfully stayed away as the only option for preserving his life. Baba informed me that my clan name, Mucina, came from his junior mother, Amanat. At first, I thought she was the younger sister of Falacon, Baba's birth mother, but Dadakazi says she does not know where the name Mucina came from. A few days before we left Zimbabwe for Malawi, Baba had this to say about the Mucina clan name:

> My junior mother told me to take her clan name of Mucina and make it my own. My younger brother was given the clan name of Komba and I as the elder child was given the name of my junior mother because she did not have any children and she wanted to ensure that her clan name was used beyond her by ensuring that

Figure 6. A few members of my maternal family, who live in Zimbabwe. Even though I was born among them in Zimbabwe, I know very little about them and they are even more silent than Baba about our separation.

a family male had this clan name. Let me also say that my mother did not die of natural causes and the family members that were responsible caused me a great deal of suffering. This is why I was reluctant about going back to Malawi but, after some reflection, I know these people are long dead. I am also worried that if I leave Zimbabwe I will lose contact with my children. (Baba, personal communication, 6 August 2008)

Let me start by responding to Baba's last point. Baba states that one of his fears about leaving Zimbabwe is that he will lose contact with his children. I understand his fear from a Ngoni and a Shona cultural perspective, which conveys that if a man has not paid the bride price for a woman then, in the eyes of these two communities, that woman and that man are not married. Children from this co-habitation belong only to the woman, and the man has no rights in relation to these children. These children cannot be given the father's clan name and are only allowed to have the mother's clan name. Regardless of age or the wishes of these children, they are strongly encouraged to stay with the mother's family until the bride price is paid. The general message here is that if the paternal family wants children to carry their names from one generation to another then they must thank the maternal family and the woman for this right. In our Ubuntu cultural case, this is done through the bride price. It is hoped that the bride price is set within the means of the paternal family, which is reflective of the Ubuntu relational spirit. Baba never introduced himself to the family of his children when his new wife was alive, and I cannot imagine how he would have approached the issues of bride price for a woman who had gone to the ancestor world. The process of asking for a bride price across cultural difference is hard enough without adding crossing over into the realm of the living dead. This explanation does not begin to address, however, the fact that Baba had no resources for starting this process.

Before Baba went to the ancestor world, he received the news that Lee, my brother from his new younger wife, had died. This news hit Baba especially hard, as he felt that all the families that he had started were always being fragmented by the colonial capitalistic power structure, which took so much from Indigenous peoples and gave nothing back in return. Here I am specifically thinking of the fact that they took on the lands and our labour, and in return we have gotten an education on how to become an imitation of white settler society, but even white settler society rejects our imitation of white supremacy (hooks 2004). Notions of reciprocal relationships in the colonial capitalistic power structure are counterproductive to its aims. Our ways and our families are always being disregarded as primitive in colonial ventures of accumulation of capitalistic wealth. White supremacy views our participation in its colonial structure as an invitation to disembody us from our Indigenous knowledge. To counter such colonial behaviours, we need to responsibly decolonize and practise our Indigenous ways. Centring our Indigenous ways is an act of creating healthy resistance that does not create colonial toxicity while nurturing all our relational spiritual bonds with all elements (Green 2017).

The other part of Baba's orature shows how a problem can change cultural practices and, therefore, perhaps, change is the only constant. Baba took his junior mother's clan name (it is not common for Ngoni children to take the name of their mother) in an effort to ensure that this name among the paternal family was not lost. It is also possible that Baba took the Mucina clan name because he felt stripped of the dignity of his family name when family members threatened to kill him over his inheritance. It is under this mystery that I share the surname of Mucina with Baba. Either way, through this name change, Baba was able to distance himself from the shameful acts that were associated with his family name in Lizulu. This, to me, conveys clearly that among the Ubuntu, when a name becomes associated with shameful acts, family members try to disassociate themselves from the stained name because, as Baba told me many times, "A name tainted is a name forever lost." This is how our family cohesion crumbled. Still, honourable individuals can transcend a tainted family name through the collective will of the community to immortalize such individuals. For example, Baba has never let me forget our clan totem name of Komba, which connects me to the spirits of my paternal communities beyond our family name. Also, my grandfather's name of Dee has special significance to me; when I pray to my ancestors, I see him as a conduit that directs my prayers to the great spirits of my Seano (totem) of Komba[3] (bush baby).

Other important spiritual ancestors for me are Gogo (Grandmother) Falacon Mlangeni, she gave birth to my Baba but died shortly after his birth. She comes from a line of fierce warrior Ngoni Queens (Phiri 1973). She watches over me, she gives me strength and counsel when I need them. I am because she is. Gogo Amanat Mucina is another important spiritual ancestor, and it is my sense that our ancestral and familial bonds are deeper than was communicated to me. Baba addresses her as mother. Without asking Baba, I changed my surname from Dee (my grandfather's name) to the praise name that Baba used to honour me, Mucina (Gogo Amanat's name). I will admit that, in the beginning, this change was hard for folks from my paternal family but, after having their questions answered about the name change, these family members became more comfortable addressing me as either Komba or Mucina. This also shows that names are not static and can be changed. Whether we welcome it or not, change is coming. At times, change seems to be taking us away from our traditions when, in fact, it is taking us toward our traditions, and when we are comfortable in traditions, change quietly lets us drift away from traditions. This is one of those puzzling mysteries of life (Okri 1997).

My names reflect where I have been and who I have been in connection with, but for Baba, when his name marked him for forced erasure, that name became nothing. Such a name I will allow to remain silent, too much has fragmented us. It is time to focus on that which unites us. Yet, when Baba took me to our village, it was our family name that connected us to the family I never knew I had. It was a name that gave me new familial relations in Swaziland. The power of a name is sacred when all is as it should be, but in our relational political colonial world, for the most part, a name is a peculiar thing that reflects tensions and connections. Sankofa, Sankofa, Sankofa, I am going back to reclaim my past before the great Maafa.[4] Most things that need to be located have now been located. In the next Millet Granary, I will engage

Figure 7. My Dadakazi (female father), whose leadership is helping me understand some of the silences in our paternal family. Dadakazi, your Ubuntu spirit inspires me, thank you Indovukazi (great female elephant).

my Amai (mother) as truthfully as I can. As I write to Amai, I am motivated by love, which has been gained by confronting colonially created fears of abandonment, isolation, and false notions of manhood embedded in colonial toxic masculinities (Tengan 2008). My motivation for sharing is grounded in creating familial relational pathways to each other and not in creating academic trickery, which furthers colonial goals.

How are you accountable to your words?

Who is silenced by our relational Ubuntu accountability structure?

Is relational accountability among the Ubuntu only determined by blood ties?

A Letter Across Many Borders to Amai

Methodological questions that guided my writing of this Millet Granary:

1. *How do I open myself up as an Ubuntu man to the realities of Ubuntu women?*

2. *How do I honour my Amai's courage and bravery and hold the hurt and isolation?*

3. *How do I use relational Ubuntu philosophy to engage questions of gender equity and social justice?*

4. *How do I express a hurtful thank you to my Amai?*

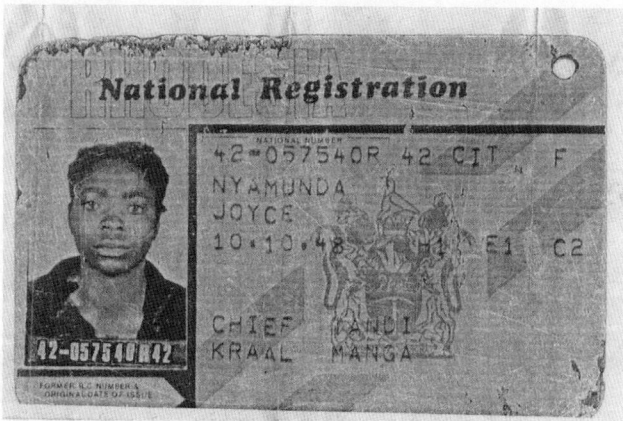

Figure 8. This national registration card is the only photograph I have of my Amai.

Sanibonani Amai,

In my search to find my way

I cause you endless troubles

As I ask you to hear this challenge

Answer this inquiry

All the while expecting unconditional love from you

Yet there is no love for you

My mischief does not let you rest peacefully

But today I will try to open myself to hearing from you

Because I am starting to understand that your act of abandoning me

Was an act of painful courageous love

This kind of love can only be seen in retrospect.

Amai, during a discussion with Njoki Wane, an Indigenous African feminist scholar, she mentioned that the Ubuntu family is one of the basic foundational units that makes up the Ubuntu governance structure. Wane communicated to me that the health of the Ubuntu family is reflective of the health of Ubuntu governance. As I reflected on those words, I was struck by how colonialism had fragmented our family and, in so doing, had undermined the health of our family. My family orature is of the Ubuntu reality, but it does not and cannot capture the whole Ubuntu experience with colonialism. Yet it does tell you how colonialism has fragmented my family and that conveys a reality shared by many Ubuntu communities, which, by extension, is a reflection of how colonialism has fragmented Ubuntu governance on a macro level. As a social being, I share my political reality as a way of reaching out further to our larger Black Indigenous community because my orature is one of their oratures, which reaches out to them in a sharing manner.

Ubuntu theory and Indigenous African feminism, like other theories that seek to communicate the human experience truthfully, have at times created tensions for me between the oratures I knew about you, Amai, when I was a child and the ways I am learning to discover you as an adult. For me, it is this experience of living in these tensions of colonialism, Ubuntuism, and Indigenous African feminism that has caused me to be reflective of how I am living in our social world. In an effort to honour and communicate with you, I write this orature to you. Yet, through this letter, I struggle to speak to you because of the pain. I am writing to the invisible you while reflecting on the past visible you that was never there to comfort me in the nightmare created by white supremacy. I am not sure this is fair, but I do this in the hope of making us a happier and a less nervous people. Truthfully, Amai, I write this letter as a way of speaking to you beyond fragmentation. To be respectful of you while also being mindful of my positionality as an Indigenous Black male, I use Indigenous African feminism to try to help me centre your positionality as an African Indigenous woman (Wane 2009; Crenshaw 1991). In her novel orature, titled *The Joys of Motherhood*, Buchi Emecheta (1979) has this to say through one of the characters, "They are all slaves, including us. If their masters treat them badly, they take it out on us. The only difference is that they are given some pay for their work, instead of having been bought" (51).

Bought like meat, my Amai (mother); it is not a thought that I have ever seriously considered, but when scholars have made comparisons between bride price and buying of people, I have always scoffed at their ignorance of Indigenous traditions. But it is possible that my African male privilege and context kept me from seriously exploring how traditions like bride price, in the context of material capitalism, has led to the exploitation of women's bodies (Hill Collins and Bilge 2016; Vera 1992; Crenshaw 1991). As a man, I have never had to contemplate the threat of being married. The thought of being forced into marriage because of monetary gain is inconceivable to me. But if you speak about marrying someone in order to escape poverty, my Black African male ears hear you very well. In Amai's silence, the quote from Emecheta's story has left me questioning, was my Amai bought against her will? Could such a happening explain her actions of allowing my maternal family to give custody of me to my Baba, especially when the orature by Yvonne Vera (1992) in *Why Don't You Carve Other Animals* communicates the following about the experience of Zimbabwean women:

> There are so many women with no husbands but with a lot of chil-
> dren. I do not want to be one of them. The country is in a state of
> confusion. Who knows what the rules are anymore? Who knows
> what to do? Who knows what is really important? We only know
> our loss and our fear and our silence. We know we are women asked
> to bear children. We know that to bear children will bring us suf-
> fering. This land must be watered with the blood of our children
> and with the saltiness of our tears before we can call it our own.
> What shall I tell my child about his father who is absent? (44)

When I first read those lines, it was as if a traumatic fragmented memory had been given back to me. I cried because I knew those women's pain; I had been the child in their arms; I knew their fear because it was my fear; I knew their desperation because it was my desperation. Amai, you let me go adrift, believing that any other place was better than the colonial context that you faced. I survived because of your brave actions, which I know I could not take with my own children and never have to because you did it for me. I am learning through Ubuntu spirituality and through other scholarship that you are in me as I once was in you (Cixous 1998). We share a painful fragmented love. As I open my heart to African feminism, I know you in a broader context. Albeit in spirit, I am coming home to you, and I want you to know your grandchildren, Khumalo and Nandi, and your daughter-in-law, Mandeep. We have survived and we are now focusing on ways of thriving and regenerating beyond an imposed white supremacy colonial reality.

Sanibonani Amai (1948–2003),

I open my mouth to speak to you but my throat is dry

My stomach is cramping up, my head is throbbing with pain

Yet my sweat is icy cold

What is this obnoxious smell that I emit?

Could it be fear?

Could it be frustration?

Could it be love?

Could it be hate?

I pick up the pen to write to you

I remember that I am dyslexic

I set up my laptop

But I cannot abandon the pen

It is the security officer of that which is in my head

So I dictate when I cannot get the brain and the pen to
co-ordinate

But right now I cannot get to the problem because my throat
hurts

My stomach is cramping up

My head is pounding away

And

My armpits are trickling with icy cold sweat

And yes, I am unsettled by my own smell

But There Is So Much To Say.

Yet I cannot start with my own words, so I will start with the words of the Indigenous African feminist scholar Kuwee Kumsaa:

> Oh, the flesh of your flesh and the blood of your blood is yearning for you. The splinter of your bone is craving for reunion, Aayyolee. Like when I was a child, I'm hungering for the caresses of your hands and thirsting for the whispers of your love. I long for you like one in darkness longs for daylight. I crave you like a starved body craves food. I long for the sight of you like a thirsty person in the Sahara longs for the sight of an oasis. I reach out for you but this cold winter grips me harshly. And my heart bleeds. Yes, my heart bleeds, Aayyolee too! Why should this ugly hateful curtain of mist drop between us? Why should this eternal-looking darkness swallow us? When will this enveloping and choking night dissolve away? When will we rejoice in that magical togetherness and be lost in our familiar bliss once again? (Kuwee Kumsaa 1994, 23–24)

Amai, let us thank our dear sister Kuwee Kumsaa because she has given me the motivating energy to articulate the start of this letter and, as you know, the start of generating the directional path of any dialogue is always the hardest part. Now that sister Kuwee Kumsaa has opened the way, let me continue.

The earliest image that I have of you, I have learned is not of you. I was telling Maiguru (your older sister) that I have a memory of you carrying me on your back in a shawl towel. I am looking at the back of your head and I am amazed by the beauty of your Black hair that is braided in cornrows. The contrast of the pink and white dress on your beautiful Black skin is mesmerizing. As I am telling this orature, I noticed that Maiguru and Sisi (sister who is the daughter of Maiguru) exchange a knowing look. I ask if something is incorrect and Maiguru tells me that the image I have described is not of you. It is of Sisi, who cared for me, as is the traditional Shona way. Njoki Wane (2000), in her work titled "Reflections on the Mutuality of Mothering: Women, Children, and Other-mothering," talks about how other women (and men in some situations) care for children in our communities. She makes it clear that mothering is more than the biological act of creating a child and it is more than the gender roles society prescribes. Wane informs us that "our mothers, aunties, sisters and community mothers carried us on their backs" (108), and this community mothering she calls other-mothering. Meaning, we are all responsible to mother beyond our own biological children. Wane (2000) has put it thus: "Within African communities, mothering is not necessarily based on biological ties. Established African philosophy suggests that children do not solely belong to their biological parents, but to the community at large. This philosophy and tradition inform what we refer to as 'other-mothering' and 'community mothering.' Significantly, even in the face of Western conceptions of mothering, which often view community-mothering practice as deviant and negligent, African understandings of mothering continue to thrive. Throughout the African Diaspora, Black women care for one another and one another's children regardless of their cultural backgrounds" (112). This scholarship highlights my experiences of being at times other-mothered across racial lines, which again exemplifies the contradictions that exist in our racist contemporary Canadian society. Just when I am comfortable seeing the racism of compulsory white supremacy, very small and at times large individual acts challenge me to have hope. How can I be silent about the many white women who have other-mothered and at times exposed me to racist micro-aggressions? I guess I could say that slowly the racist white world is changing; in 2008, my Baba reminded me that his experience of compulsory able-bodied whiteness was not the same as mine. Baba's point has implications for mothering in the Canadian African diaspora. Again, I return us to Wane's work on other-mothering. She informs us, in the Canadian context that, "although I focus on Black women who mother children and one another, such practices exist beyond gender and racial boundaries. It is not unusual to find young boys mothering their younger siblings and uncles and fathers mothering their nieces and/or nephews. My mothering experiences in Toronto have also shown that women from different racial backgrounds may step in as other-mothers or community other-mothers" (12). I have used Wane's scholarship to shed light on the nuance of mothering and other-mothering in the African context. Yet this truth does not erase or ease my pain and disappointment of learning that I have no memory of you. I have nothing that connects me to you in a way that is born of my memory. For the longest time I blamed you for this erasure. How was I to know that this was the insidious trickery of colonialism that fragmented our family and then pitted us against each other (Fanon [1952] 1967)?

All this was achieved through the harshest, most humiliating manner to ensure that we draw less and less from our past Indigenous memories. Albert Memmi asserts that the colonial reality makes it seem like we, the Indigenous people, are doomed to lose our memories because our "memory is not purely a mental phenomenon. Just as the memory of an individual is the fruit of his history and psychology, that of a people rests upon its institutions. Now the colonized's institutions are dead or petrified. He scarcely believes in those which continue to show some signs of life and daily confirms their ineffectiveness. He often becomes ashamed of these institutions, as of a ridiculous and overaged monument" (Memmi 1965, 103). Amai, in my bid to be accepted in the white supremacy structures of governance, I was ashamed of our Indigenous ways and I was ashamed of you. I hope you will forgive me for not seeing beyond the colonial façade and for doing the bidding of compulsory white supremacy through each moment that I denounced you, denied my connection to our Ubuntu languages, and used European religions to denounce my African spirituality. Baba, who is both a victim and a survivor of colonialism, could not see beyond his own suffering, or was it too painful for him to face your hard truth and still go on living? So much is unknown on the personal level, yet so much is known of our social political realities, so we struggled to put faces to our oratures so that they are not just dry facts that overwhelm us into a traumatized silence (Mucina 2013; Richter and Morrell 2006; hooks 2004).

Amai, I cried for you because I wanted you, needed you, desired your warm touch, and because I was lost without your motherly wisdom. But Baba's response to my cries for you was always the same in its substantive content. Baba had one of two responses: he was either icy cold about you, which in my books qualified for the gentler side, or he erupted like a scary volcanic mountain, which, in its fury of manifestation, threatened to consume me to the point of nothingness. In his orature titled, *Kaffir Boy: The True Story of a Black Youth's Coming of Age in Apartheid South Africa*, Mathabane (1986) clearly conveys how white supremacy and its governing colonial structures also turned his Baba into a threatening fury because he enacted the structural colonial violence that he experienced upon those he loved. At times like this, I only wished I had never brought up the subject of you but I could never stop myself because you are my bones, you are my flesh, you are my heart and, most importantly, you are my soul. I do not believe you could find the point that distinguishes you from me because I am of you. I was in you as you are now in me (Cixous 1998).[1]

Yet, Baba would say metaphorically: "You and I are like a pair of trousers and a belt. We need each other, we support each other. For how can a pair of trousers stay up without a good belt? I am the trousers and I am dependent on you the belt to keep me up" (Baba, personal communication). I wonder what Baba would have said if I had pointed out that a pair of trousers and a belt could not stay up without a body. Thus, the three (trousers, belt, and body) make one and this one makes three. Regardless of the play on words, it was his inevitable next attack, which always silenced me while making me the follower of his party line: "She was a whore who killed my babies but she did not do it alone. It was her parents' fault. They could not stand to be out of sugar, so they made her sell her body" (Baba, personal communication).

Amai, let me state that the telling of our oratures is an important step toward our healing from colonial oppression as it allows us, the peoples who have Ubuntu knowledge and are struggling to live it because of the imposition of colonialism, to have the space to analyze these experiences and speak about them from our own philosophical and theoretical perspectives (Somâe 1994; Douglass 1989; p'Bitek 1984). In my writing, I directly and rightfully blame our spiritual and physical injury squarely on colonialism. I take such bold steps, Amai, because I still remember the childhood hurt of loving an absent you; I yearned for your love, but the lack of observable reciprocal evidence of the love that I had for you threatened to destroy me. So, to survive your absence I started to accept the oratures that Baba bombarded me with, because at the time they were easier to live with than the truth. What would I have done knowing that colonialism was responsible for the fragmentation of my family? Could Baba have believed that he was giving me the lesser of two evils? Could I have survived the truth? Dearest, dearest, dearest Amai, how did you survive this colonial nightmare? Did you direct your blame on Baba like he directed his on you? Did you see the true cause of our suffering as colonialism? Was your suffering so intense that giving it an analysis was only adding salt to an already throbbing and festering wound? Do you feel a sense of solidarity and less isolation knowing that many Indigenous women across the world shared your fate? They, like you, had to set their children adrift into the unknown abyss in hopes of saving them from certain death and others had their babies forcibly plucked from their hands by colonial governance structures (Hill Collins and Bilge 2016; hooks 2004; Vera 1992; Crenshaw 1991). How do you heal from such pain, especially when the son you tried to save now points an accusatory finger at you and has the audacity to question your womanhood?

Amai, I am sorry for the hurt I have caused you. As a child, it was easier to project my suffering as the result of your lack of maternal mothering. My questioning of your womanhood, from my position of suffering as a boy/man without ever contemplating your position as an Indigenous African woman fighting the brutality of colonialism while trying to nurture my life, communicates my male chauvinistic privilege (hooks 2004). The truth, Amai, was too ugly to face because it reflected my weakness and vulnerability as perceived from a colonial and Indigenous masculine positionality. As a child and as a young man, my only relief seemed to materialize from my anger, but my anger was born of colonially induced isolation and fear.

When Baba was accused of disrespecting you and other Indigenous women who were forced to give up their children, he would respond by saying: "If my son is to survive this hard cruel world he must learn to deal with the ugly facts that make up our reality and truths" (Baba, personal communication, 1980–1982). I know I took part in humiliating you publicly, so it is only fitting that I publicly apologize for my behaviour. Now that both you and Baba are in the spirit world, you no doubt see the truth and forgive each other for the misdirected hurt you caused each other. I, for my part, write this orature to you now acknowledging my failures and begging your forgiveness. Amai, if I am asked how colonialism is implicated in our spiritual and physical injury, can I share this orature?

I wonder if Baba ever spoke the truth about his colonial experience with you. I wonder if he ever talked about how he was emasculated by colonialism, and I wonder if he ever drew links between your experience and his experience. I wonder if he was aware that he was reproducing the same oppression that he experienced at the hands of white settler society with you. Did he ever tell you why he could not send money to you, besides telling you that he could not find work? Well, I heard one of the reasons when he was trying to explain how white settler society dehumanized and humiliated him. Whenever all the neo-slaves (domestic servants) started to share their oratures about colonial exploitation, Baba would share numerous oratures about how he was exploited. But this orature always stood out in my mind, and it is only now that I'm seeing the connection that it has to your suffering and the heroic acts that you did in order for me to survive (Crenshaw 1991). I remember Baba saying:

> After searching the different white neighbourhoods for any kind of work, for over a year and a half, I found work as a gardener and a laundry wash boy. The promised work pay was great and, on top of that, this Madame and Bass [Boss] were providing me with

food as well. This job was evidence that my ancestors were watching over me and I was sure I would now be able to put something in my family's hands. My manhood was restored and I made sure I was early for work every single day and I stayed late on the job until they sent me home. I made sure that when the Madame or Bass called I was there in less than a minute and I was especially attentive to the needs of the Madame because if she was not happy there was no possible way that I would keep my job. If the Bass likes you and the Madame dislikes you, then you lose your job. The Madame must be happy at all cost.

So when she started to put her underwear as laundry I was a little surprised because usually white women do not like Africans touching their panties. They are happy to have you wash the husband's underwear but will not allow you to touch theirs because this is like touching their womanhood. But I did not care what I did as long as I had a job. Every now and again the Madame would come and watch me do the laundry and at times she would chat with me while I did the laundry or the gardening. It was therefore not unusual or alarming when she came to talk to me while I was washing her panties. Still dressed in her bathrobe, she asked me to stop the washing and come and help her in the house. When we got into the bedroom she dropped the bathrobe and, while standing naked in front of me, commanded me to remove my clothes. As this was not the first time that this had happened to me, I simply fulfilled my male role and went back to work. Whenever the Madame had an itch, I just simply scratched it for her and went back to work. But Madame was not happy with the services rendered. She also felt that I needed to pay her my whole monthly earning as a sign of my honour and privilege for serving her. When the Bass asked why she was taking my money from me, she simply responded by saying, "I have given him a loan to build a home in his village for his family. So we have calculated that for the next four years he will have to give me all of his earnings." This of course meant that if I left her services or misbehaved she could now get the police after me. As if she needed a legitimate reason to get me arrested. (Baba, personal communication, 1980–1982)

Baba became their slave through their governmental structures that allowed for heinous laws like the Master and Servants Act to exist (Meredith 1979). Baba highlights this orature in part to demonstrate how he was emasculated because, as an African man, he would never have touched the underwear of Amai, as this was not a man's work. As to why this was not an Indigenous man's work, Baba never elaborated, but from my understanding of colonial masculinity, his doing women's work was an act of emasculating him and other Indigenous men as being women in the hierarchy of colonial masculinity. Many laws like this made it a criminal offence for a Black employee to disobey his/her white employer. On the other hand, you, Amai, were forced, through the colonially enforced Land Apportionment Acts, to live on reserves that the government had created after stealing your lands (Meredith 1979). Meaning, colonial white settlers took our arable lands so they could profit off our dispossession (Harvey 2005). To placate the threat that our dispossessed ancestors posed to white supremacy, white settlers turned to their kith and kin, who had developed a workable solution for dealing with dispossessed "natives" in Canada (Cook and Lindau 2000). The Canadian solution for dispossessing and disconnecting the "natives" of their lands was workable because the white settlers could identify the "natives" through their colour, which differentiated them as non-white. Therefore, the settlers' solution to us being a problem was to place us on reserves (Cook and Lindau 2000). The immediate benefit of their solution was that we stopped being a major threat to their need to access our land and water-based resources. Having us on reserves made it easier for them to control our marked, Indigenous bodies while justifying their wickedness to themselves and the rest of the world as civilizing actions.

To this day, the colonial reserve systems of control keep us busy through neo-colonial capitalistic governance structures. Hence, as we focus on colonial goals, we are drained of the energy we need to work toward our own total directional Ubuntu destiny. We the Ubuntu people have suppressed the fact that we are of the complete African continent. Colonialism has limited our identity and our vision of relational bonds to colonial boundaries and, in so doing, compulsory white supremacy has taken our people, who were able to sustain themselves, and turned us into exploitable dependants so that we do not think outside white supremacy and its governing structure of colonial capitalism. Boaduo and Gumbi's (2010) article "Classification: Colonial Attempts to Fracture Africa's Identity and Contribution to Humanity" captures the insidious dehumanization and commodification of Africa and its people. In this colonial carnage, Amai, you and Baba did what was necessary to survive, even though the colonial system was stacked against both of you. Amai, could I share this orature as evidence of how colonialism has stolen our lands, controlled our actions with its laws, enacted violence upon us, treated us as sexual objects and, in its actions of oppression, has further divided us against each other which has only advanced spiritual and physical injury upon us?

I now see that it was the oppressive structural practices of white settlers in Zimbabwe that led to the African uprising against the colonial system. I, who was born to you during the liberation war, now have these questions. What made you marry Baba, one of many migrants from Malawi in Zimbabwe? Did you know that these Malawian migrants who were in Zimbabwe were perceived as "Uncle Toms" (traitors to the liberation cause)? Why did you risk being perceived as a traitor for marrying a Malawian migrant labourer who worked for less when the leadership of the Black liberation struggle was asking the Zimbabwean people to resist being exploited by colonial structures? It was clearly understood around the rural areas that death was the fitting penalty for any Zimbabwean who embraced these migrant traitors. Frantz Fanon, in *The Wretched of the Earth*, illuminates our self-destruction when he reminds us that: "While the settler or the policeman has the right the livelong day to strike the native, to insult him and to make him crawl to them, you will see the native reaching for his knife at the slightest hostile or aggressive glance cast on him by another native; for the last resort of the native is to defend his personality vis-à-vis his brother [and in this case wife]" (1963, 54). We took hell from colonial settlers, but exploded at the slightest provocation from our own brothers and sisters. Fanon asserts that as a last resort we defended ourselves more vigorously against the less threatening acts of our people because their actions did not pose a totalizing destruction and in some measure allowed Baba and me to still exhibit a measure of violently exploitative masculinity vis-à-vis those we loved.

Amai, what was it like to try to raise children while a war was raging around you, having no home of your own, struggling to feed your children without any source of income? Let me say, Amai, I am ready to hear your orature because I am learning to live with these scars while also learning to renew beyond these colonial scars. In a way, I am trying to understand the circumstances and motivations that guided your actions, but I do this lightly, because if I do it heavily, I will want answers to questions like, "What was behind your decision for not coming to visit me when I did everything possible for us to meet? Did you know how much I wanted and needed you? Why did you not come, why did you not come, Amai? Did you know I made Baba send you that money so you could come but you never came; why did you torture my heart? You sent your brothers and your sister when I wanted you. Did they tell you that their presence only further confused me, because I did not want them and I only wanted you? Did they tell you that they could not quench my thirst because I wanted my mother the proof that I am because she is?" What Hélène Cixous (1998) conveys about her mother is reflective of what I want to convey about you. She states: "My mother the proof, my mother who circulates within me, my mother who was in me as I was in her. . . . Here, in the invisible inside, I no longer know if I'm the subject of the verb in the past tense, in the present, or if today is really the day before yesterday whereas erstwhile is a part of the future. . . . The most surprising is not that I, I will die, it is that I was born, that I am not you, and that I am me. I would like very much to know that me [which is you]" (86–7).

Amai, did you know that my relationship with Baba was volatile from the start and, as I grew older, he tried every trick to mould me into a perfect Black English boy because he believed my survival was dependent on my ability to assimilate into white society? I had to learn how to be acceptable to white society. Baba used all means necessary to ensure that I embodied compulsory white supremacy in my behaviour, and I am sure that if he could have changed my pigmentation to make me white, he would have done it (Fanon 1963). He would demonize all that was Ubuntu and praise all that was Christian and white. Any resistance that I put up against his efforts would result in the severest form of verbal abuse and, on a number of occasions, he beat me until I was unconscious. I guess this is how you preserve a Black body marked for destruction by white supremacy (hooks 2000; Césaire 1972; Fanon 1963). My Baba enacted so well all the ways my body could be destroyed. I was left confused about who the enemy was. At some points, the white enemy seemed more human than Baba (Boaduo and Gumbi 2010; hooks 2004; Césaire 1972).

Amai, I am not claiming that I was an easy child to father. I know my ancestors gave me an unbreakable spirit; I embody resilience and resistance. I am because my ancestors are me; without my ancestors there is no me and without me there are no ancestors. Our existence is one and the same. When I ran away from home, I was resisting being whitewashed, and because I ran away, I had to stay away as a way of preserving my life. Alone, in the middle of the night, fear would threaten me and, as terrified as I was, I knew my life was in the hands of our ancestors. Due to the imposition of Christian spiritual colonialism, there were times when I would pray to our ancestors and, for good measure, I would also pray to Jesus to do his thing because I was afraid of going to his hell. Amai, by the time I was seven years old I had learned how to sleep alone in the bushes, on the streets, and in wastepaper bins. I ate food from the garbage bins and, when I needed to, I stole food from wherever I could find it. All this I did in order to survive. I guess you had imprinted onto me the blueprint for survival.

In 1981, I was picked up after a grocery store owner had reported that I was sleeping in the shopping mall's wastepaper bin. The social workers who took me off the street soon learned that I was not safe in the care of Baba because, when they took me home, Baba openly threatened to kill me. The social workers placed me in an orphanage called St. Joseph's House for Boys while they assessed my case. On 2 April 1982, the Harare Juvenile Court, using the doctrine of the Children's Protection and Adoption Act (chapter 33), admitted me as a ward of the state under section 21 (1) (a) of the Child in Need of Care Act. The Harare Juvenile Court named St. Joseph's House for Boys as my legal guardian. Once I was in the orphanage, which primarily cared for European and mulatto boys, I did everything possible to reduce my Black connection as I was trying to fit in with the other boys who only highlighted their white connection. The European worldsense that Baba had tried so hard to make me assimilate into now became the barrier, which was a reflection of his neo-slave status. I do not know why Baba had left the responsibility of trying to keep in touch in my hands, because I perceived his neo-slave status as a threat to my upward mobility in white supremacy structures (Fanon [1952] 1967). So I made no efforts to keep in contact with him. Even though we were only a few kilometres away from each other, with each passing day the distance between us became greater and it felt like we were worlds apart. Contradictorily in the orphanage, the more I tried to integrate into white settler society, the more it reminded me that I could never be a part of it. Yet the lies of colonialism still made me want acceptance from it, and being in this position made me vulnerable to white sexual predators. Thus, in the orphanage, all of us during the day were the scorn of white society, but under cover of night, we were potential victims of their sexual abuse and exploitation (Boaduo and Gumbi 2010; hooks 2004; Césaire 1972).

Amai, in the orphanage the warden, who we shall call Dianne because that is her name, taught me that I was either a usurper or the usurped, but I also came to realize, through experience, that a good usurper must know first-hand the humiliation of being usurped, because it makes you merciless in your usurpation efforts. Let me give you the context. This particular white female warden had been brought into the orphanage because of all the forms of abuse and sexual exploitations that white male wardens had performed on the boys. Under her welfare, we were supposed to be safer. I was a thirteen-year-old who was disconnected from his community and family structure. Thus, the special attention that Dianne paid me made me feel wanted and more manly than the boy I was.

It all started with after-dinner invitations to her apartment under the guise of discussing the structural issues of the orphanage from my viewpoint as a boy in the orphanage. At first, we did talk about orphanage structural issues, but very soon, Dianne was sharing her private life with me. At the time, I felt honoured with the fact that she trusted me with such intimate details about her private life. I had never had such an intimate relationship with an adult, and I valued our friendship and relationship very dearly. Every Friday night she began to make me dinner and, when I came back late from school, she would have snacks for me in her apartment. Food was always a big deal in the orphanage, as there was never enough, so I was amazed at my good fortune. I had a mother figure who was a great friend and she fed me the most amazing meals. At the time, I believed this was as close to heaven as I could ever be. Dianne even started giving me driving lessons and coming to all my rugby games. She knew all about my relationship with Baba and had assured me that, when my court review date came up, she would make sure the social workers and the court understood how important it was for me to stay in the orphanage so that I could continue to thrive and reach my potential. When the social worker recommended that I spend more time with Baba, Dianne told me we could just disregard this, as there were not enough social workers to enforce and follow up on any recommendations made about any of the boys' care.

You, Amai, on the other hand, were demonized in the most severe manner possible. Dianne always informed me that if she had had a son like me, she would never have given me up. How strange is this, a white woman telling a Black child that she would never have given him up? Yet, strangely enough, she in reality had done the very act she condemned you for. Speaking from a white-privileged position, Dianne stated that her reason for leaving her son with her husband was to ensure that, through her husband's wealth, her son got every single opportunity that she was not able to provide as a single white female. Could you have given me to Baba because you believed he was in a better position to save my life? On this point, Dianne could not extend her white feminist thinking to you because you, as a Black woman, were not worthy of white reflection. Dianne, instead, validated her reality as real and meaningful while dismissing your reality as pointless. You were a nobody to her and, therefore, we were better off not thinking about you. But you, Amai, I now believe, sensed the danger that I was in so you made Baba bring you to the orphanage. Did you know that this was the first time that Baba had ever visited me at the orphanage? After so many years of craving you, I had learned to live and do without you, but here you were expecting me to welcome you with open arms. You wanted a relationship. You wanted to change my world again. Amai, I know this letter is divulging all, but bear with me, because deep down I know you are part of me and you know I am part of you. Allow me to continue, Amai.

Do you remember that, by the time you decided to connect with me, the gap between us had widened so much that I did not know you and I did not want to know you? Or did I want to know you? My world became overwhelmed with confusion and the only thing that was clear was my anger, so I denounced you as my Amai, but my anger was my expression of my fear. What would it have meant for me to open myself to you, without any guarantees? How was I to love when I was most familiar with abandonment? It was easier to tell you that you had let too much time go between the time when I actually needed you and now, that I had learned to cope without you. I remember you cried as I spoke these harsh words to you. Your only response was to say, "Nothing I did was easy; I tried to raise three children with nothing" (Amai, personal communication, August 1989). After this, you left and I imagine you probably felt disappointed but, unbeknown to both of us, our spiritual connection had been re-established and this shared spirit would guide us in future interactions.

Feeling distraught and confused about my encounter with you, I went to Dianne to seek comfort but she rebuffed my calls for support and understanding. In fact, she spoke more intensely about herself and her family problems. She talked incessantly about how her marriage had fallen apart because she had fallen in love with a former boy from the orphanage. She also told me that as soon as the ex-boy had found out about her pregnancy he had wanted nothing to do with her. As Dianne could still sense that my mind was on you, she shocked me into focusing on her totally by saying she was sure that she was having a miscarriage. I, wanting to help, offered to drive her to the hospital, but she told me that it was too late, as she could not save the child. I asked her what I could do to help her and she told me she just needed me to be a good friend and be there when things got tough. Wanting to demonstrate my friendship and manliness, I began to spend all my extra time with her and, in return, she made sure that if any trips or events were offered to the boys from the orphanage I was given special treatment. Meaning, I was offered all possible opportunities made available to the boys by the communities first before any other boy was considered. Unbeknown to me, I was being ambushed for sexual abuse. I have heard that to ensnare a monkey in a gourd, you need something shiny to attract it. Happily, I walked into the trap. Amai, could I share this orature as evidence of how colonialism has fragmented our family, undermined our memories, tricked us, humiliated us, and pitted us against each other after abusing us emotionally and physically?

As part of my special treatment, I was chosen as one of four boys to go on a Lions Club trip. We went to Kariba and, after being away for the whole weekend, Dianne was so excited to see me that she made a special dinner, which she served with an expensive wine. As the evening was ending and I was ready to go to bed, Dianne asked me if I thought it was okay for friends to kiss. I told her of course it was okay and I went over and kissed her on the cheek. Dianne held my hand and drew me in front of her. She then told me that she meant very passionate kissing on the mouth. I will admit that when she started kissing, I did not resist and in fact enjoyed it immensely. The only thing that was missing was that I wanted the other boys to see my experience and share with me my good fortune. I knew the other boys would never have believed that the warden had kissed me and let me fondle her everywhere. The further we went, the happier I was because I knew this was the stuff that made for great manly oratures in the colonial context. However, as I was leaving, Dianne told me that I could never tell a soul about what had happened because she would lose her job and go to jail and I, on the other hand, would end up in reform school. Everyone in the orphanage feared reform school because there were oratures about boys being beaten and raped on a daily basis. I, therefore, kept my mouth shut.

By the time I was one of the senior boys, Dianne made sure I had a room right above her apartment, as this made it easy for her to call me down. She also made a copy of her apartment key so I could get in and out without being easily observed. But, needless to say, one cannot keep a secret in a home of fifty-five boys and eleven staff, so we will just say that everyone kept their mouth shut and purposefully ignored our social relational responsibility to one another. It seemed like I had a win-win situation. She gave me money, food, and sex and brought me things from the UK as she made frequent visits to see family. My best friend in the orphanage, who made it clear that he had figured out what was going on, was given a special apartment with a self-contained kitchen so that he could entertain his guests. He also had free access to any of Dianne's three Volkswagen vehicles.

Amai, it is amazing how bribery can buy loyalty. Dianne had also told my friend that, when we graduated, she was going to buy a house in which we could all live together and we were not to worry about jobs because she was confident that, through her network in white settler society, she would get us jobs. When I started to see that the relationship was built on abuse and exploitation, I began to express doubt. To keep me in order, Dianne exerted pressure through intimidation, which she directed at me and at my friend. After a while, she realized that intimidation and fear did not work so well on me so she went back to the old trick that had always worked on me. This was my fear of being responsible for another human being's suffering or death. Knowing this fear of mine, Dianne made me believe that, if I left her, she would kill herself or go crazy.

Not wanting to be responsible for the death of anyone but also knowing that I could not play this game anymore, I dedicated my time to finding a way out of this craziness. Even my high school headmaster had suspected that the warden was sexually abusing me. To the headmaster's credit, he called me into his office and asked if anything was going on between her and me. I remember my headmaster saying: "If you have any problems, I can only assist you if you disclose to me what is going on; I cannot act on suspicion alone when the consequences of my actions have great ramifications" (Headmaster, personal communication, November 1990). Knowing my headmaster, I knew that if I disclosed to him the truth, he would take decisive action, but I could not determine the outcome of his actions. Believing that if I disclosed the truth I would end up in reform school, I chose to deny that anything was going on between Dianne and me.

Amai, I therefore suffered quietly but unbeknown to me, the situation with Dianne was having a negative impact on my health and I only became aware of the severity of my problem when I went to see the doctor because I had tonsillitis. At this doctor's visit, it was discovered that I had high blood pressure and, after monitoring my condition without any improvement, I was started on a medication regime to control the high blood pressure. Counselling sessions were also arranged but none of these interventions could help me because I could not disclose my real problem due to fear. So out of desperation I began to track you down. Is it not interesting to notice that at the highest level of my distress I came looking for you? Is it not also interesting that Baba and I shared the same fate of being helpless at the hands of white women? Amai, could I share this orature as evidence of how colonialism has stolen our lands, controlled our actions with its laws, enacted violence upon us, treated us as sexual objects, and, in its actions of oppression, further divided us against each other, which has only advanced spiritual and physical injury upon us?

My search for you, Amai, led me to Maiguru's (maternal aunt's) home; she then connected me to the rest of my maternal family. My meeting with my Ambuya (maternal grandmother) was a bittersweet experience, as I did everything possible to make her sense that I was still very angry for what I perceived as her abandonment of me. Before I left to find you, Ambuya told me that she would ask the ancestors to show me the way and she added that she was confident that the ancestors would do their job because was I now not standing before them? Sekuru (maternal grandfather) did not say much to me. When I arrived, Sekuru asked me to come and stand in front of him so that he could see me (even though he was blind). As I stood in front of Sekuru, I heard him say, "Is this you, Peter?" and I respond by saying, "Yes, Sekuru, it is I."

After a moment of awkward silence, I noticed that Sekuru was crying and I knew that I was loved. Sekuru did not need to say anything, his tears honoured me and made me feel that no one had wanted our family to fragment, but we had all done what we needed to do to survive. I will not say that everything was forgiven and forgotten, but this exchange with Sekuru spoke to me on a spiritual level that allowed me to have a certain amount of empathy for my maternal family. Before I left, Sekuru told me that he and Ambuya were now ready to go to their ancestors with not so heavy hearts. He also told me that time would lead to healing through the understanding that I gained with age. Amai, if I should be asked how orature, truth-telling, and the act of seeking forgiveness create healing, re-establish familial bonds, revive memory, support understanding, move us beyond anger, give us voice to fight against injustice, bear witness to our survival, bring hope to our fragmented families, and ensure that an evil is not repeated by forgetting about the past, can I share this orature?

Amai, after visiting with you I know that I came back to spend a night with Sekuru and Ambuya, but I cannot remember that experience. I have no image or memory of it, but I remember coming back. Could it be I do not remember anything because all that needed to be remembered had entered my soul already? Amai, if you can see Sekuru and Ambuya, thank them for me for understanding my childish ways. I am still trying to digest the meaning of all their words and, because I have written them down, I find that I can worry more about meaning than trying to hold them whole in my mind. Yes, I am transformed, and yet I am still naming the ways in which I am transformed because the process is still ongoing. Yes, I am still learning from my engagement with Sekuru and Ambuya, and their oratures are still working on me, they are still healing my spirit. I believe when I am ready and I have worked through the sections of their oratures that are healing me, I may remember the missing gaps.

The morning that we set out for your home, Amai, we left at four o'clock in the morning. Dark as it was, we were able to find our way because the stars were so bright. After eight hours of hard walking in the blazing sun, we arrived at your home just after noon. We were all starving and very thirsty for water. Very nervously, you invited us into your hut and, right away, I noticed that your hut was poorly constructed, using corns stocks as walls. Sitting inside your hut, I could see outside very clearly. There was nothing in your hut that the poorest thief would have taken. I had never seen such poverty, never even imagined it possible. From the dryness and isolation of the land, I could not imagine where you got your drinking water from. For miles and miles around you there was not a single being, because this was hushed territory and here you were alone with a baby. If I had any questions for you, Amai, the reality of your surrounding robbed me of my voice. When you gave us a mug of water to share, I became acutely aware of how precious water was in this place. As I drank the water, I became aware that I was not as thirsty as I had imagined. From the single pot sitting over the fire in the middle of your hut, you spooned out a few kernels of corn and placed them in each of our hands. I knew that each kernel of corn that you gave us compromised your reserves but I could not turn down that gracious offer that you were using to re-establish our familial bonds. As we ate, I knew that there was no place for us to sleep and there was definitely not enough food to feed all of us. So when you asked when we were leaving, I knew that we had to leave right away.

Even though the full impact of that visit did not manifest itself until some years later, I believe when I went back to the orphanage I was not the same person, because you and the context of your reality had transformed me. You had opened my eyes to a reality that you had protected me from. I am sorry that I did not get my act together sooner so that I could have helped alleviate some of the poverty that ultimately killed you. Amai, if I should be asked how orature creates healing, re-establishes familial bonds, revives memory, supports understanding, brings hope to our fragmented families, and ensures that an evil is not repeated by forgetting about the past, can I share this orature?

It seems my visit with you, Amai, made me more willing to confront confidently the exploitation of white supremacy on a personal level. I knew then that I would not let the governance structure of white supremacy or the actions of white settler society destroy my spirit. This new state of being, combined with my growing maturity, was supported by the life skills I was gaining beyond the orphanage community. For example, I was involved with a disabilities group, which toured around Southern Africa; I was on our high school rugby team, which toured England; and I was on the schoolboy provincial rugby team. These activities exposed me to the world beyond the orphanage and, through these exposures, I became more critical of my positionality, which meant I started to see everything anew and questioned everything from this broader social location, which I had gained through travel. Travelling with a disabilities group made me aware that I was more than my label of having a learning disability, and the success I experienced through playing rugby made me believe that I could build personal and professional relationships beyond the influence of the orphanage, which was controlled by Dianne. Crowe (2004) captures this kind of work in her essay "Crafting Tales of Trauma: Will This Winged Monster Fly?" Dianne's exploitative and abusive behaviour, which also violated child and youth care ethics of relational care, could not keep holding me down. My increased confidence and awareness inspired me to strategize ways to keep me away from Dianne until I left the orphanage. Thankfully, I had built enough of a community of support around myself that I managed to stay away from Dianne for the most part. I still went back to Dianne because the relationship was not all bad and there were things I still believed that I depended on her for, like unquestioned access to sex and financial resources; but of course going to her always put me at risk of being entrapped again. I guess the point I am making is that I was not able to break away in one swift move after being in this exploitative relationship for over four years.

Because of the distance I had to place between Dianne and myself, I started to learn that I was not one of two boys that Dianne had sexually abused but, in fact, there were several others. Sadly, as I was pulling myself out of this position, other boys were being set up to be exploited and sexually abused. These boys, like I had, would quietly accept this reality of sexual abuse because they too saw no other way of accumulating capitalistic power (hooks 2004; Fanon [1952] 1967). The more I learned, the more I was able to break away from Dianne's control—as Francis Bacon pointed out in his 1597 work *Meditationes Sacrae and Human Philosophy*, knowledge is power (Farrington 1966). The board of the orphanage was so proud of my rugby achievements that they decided, under the guidance of Dianne, to send me and another brother, who was academically strong and had also made the provincial athletics team, on an Outward Bound course donated by the Lions Club. The knowledge I gained from going on that Outward Bound course was more like a confirmation of the fact that I was a good leader. At the end of the Outward Bound program, the director of the program invited me to apply for a position with the school when I was ready, as they would welcome my application.

Because I had failed my high school and was not taking full advantage of the opportunity I had been given to return to school, I was given six months' notice to leave the orphanage. I used that time to apply for a job with Outward Bound Zimbabwe and, to my delight, I got it. Unceremoniously and unannounced, I left the orphanage. My power to act came from the knowledge of knowing that I had a job and a place to stay with Outward Bound Zimbabwe. Unfortunately, through my experience with Dianne, I had gained the skills of usurping other people. I am not sure if my actions were motivated by unconscious vengeance or what I perceived as a soft target in the hierarchy of white supremacy. Whatever the reason, European white women became my target for usurpation. I became a taker and only one objective motivated me, self-gratification at all cost. I suspected that all women were trying to use me in some manner for their own capitalistic accumulation goals and therefore it was my goal to use them before they used me. At least this is how I justified my colonial actions of usurping. So when I met the Canadian white woman who had travelled all the way to Zimbabwe from Canada, I was impressed because not only had she travelled so far, she actively worked hard to be a part of the Zimbabwean Outward Bound community, and I read her as being carefree and adventurous seeking. I wanted to be that too, and so I worked at seducing her, because I had learned that my Black embodiment was a desired sexual commodity among white women travellers. We eventually married, but I want to be clear that I was not marrying this woman, I was marrying an idea that I believed she embodied. I was also marrying an idea about a life in Canada (hooks 2004). I also did sense that she was a good person, so a part of me was hopeful that, over time, we would grow to know each other and I would grow to love her. Nevertheless, I soon learned that I was unwilling to be intimately vulnerable with another person. I also did not know how to open myself to loving another person without losing control, and I perceived loving vulnerably as a sign of weakness. I had learned to value taking as a sign of strength, and nothing in my experience had demonstrated a loving partnership as a desired strength (hooks 2004). Therefore, when the relational work started, I left the marriage. We were married for less than a year. I share this knowledge with you, Amai, because I wonder if you married out of forced necessity. So much has changed, but so much is the same. You are in me as I once was in you.

I have so much to talk about, Amai, but mostly I want to say thank you for your fighting spirit, because without you there would be no me. In retrospect, it would seem to me that I am picking up the fight where you left off. Colonialism has fragmented us as a family, co-opted us, and pitted us against each other. By undermining our memories, it has undermined our ways of knowing. While we point fingers at each other about who has transgressed what boundaries and who has undermined what family values, colonialism takes advantage of this confusion and continues to decimate all our Ubuntu governance; but we will not let this happen anymore, because we are now aware of the insidious nature of colonialism, and we will not let it fool us again. Our talking about colonialism's insidious nature is itself a step toward creating solidarity and bringing our families together. I thank you, Amai, with all our other ancestors who paved the path of struggle, because your efforts of liberation have taught me that we cannot use colonial structures to determine our future without reproducing colonialism (Fanon 1963). I hope, Amai, I learned to love as deeply and as bravely as you do. I know you are with me because I have felt your presence in all the great women (African, Black, brown, yellow, red, and white) that have been Amai to me when I needed you. As I centre Indigenous Ubuntu ways, I am also starting to realize that you always came when I needed you. I just did not recognize that you were the spirit guiding the arrivals of your brothers, Uncle Samuel and the other uncle, whose name I cannot remember. How could I not have seen you in the arrival of Maiguru (your older sister, who is traditionally referred to as my older mother)? If I had understood tradition back then, I would have known and seen that my mother was everywhere present with me. May we be whole again because you are my bones, you are my flesh, you are my heart, and, most importantly, you are my spirit. I do not believe you could find the point that distinguishes you from me because I am of you. Sanibonani Amai, I clap my hands as a way of welcoming and honouring your spirit. Let us be one in addressing our deep pain, because this pain is fragmentized love. In a daydream, you once asked me what I had to say. Well, I have spoken, and now I respectfully ask you, "What do you have to say, Amai?"

Your loving son,
Dr. Devi Dee Mucina Komba

Amai, in this blank page may you inscribe your spiritual wisdom to me.

For Amai's voice

Amai, I am learning from our orature, which is why I want us to keep this dialogue open as I welcome Baba into it. In the next Millet Granary, I speak to Baba in another letter.

Why does African feminism offer a good entrance into understanding Ubuntu women's reality?

What is the danger of Ubuntu men telling the orature of Ubuntu women?

What actions of Amai stand out for you from this orature?

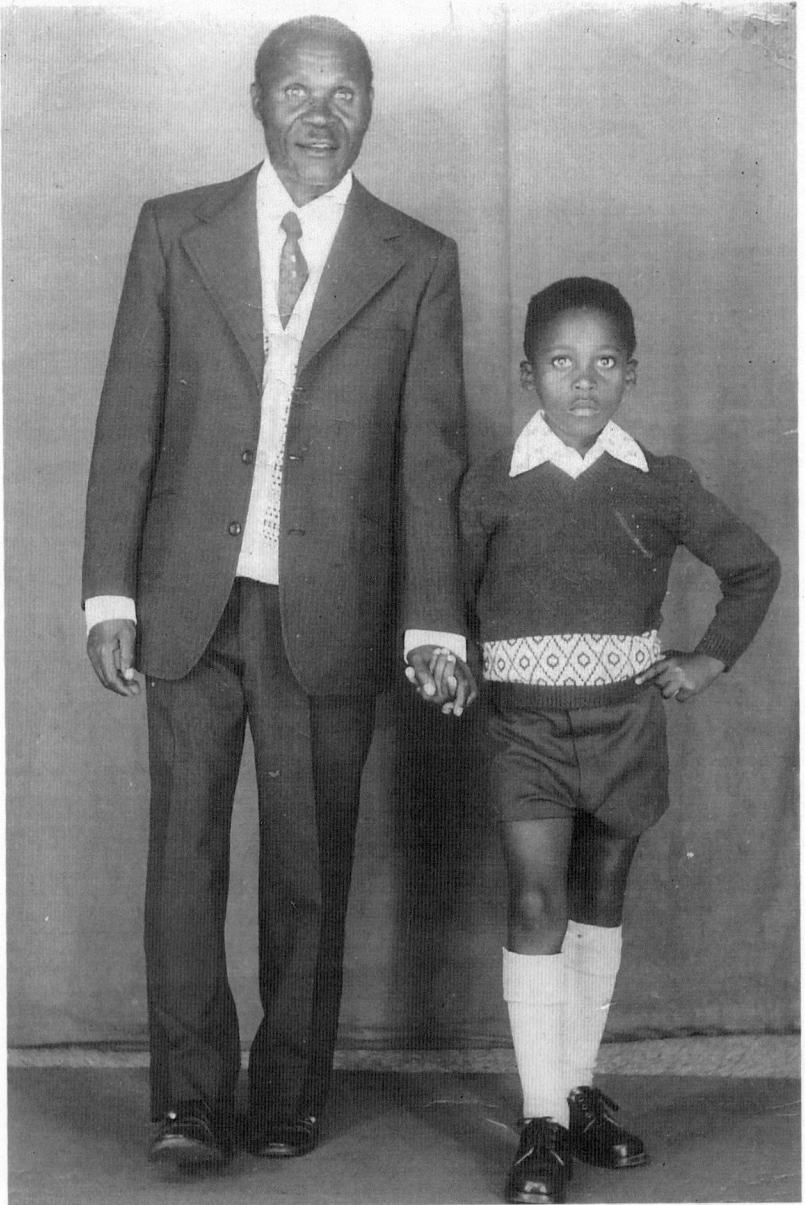

Figure 9. When this photograph was taken, I was upset because I had to go to church with my Baba and, on top of that, I was forced to hold his hand in this photo pose.

Finding Baba, Finding Our Fragmented Family

Methodological questions that guided my writing of this Millet Granary:

1. *How do we start decolonizing Indigenous masculinities with our fathers?*

2. *What do you identify as Baba's strongest resistance to colonialism?*

3. *How can future generations of Ubuntu use these oratures to decolonize from the power of colonial toxic masculinities?*

Sanibonani Baba (1920?–December 2009),

Before I can start to create dialogue, I must face some truths. For example, my motivation for finding you in 2003 came from my desire to confront you about the injustice I perceived you had committed against me. My perception was unlike that of Mark Mathabane (1986) who, in the preface of his autobiography orature titled *Kaffir Boy*, has this to say about his Baba: "They turned my father—by repeatedly arresting him and denying him the right to earn a living in a way that gave him dignity—into such a bitter man that, as he fiercely but in vain resisted the emasculation, he hurt those he loved the most" (x). Such understanding demonstrated by Mathabane toward his Baba's struggle within the colonial masculine power structures of compulsory white supremacy was beyond me. Ta-Nehisi Coates (2015) in *Between the World and Me* also communicates that, in the power structure of masculine compulsory white supremacy, which aims to destroy the Black body, our parents were scared into enacting violence on our young Black bodies as a way of communicating the imminent threat directed against us by white supremacy. I lacked this kind of understanding expressed by these two authors for their parents because I only wanted to respond to my own pain. Like a lawyer, I had prepared my opening statements, which I was confident clearly showed your guilt, and I was well prepared for any rebuttals that you offered as justification for your actions. For many years, I had rehearsed this confrontation, and I was certain that victory and vengeance would be mine. Yet, when I arrived in Zimbabwe in 2003 and found you, the realities of your life in a so-called ex-colony manifested themselves in ways that tempered and undermined my plans for vengeance.

For starters, I was informed by those who knew you that you were living in the bushes and relying on the charity of others because you were so poor. I learned that your common-law wife (meaning you had not paid for your wife's bride price and therefore had no claim to your children) had died of AIDS on the reserve of Nyamapanda. I learned that your children with her were struggling against poverty with little support. Such ex-colony realities were weakening my desire to exercise my vengeful voice. When I first saw you, I could not believe you were the same man, because age and poverty had shrunk your stature. Our lack of communication over so many years left you speechless as I stood before you. The spectators in attendance had to coax you into speaking again. I could tell you were wearing your best clothes even though they were worn out to the point of being rags. If I had poisonous venom about how you had parented me, it kept dissolving away. After the formal public greetings, you and I went for a walk and, while we were walking, you looped your hand around mine and asked me: "Baba,[1] what has kept you away for so long?"

Baba, I had not planned for you to confront me with gentleness and I could not respond with anything else but truth. I remember telling you that I had stayed away from you because your desire to make me a Black Englishman made me feel like the idolized image you had of me was more significant to you than the actual me (Fanon [1952] 1967). I also told you that the dominant memories I had of you were of you beating me until I was unconscious; you threatening to kill me in front of the social workers; and you willingly giving me up to the state in a court of law. Interestingly, without me elaborating any further, you turned to me and said, "I am sorry for the pain that I have caused you." Baba, your honest few words have liberated me (hooks 2004). They have satisfied my need for justice from your marginal location in the matrix of colonialism. Your apology has started to give me the power to focus more on love and less on hate (hooks 2000). I only wish I had been wise enough to apologize to you for your suffering under colonialism when you were here in body. Baba, I could now say: "I am sorry for the scars colonialism left on your heart and, if you will speak about it, I will now listen."

Baba, do you remember how, for the rest of the visit, we shared with each other oratures about the gaps that were between us? We established a plan for how I was going to get money to you in a reliable way. You seemed truly proud and happy to hear about my plan to start doing a master's degree, and the only disagreement we had was over my refusal of your suggestion that you start arranging a marriage for me, as I had already found the woman I was going to marry. You were especially perplexed when I showed you a picture of Mandeep. I remember you, Baba, saying: "Why don't you keep her as a girlfriend and marry one of our own?" This could have been your way of conveying that, for the most part, South Asians in our African colonial context have a history of separating themselves from us (Mandela 1995; Kenyatta 1962). M.G. Vassanji (2003) in his novel orature titled *The In-Between World of Vikram Lall*, highlights the separation that exists between South Asians and Africans within the African context and this has made love seem like a foreign concept among our two communities. Nevertheless, Baba, you know that in matters of the heart, sometimes political realities are ignored. This is what Mandeep and I did. By the time I left to come back to Canada, you were joking about having an Indian daughter-in-law and that is when I knew that our colonially fragmented familial bonds were being established again. We are changing our family structure from forced fragmentation to chosen relational engagement (hooks 2000). I hope that in the afterlife our ancestors keep helping you heal beyond our family fragmentation.

I hear the ticking of colonial white supremacy time

You are waiting for me and I am waiting for you

Before us and between us colonialism has established foreign ways

And colonial white supremacy time keeps ticking

You and I struggle to speak to each other in these foreign ways

And colonialism has made us believe that our time keeps ticking away

Where is the cultural dialogue, which allows us to speak to each other?

Where is the path that leads to you?

And why, Ubuntu Ancestors, does this colonial white supremacy
time keep ticking?

In the matrix of colonial white supremacy, we are familial strangers
to each other

Where will we meet while this colonial white supremacy time
keeps ticking?

Should we meet in the middle or should I come across to you?

I cannot think because there is this colonially white supremacy
ticking sound that keeps me running

Where I run to I am unaware

Why I run I am unaware

Oh Baba, dear old Baba, what has become of our world?

Colonialism has taken all while leaving us its ticking idea of
frantic colonial white supremacy time.

Tick, tock, tick, tock

How do we remember with all this ticking?

Fred D'Aguiar (1994) in his orature novel *The Longest Memory*, has helped
me envision what I imagine to be your responses to my questions: "Memory
hurts. Like crying. But still and deep. Memory rises to the skin then I can't be
touched. I hurt all over, my bones ache, my teeth loosen in their gums, and my
nose bleeds. Don't make me remember. I forget as hard as I can. . . . So I look
with these bloodshot eyes that see without seeing, witness without registering
a memory or sensation. . . . My memory is longer than time. I want to forget.
I don't want to see any more" (2, 4–5, 26).

Baba, I now know how much your memories hurt because I now hold
your memories. In this letter, there are many memories of many things but the
sweetest memory is from August 2008 when I was thirty-five years old and you
took me home for the first time. This is the memory that gives me strength to
talk about the early memories that are harder to talk about. Baba, I am giving
you this letter as a way of putting some of those early memories to rest so that
we can focus on love (hooks 2004). There are so many memories I could use
to start this orature, but for this letter I want to start here.

I was probably around five years old. You and I lived in the servants'
quarters, but I was your little hidden secret, as Black domestic workers were

not allowed to have their families in the white communities that they worked in. Like a curious cub, I wanted to explore my environment and you, like a protective lion, tried to establish in me the ability to distinguish danger. You had taught me to hide whenever I saw a white person and, from your teachings, I understood that they posed a danger to our survival (Coates 2015; Somâe 1994; Mathabane 1986). However, my need for play led me to explore the back of the servants' quarters, which was out of sight from the main house and its sprawling gardens. It was when I was returning to the servants' quarters from my secret play area, before you returned for lunch, that I noticed from the periphery of my vision something yellow moving. Instinctively, I hid myself behind a bush. As I watched from behind the bush, I saw an older and much bigger white boy who was wearing a yellow Speedo (swimwear). It was evident that he had just come out of the water, as his body was still dripping wet. From the way he looked around it was clear to me that he was making sure that no one was observing him and, when he was satisfied that no one was watching him, he hid a key under the garbage bin near the main gate. Satisfied that he had accomplished his mission, he went back to the main house and, about an hour later, you came to the servants' quarters looking truly terrified. You searched all over the servants' quarters and when I inquired what you were looking for, you would not answer me back. It was when I offered to help you find what you were looking for that you told me about the missing house key.

I immediately told you that I had seen the white boy in his yellow Speedo hide a key under the garbage bin. At first you would not believe me and were convinced that I was mistaken, but I insisted I knew what I saw and offered to take you to the key. You asked if I could show you the location of the key from the entrance of the servants' quarters and I did. You went and got the key. As you picked up the key, I could see and sense your relief, but as you turned to go to the main house, I could tell that you were angry at how unjustly you were being treated. I now imagine as you were walking up to the main house you realized that this white family was reflective of the settler white government, because they did not care about your needs. The colonial system only responded to Black needs if such action served their greater interest (Mandela 1995). As I watched you, I noticed you pause, turn around, and come back.

You packed up our few belongings into one suitcase and in your other hand; you took my hand and led me up to the main house. You gave the madame her key back and in your broken English said, "My children see your children hide the key. I think your children do this because you tell him to do this thing."

I do not remember the rest of the conversation, I do not remember leaving that beautiful property and I do not remember going around with you seeking help as we had no place for us to stay. But I do remember crying because I was hungry, tired, and scared of walking in the dark. As we stood on Westminster Avenue's bridge behind Ellis Robins School, you suggested we go under the bridge to rest, as it was out of the way and therefore less likely to cause us to be spotted by the police or community watch patrols. As it was the start of winter, the stream under the bridge had a small volume of water flowing through it, so it was safe to be under the bridge. You sat your suitcase down and broke me a piece of bread while we shared a half litre of buttermilk for dinner. When we were done dinner, you invited me to sit on your lap and covered me with your jacket for warmth. How many nights we spent under that bridge I do not remember or know, but in your efforts to care for me you sent me to live in Black townships. You had to keep moving me from one kind family to another in order to ensure I was not too much of a drain on their meagre resources. For how long this went on, I do not remember, but I remember you telling me that, when you were finally able to take me in, you still had to keep me as your little secret in the white community that you worked in because Black families were not allowed in white neighbourhoods (Mathabane 1986; Mugabe 1983).

To address my sense of fragmentation and disconnection while still building up my attachment, you gave me a whistle and told me to put it in my mouth when I went to sleep. I remember you saying: "Now you can get my attention at night when you are feeling sick, afraid, or confused." When I did get a cough you did not seem to get disgruntled by the whistling noises that I made in the middle of the night. All this we communicated in Shona, Nyanja, and some Zulu; because you wanted to ensure that, I knew how to speak our Ubuntu languages, and this action of yours has helped me stay connected with our people and our histories.

Baba, I may fault you for many things, but I can never say I went hungry when you were with me. I remember seeing you go hungry so I could eat. I remember seeing you beg so that I could eat, and I remember saying to you: "I will take care of you when I grow up." So how did we change from showing each other so much love to showing each other outright hostility? Do you remember that, right up to the time I went into the orphanage, you openly expressed your reservation over whether I would be willing to care for you in your old age, as is part of our Ubuntu custom? Even when I was in the orphanage, you would remind me, on the infrequent visits that I made to you, about our Ubuntu relational actions as a way of reminding me that you expected me to care for you. Why, Baba, did you need to remind me of that which was common knowledge and why, Baba, did I not want to care for you?

I am making explicit these questions of confusion, which are situated between us because they are the creation of colonialism and white supremacy. Baba, I am sharing this orature with you because I am recovering our unknown oratures before, between, and after colonialism as a way to move forward in a positive manner (Somâe 1994). Baba, let me continue this orature before you offer your judgment.

When your new employers found out that you had me (a Black child) on their property, they were upset and would have fired you if it was not for the fact that you were the best "house boy" and "garden boy" that they had ever had. Therefore, they agreed to keep you employed temporarily until you proved that you could care for an African child without causing any problems for the white community. On your occasional Saturday or Sunday off, we would go for walks together. These times make up some of my happiest memories and also mark some of my most hurtful memories. For example, I have memories of us going for walks, holding hands. I remember your rumbling laughter. Your infectious smile, which always made me smile too. You radiated so much love that even when our home was packed with strangers and community members in need of your healing services, I never felt forgotten or loved any less. It was only when you were navigating the colonial white system that you became someone else. It was that someone else that I feared because he was unpredictable. His rage against whiteness could at any point be turned against my Black body and our familiar bond offered little protection against his brutality.

I too felt your rage, I too felt my own rage, but you were never vulnerable to my rage, I have always loved you deeply. I judge you without having to navigate the colonial system at its lowest level. I have not felt the kinds of colonially created inadequacies that you have experienced. You left my mother to watch over my two elder siblings as they died from malnutrition and poverty. So how could you have been surprised when some years later, the same predicament of death by malnutrition and poverty threatened my life? The burden of my death was something that my maternal family was unwilling to hold alone again. Especially as your participation in the colonial system as a house servant threatened the existence of your in-laws, who were harassed by the colonial white soldiers for possibly supporting the Black guerrilla fighters and, on the other hand, the Black liberation fighters hassled them for welcoming a sellout (you) into their family (Mugabe 1983; Meredith 1979). My maternal family evaluated that the risk you posed to their family, as a whole, was greater than the meagre resources you offered them. My maternal family, therefore, did not feel they could justify risking their whole family for you. In the wretchedness of this colonially induced poverty and hardship, your marriage broke apart and you were left isolated from all familial bonds. In this state of loneliness, the colonial spirituality of the Watchtower community welcomed you as a Jehovah's Witness, on the condition that you denounced all that was Ubuntu (p'Bitek 1984).

Desperate for acceptance and community, you agreed to their conditions, but as you established yourself beyond their community, you began to question their Watchtower religion. This is when they told you that if you ensured that I walked the righteous path, meaning I remain in the fold of the Watchtower community and was a Witness for Jehovah, you would gain admission into the Kingdom of God. It is possible that you believed in the teaching of the Jehovah's Witnesses or that you thought "new times, new religions." Whatever it was that motivated you to take the steps that you took, it made me feel like a religious sacrificial offering. Right from the moment you introduced Watchtower to me, it felt like you were making me convert to this new religion for your own benefit or because of your trained colonial fear. The Jehovah's Witnesses made you believe that you risked damnation for your beliefs in traditional Ubuntu ways and, because you believed them, you wanted me to become your tool of this colonially promised Watchtower salvation (Somâe 1994). All I had to do was believe in the righteous path of the Jehovah's Witnesses but, even as a child, I could not do this. This was not my religion. It was a foreign religion and I could not follow it.

My refusal to follow in the fold of the Watchtower as a Jehovah's Witness was the start of our volatile relationship. When I refused to go to the Kingdom gathering (because at that time that Jehovah's Witnesses fellowship did not have a hall), you forced me to go by threatening to beat me if I did not go. As a side note, I now wonder where the white members of that Jehovah's Witnesses fellowship met when the Black members were meeting in the bushes, because they were not there with us. It would seem the white brothers and sisters were happy to talk about a multicultural Kingdom Come while participating and perpetuating racism in our communities. I never heard the white Jehovah's Witnesses condemn colonialism as the evil we all needed to stamp out together. However, I can tell you that through the Black leadership, as directed by the white leadership, the message was clear that political activism was diametrically opposed to the will of God (Césaire 1972). Therefore, we, as Black people, were meant to suffer quietly in this physical world while preparing our spirit for the spiritual world through the Watchtower religion. I do not know whether it was my political ancestors guiding me to awareness or if it was my desire to play and have fun with other kids that made me start lying to you about attending the Watchtower services. As you hardly ever went to these services, I was confident you would not find out about my lack of attendance.

My luck ran out one Sunday when you had sent me to the Watchtower service but I had gone to play. On returning home, I failed to notice that you were dressed in your Sunday best suit, which would have been a clue that you had gone to the service. Following my past pattern of lying, I started as usual to give you a fictitious orature about the service, as I removed my Sunday best clothes. I remember turning to face you when, without warning, your fist hit me on the side of the head. I flew into the old dresser and its door broke in half. All I remember is the top half of the dresser hitting me on the head before I passed out. How long I lay unconscious, I do not know, but when I did gain consciousness, I had problems maintaining my balance. As I could not focus on anything, I closed my eyes and went to sleep. The next morning, clear fluid was coming out of my ears and you had to take me to the clinic, and when the nurses asked me what had happened, I told them that the fluid had just started coming out by itself. Without you telling me, I knew I had to protect you in the same manner you protected me from the colonial white supremacy system, but there was no one to protect me from you (hooks 2004).

Baba, as I now reflect on our relationship, I can see that it had started to fragment before the Watchtower incident. The drifting apart of our relationship started when you began trying to mould me into a perfect Black Englishman, because you wanted me to escape some of the colonial exploitations that you had endured as a poor and illiterate Black man (Fanon [1952] 1967). To change my fortune, you encouraged me to make friends with white kids and you were very proud when I started to speak English better than our own languages. I even remember the orature of how I made my first white friend. It was around nine o'clock in the morning when I touched my first white person. I was playing on the main gate of your employer's property when a white boy came up to me. He began to try to communicate with me but I could not understand him because he spoke English and I spoke Shona and Nyanja. An even bigger problem was the fact that I was afraid of this white boy. I had seen your employers from a distance and I had no wish of knowing white people up close. To me, his white skin looked like what I would expect to see when a person had been skinned. I was also scared that, if this white boy touched me, somehow, I would end up with my skin peeled off too and I just did not want to look like that. I was also sure that being white hurt. Somâe (1994), in *Of Water and the Spirit: Ritual, Magic, and Initiation in the Life of an African Shaman*, expresses a similar fear when he first encountered white people. I wonder how young white children react when they first encounter Black people.

As a son of a neo-slave in the colonial settler context of Zimbabwe, my fear kept me safe from the destruction of white supremacy (Mathabane 1986), but to my surprise, my aggressive posturing of unfriendliness (trying to hide my fear) did not deter the white boy in any meaningful way and strangely seemed to motivate him more. What I did not know then was that fear was not the central teaching or central mode of operation for him. Curiosity and discovery were his central teachings (Mandela 1995; Mathabane 1986). Our parents were employed to ensure the safety and uninhibited flourishing of white children as they discovered the beautiful world. The safety of white people was our problem, yet this was not a reciprocal relationship, because every day my Baba warned me about the dangers white people posed to my Black body (Coates 2015; hooks 2004). This is why the white boy had no problem reaching over the gate for my hand. Even though I jumped off the gate in fear, he was not deterred but simply continued to climb over the gate. Afraid and out of ideas for keeping that little white monster at bay, I began to cry. Your employer's dogs, on hearing me cry, began to bark. On hearing this uproar, you came to inquire about the problem and the first words out of your mouth were, "Do you want me to lose my job?" Not knowing how to explain the white boy, I just pointed at the problem. You looked at the white boy and then said to me, "You fool. He just wants to play with you."

I told you I was afraid of him and did not want to play with him, but you said angrily, "Either play with him or go inside, but I cannot have these white people complaining about the noise you are creating." In fear of getting the curse of having what I perceived as no skin, I turned and began making my way toward the servants' quarters. As I was walking away, I heard you speak in a foreign funny language to the white boy. I did not know what you were saying, but before I could reach the safety of the servants' quarters, I heard the white boy crying. Strongly and swiftly, you called me back. I remember you telling me that you did not need a white boy crying at your employer's gate and you did not want white people getting the idea that you were doing something to their kids. While you displayed hostility toward me, I could not understand why you were so intent on making the white boy happy. What power did these people with no skin have that you were afraid of even their children? You spoke to this white boy with the greatest respect and your actions made it clear that his social position was greater than yours because of something he had. Later in life, I would learn that his skin, which I had despised, was the recognized marker for white privilege and white supremacy (hooks 2004).

I remember you saying, "If you do not play with him, I will beat you." As I was more afraid of you than the white-skinned boy, I made my first tentative steps toward him; little did I know that I was being coerced into the culture of compulsory white supremacy. As my new friend led the way into the white community, he reached into his pockets and brought out two toy soldiers. He looked at both of his toy soldiers, looked at me with a smile, and then handed me one of the soldiers. It seems we both understood the universal language of playing war games, and my white friend had a flair for creating imaginary characters that we had to fight. As we were laughing and playing, the white boy extended his hand to take mine and I hesitated for a moment before I allowed his white hand to touch my Black hand. It was through that white boy that I made connections with other white kids from the neighbourhood. I wonder if Desmond Tutu (1994) had this kind of encounter in mind when he wrote *The Rainbow People of God: The Making of a Peaceful Revolution.* Interestingly enough, I cannot remember the name of that white boy or any of those other white kids, with the exception of one because his family took great delight in humiliating me because of my Blackness. When I reflect on those friendships, I cannot help but see their hierarchical nature. The games were always on their terms and I always had to give them the toys that I had made because their parents and you, Baba, always assumed I could make more. Yet I could never take their toys because they were too expensive and, if I did take one of their toys, I was stealing; of course, the same was never true of the white kids' behaviour.

A number of the children that I played with were British, which meant I learned to speak English with an English accent. You, believing that only a literate Black Englishman could lift us out of poverty, set out to make me a literate Black Englishman (Fanon 1963). You, with the help of your employers, had tried to enlist me in a white school, but the school had denied me admission because I did not have a birth certificate. So you decided that the best thing to do was homeschool me. The morning after the school had rejected me, the other domestic servant, the cook, was sitting on the floor with some paper and a pencil in his hands. He summoned me to sit next to him on the floor. As I sat down, I began to feel apprehensive, as I knew then that Cook, the only name I knew him by, and not you would be my teacher. Cook was a big man who commanded respect, and from the day I first met him he had not seemed very interested in me, so I was taken aback to see him so interested in my education. As we settled down to the lesson, I noticed that you had seated yourself in a chair as if you were some expert on colonial educational training. To facilitate my learning, Cook had written on each single piece of paper a single alphabet letter starting with A and ending with E for a total of five alphabet letters, which he handed to me. Very carefully and very methodically, he instructed me on each letter until I could identify each sound with its letter.

Cook was satisfied with our first lesson. All proud of myself, I began to get up with the intention of leaving for play. However, you were of the mind that more was better. Therefore, you tried to make me go over the lesson again, but luck was on my side. As you demanded that I repeat the lesson, your employers called for you. You told me not to go anywhere and that you would be back in a few minutes, but I was too excited about being outside with my friends on a weekend, which meant we could play all day. Cook had started to make his way to the main house so he could prepare breakfast for your white employers. Seeing as there was no one to stop me, I left and went to play with my friends, but as I approached my friends I knew my actions would have consequences and, that evening when I got back from playing, you and Cook were waiting for me. You told me to sit down on the floor and I did so without questioning you, because I could tell from your sombreness that you were in a bad mood. Cook brought out the list of letters we had worked on in the morning and he asked me to read each letter out loud. I took the list of letters from him and glanced at each letter, but I could not remember all the letters or identify which sound went with which letter. I can remember Cook looking at you and saying, "I told you that he would forget most of it."

When you heard and saw how I was failing at meeting your expectations, your dreams and hopes for me were deflated and replaced with disappointment and embarrassment. When you left the room, I knew you were going to find a stick to beat me with, but as I waited for you, it was not the impending beating that I was most disturbed by but the fact that I was not living up to your expectations. Hoping to restore your pride in me, I managed to remember the sounds A, B, and D, but could not match them to the right letters. When you came back, I remember saying very proudly, "I can remember some of the letters," then I made the sounds that I could remember in hopes that this would restore some faith in you about my ability. As you listened to me, you looked unsure of how to respond to my new sense of satisfaction and accomplishment. It was at this point that I noticed that you were as clueless about literacy as I was, which meant it was Cook whom I needed to impress and not you.

Cook then said, "If you can remember some of the sounds, then you can remember all the sounds if you try harder." I looked at you, Baba, and said, "I am sorry but I cannot remember any more." You yelled, "Get your big demon eyes off me and put them on the paper." Not knowing what to do next, I decided to show my inability to recall anything by taking your advice literally. I placed the paper above my eyes and as soon as I did this, we all started to laugh at the silliness of my action. Chuckling, Cook asked, "What are you doing, David?" and I replied, "Putting the letters on my eyes." I had started to laugh again at my joke when you struck me hard on my back with your stick. I turned to protest and you struck me again. "Read the letters," you said through a snigger, and to ensure that your snigger did not fool me you struck me again over my left shoulder. I remember challenging you by asking, "Why are you beating me?" It seems you did not take kindly to having your authority challenged, because in the next moment I could not protect myself fast enough as blows from your stick rained down on me from all angles.

As I reflect back on the ways you beat me, I cannot help but believe that I was your punching bag for the injustice you experienced at the hands of white settler society (Mathabane 1986). Still, I must ask you, how did you forget that I was the voiceless part of you in the power structure of compulsory white supremacy? I remember that you beat me so hard that at one point I stopped feeling the pain and just watched as the blood flowed from my nose and other open wounds on my body. It was Cook who finally stopped you from your violent rage. I had blood blisters under my nails and welts all over my body and, in a conciliatory and somewhat sheepish manner, you told me to go wash the blood from my face. As I wiped the blood from my face, I said to you, "Look at what you have done to me." The audacity of me questioning your behaviour shocked both you and Cook. It may have seemed that you had been remorseful for your actions, but now you were angry at me. The volatile nature of our relationship unsettled Cook and he told you that he did not want to keep teaching me, because he sensed the whole thing could end badly. On hearing this, I was thrilled knowing the teaching problem was over, but, unbeknown to me, my ordeal was far from over.

I did not have a bath or dinner that night and it was also the first night that I laid my own bedding on the floor. I rolled my sore body into my bedding and quickly fell asleep, but was soon startled from my deep slumber. At first, I was confused by the commotion, but the feeling of wetness around my lower body let me know why I was in trouble again. You were cursing at me and I was deadly quiet from my embarrassment and fear. Terrified that you were going to give me another beating, I hung onto my wet sheets. Interestingly, I felt no sense of defiance because I believed I deserved any punishment you gave me for bedwetting. As you got out of bed, I got up too and went to the door and opened it (keeping a safe distance between us). You picked up my bedding and threw it out onto the porch and yelled at me, "Behave like a dog and I will treat you like a dog. Sleep out there, that way you can pee on yourself all you like."

As I sat on the porch looking out into darkness, hearing the sounds of the night, I began to believe I was seeing monsters everywhere and, for the first time, I felt paralyzed by fear. As afraid as I was I knew it was useless to ask you to let me back into the servants' quarters, because I knew you would not listen to me. I did not know where to get help at such a late hour without getting you in trouble with the white settler community. Ben's Shebeen was an illegal house that sold alcohol, in this case in the servants' quarters, and it was my only hope of getting help. This idea seemed good to me, as I was convinced that Ben would be open to talking sense into you because he was respected for his just judgement. I was also sure you would listen to him because he was influential among the other neo-slaves. The next challenge was finding the courage to cross what seemed like a large bush area. It took me a long time before I felt brave enough to leave the porch area and walk out to the gate. A few times, out of fear, I ran back to hide under my pee-smelling wet sheet.

My real obstacle was the bush that separated your employer's property and the property of Ben's employer. All the Black people in the area knew that Ben's employers travelled a lot and their property did not border directly onto any other white person's property. This made his servants' quarters the perfect congregating place where the neo-slaves could relax and talk a little more freely. Knowing what I had to do to get help, I began to give myself pep talks, but each time I heard a loud sound, I ran back to the safety of my bedding. I repeated this process many times over, until I heard something or someone coming down the path behind me. I did not dare look because I did not want to know what monster was ready to pounce on me. So I ran through the bush as fast as I could and only stopped running when I was inside Ben's Shebeen. The place was packed with people and I could not see Ben, so I began to look around for him.

This is when I became aware that people were watching me. I could not understand why everyone was staring at me. As I made my way through the crowd, I heard Worm's[2] loud voice and I walked toward it, because I was going to ask Worm where Ben was. I was walking toward Worm and his girlfriend when I noticed that they were fighting. They were both good looking and everyone was starting to stand around, watching them fight. They both had drunk a little too much and Worm was threatening his girlfriend by saying, "I will burn those new panties if you keep opening your legs so these 'boys' can see them." In response to his threat, his girlfriend stood up and hiked her dress up and then yelled, "Burn them, baby, see if I care." Worm got a lighter out of his pocket and flicked it on. He started to lower the flame between his girlfriend's legs when another man stopped him while saying, "Do you want to do all this in front of your son?" Everyone followed the man's gaze toward me. Someone noticed that I was only wearing a vest without any pants and yelled, "I wonder if Worm burnt them off!" The group broke out into roaring fits of laughter. Before I could move away from them, Worm yelled, "Do not laugh at this boy" and, as quietness fell over the group, Worm pointed to my penis and yelled, "This is our manhood being put on display by the white man. You see this boy's fear. It is our fear. They have grabbed our genitals and have put them on display; how can we fight while they are squeezing our balls?"

In the restrained silence of this colonially created reality, I felt a lump building up in my throat. I fought back the tears that were building up in my eyes, as this would have betrayed how embarrassed and belittled I was at that moment. I wanted to get out of this mean place and I intensified my search for Ben. At last, I found him on the other side of the room and within a few moments, I was pouring my heart out to him. I will never know how he made sense of the situation as I did more sobbing than talking, but somehow he got the point that I needed him to take me home and help smooth things over with you. Ben, being the businessperson that he was, looked at me and said, "Sorry, kid, I cannot take you home, there are a lot of drunken people here and I need their money. How about I get JJ here to take you home?"

JJ took my hand in his big hand and we started for home across the bushes. I felt safe and confident that nothing could get me with JJ by my side. JJ was a big man, but when we got to the front of the gate, JJ would not go any farther. From the look on JJ's face, I knew that he was afraid of facing you. I could not understand why a big man like JJ was afraid of a small man like you. To this question, JJ replied by saying, "Your father is a respected healer and if he has the power to do that then he has the power to hurt you too." I tried to argue against his logic, but JJ just said, "Sorry, kid, I cannot mess with the likes of your father. However, I will tell you what! How about I watch you from the gate here until you get to the porch area and then I will leave." I could tell this was the best JJ could offer and that trying to explain my orature to him was a waste of time. I was sure nothing could or would change his position, so I started the walk toward the porch alone. I walked very carefully, turning toward every sound I heard while praying to the spirits to protect me from all evil. I could hear my heart pounding in my ears and as I made it to my bedding, I pulled the one sheet over my head and closed my eyes. As soon as I closed my eyes, everything started to spin and I began to see different colours flashing. I felt sick, so I pulled the sheet off my head and opened my eyes. Opening my eyes helped me not feel sick. As much as looking into the darkness was scary and hard to do, it was better than feeling sick. To comfort myself in the darkness, I kept telling myself, "Nothing will get me because you, my great ancestors, are watching over me. You are watching over me because I am of you and I am living because this is your will, great ancestor spirits." I would recite these words over and over again that night; little did I know that these words would cross my lips many more times in the future.

As I sat wide awake from fear, I watched the darkness and learned all her sounds. That night I saw the many faces of a single night, from the pitch-black darkness of night to the break of light as dawn approaches and finally the rising of the sun, which announces the beginning of another day. That night I was forced to face the dark monsters of my mind. In my mind, I had proven that I was a true Ngoni. My victory over my own fears seemed to make me feel connected to the natural world in ways that I could not explain. I could see the miracle of life and the beauty and wonder of the world. As I sat with my face turned toward the warmness of the sun, I felt powerful because the world had witnessed me triumph over fear. So when you came out of the servants' quarters, I was at peace with my surroundings and I did everything to make it appear like the whole process had been easy for me. Why I had to always get under your skin, I cannot adequately explain, but I think it had something to do with my wanting power. Sadly, because of your low parenting skills all my provocation led to greater degrees of violence, as you too wanted power (Fanon 1963 [1952] 1967).

We were locked in the cycle of violence and, at times, I would run away as a pre-emptive measure before you found out that I had done something wrong. The advantage of this move was that sometimes I avoided being beaten, and the disadvantage was that it made me appear as if I was suffering from delusions. I would live in the street alleyways, bushes, and wastepaper bins, and at other times I would break into abandoned buildings and live there. I had no problems searching for food in garbage bins or begging for money on street corners. If I made a lot of money, I would use it to buy groceries to use as a peace offering or as a bribe to get you to let me come back to you. It was fairly common for me to run away for months on end and then not remember or know why I had run away from you in the first place. At times like this, I would come back to you genuinely confused about why I had run away and sometimes you would show extreme tenderness and understanding. I remember a number of times you performed ritual ceremonies to cleanse me of evil spirits. However, there were other times when all you wanted to do was get your hands on me so that you could beat the hell out of me.

Baba, I do not believe that when you hit me with your Ngoni club so hard that I could not stand up that you were teaching me any lessons. I do not believe either that when you threw that brick at my head you were trying to discipline me. I think at that point you had given up on me and you wanted to get rid of me. I remember you telling the social worker that it was better for her to take me before you killed me, but when you said this, I was not offended because I understood that you were still angry at my behaviour. But I was shocked when, after some months had passed, you stated in a court of law that you did not want me. You told a judge you could not care for me anymore and that is how I ended up in the orphanage called St. Joseph's House for Boys at the age of eight. Once I was in the orphanage, I saw less and less of you. You even started another family and I became more disconnected from you. However, I did not let any of this worry me because I believed I had entered the world of whiteness through the orphanage.

When I arrived at the orphanage, St. Joseph's House for Boys, it had about thirty-five boys there. Of this number, about seventeen boys were of white descent and thirteen boys were of mixed race. The mixed-race boys, for the most part, identified with their whiteness, as it was associated with wealth and power. I, being one of five Black boys admitted into the orphanage, saw it as my entrance into whiteness and felt privileged to share clothes with white boys, eat the same food as they did, sleep in the same dormitory, and share the same washrooms. I felt that the orphanage was allowing me to be as white as I could be as a Black person. I therefore did everything possible to expel my Blackness so that I was more acceptable to whiteness. I tried to limit my contact with the other Black boys in hopes to become more acceptable to whiteness. You became a reminder of the Black suffering I was trying to escape, so I limited our contact to a minimum. Even though there were reminders of my Blackness, I felt I was experiencing what it was to be white (Fanon [1952] 1967).

I had my own bed with white sheets, a full-length towel, and toiletries that I did not have to share with anyone. I was put into a previously all-white school, which was now integrated due to independence. I confirmed my own status into whiteness when I started to dream in English. This, to me, was evidence that I was one of them. Yet this happiness was punctuated by moments of isolation and ridicule because I was wetting my bed. The white schools that I had so desperately wanted admission into were now telling me that I was slow and, at worst, brain damaged. I hated those white children who I perceived as fitting the system perfectly. I went into a rage at the slightest provocation by a white child and would hit him for having white privilege and for not understanding the hardship of being Black in a racist world (D.D. Mucina 2015; Mathabane 1986). In their colonial education system, my Blackness, my behaviour, my thoughts, and my beliefs were all evidence that my mind was disabled. To fix my disabled mind they started labelling me, because this ensured that there were government resources made available to ensure my unstable mind would be fixed. Because they had started on this path, everything that I did was reflective of my unstable mind, which made me more volatile, which further confirmed their diagnosis (D.D. Mucina 2015). In my moments of silence, I had started to realize that I did not fit into their white system. Nothing in their white settler system was culturally familiar to me. I remember feeling lost and betrayed by the white dream, which spoke to me but was never for me (hooks 2004; Fanon 1963).

I soon learned that in the white settler community my limitations in reading and writing were treated as a major part of my total defining identity, which meant disability was all of me and none of my other identities could supersede it (Michalko 2002). Each new test performed on me confirmed my disability, but when they first labelled me as mentally retarded and brain damaged, there was some relief because I believed their labelling showed that my disability was beyond my control. I figured that their labelling of me as disabled would stop them from seeing me as a problem (Titchkosky 2007). I thought this process would protect me from all the criticism and humiliating putdowns, because I moved from that category of invisible disability to visible disability, but I was wrong.

Baba, at this point in my life I had started to believe that I had failed at being a part of white settler society until I realized how much they valued dominance or, you could say, targeted controlled aggression. I learned this valuable lesson in the orphanage. Part of living in the orphanage was the ritual of establishing where you ranked in the hierarchy of masculine power (hooks

2004). Thus, physical fights over dominance were a frequent occurrence. I was one of the youngest boys in the orphanage and was labelled as disabled, thus I was on the lowest rung of masculine power (McRuer 2006). Therefore, I had to ensure that my fights were vicious so that I was viewed as an intimidating opponent. When I fought, I showed no mercy. My goal was always to achieve maximum damage and humiliation for the defeated opponent, especially if I was fighting someone from my school. This communicated the message that I was not someone to mess with (hooks 2004). My fighting in school got me noticed by the rugby coach and soon I was on the rugby team. This was the first positive affirmation that I received at school and it had nothing to do with academics. It was all predicated on my masculine ability to assert physical violence against another human being (hooks 2004). I was so good at rugby I even started to believe I could transfer the skills I was learning to other athletic arenas, and I was right. I won the school's 800-metre race and, through these sporting endeavours, I became a somebody beyond my embodiment of Blackness and disability (McRuer 2006; hooks 2004).

Baba, the success and affirmation that I was getting for using my physical strength against other children led me to join the boxing club at the orphanage. This seemed like a logical step for me, especially as I had learned the fundamentals of boxing within three months of starting. I felt confident to challenge a bigger boy in the junior category of the orphanage. All the senior boys in the orphanage wanted to see this fight, as it had the potential to be very bloody. Nevertheless, just when I thought I understood whiteness, I met one who contradicted my experience with white settlers. This bigger white boy was unwilling to fight me, so the older boys and I began to taunt him. We followed him around the orphanage calling him all kinds of horrible names.

In an effort to comment on the absurdity of white cultural violence, which we embodied through our violent behaviours toward each other, the targeted white boy, without antagonizing any of us, in very dramatic fashion, began to question an imaginary figure instead of directly questioning us: "Why must we treat each other so badly? Is this not what we hope to have escaped from? So now why are we doing what was done to each of us to each other?" And to emphasize this eloquent point he began to laugh at the stupidity of all of our behaviours. For a moment, we were all stunned by the truth of his words. In that moment, the white boy had changed the white power game but I, the Black child, was not interested in his new interpretation because my sense of self was now tied to that white hierarchical power of masculinity (hooks 2004). I, therefore, did not care whether he was right or wrong and whether he made sense or not. All I cared about was controlling the white power game from the top of the hierarchy (hooks 2004). The question of whether to play the game or not was of no consequence to me. The way I understood the orphanage was that you played the power game as the only way to survive or the pressure of not conforming killed you. If you chose to survive, then, by default, you chose the game, and the game was only controlled from the top.

As you know, Baba, it is said that the tongue is sharper then the *assegai* (spear), so when I unleashed my tongue upon that white boy, I was planning on doing deadly damage. I remember looking at the other boys and asking them: "Who the fuck is this white boy talking to? All of a sudden, he believes in the spirits of the ancestors. *Roots*[3] has fucked him up or do we need to call the psychiatrist to see him again?" If the white boy had touched us with the spell of reason, then I had the antidote and I was blowing it in the direction of the four winds. The mention of calling the psychiatrist again for the targeted white boy had all the other boys howling with laughter. My verbal attack had the equivalent of a leopard attacking a lion, so I was fully prepared for a fight, but the counterattack that I received was not something I was prepared for. The targeted white boy stared at me and in that cold hard stare I read, "Do you want me to put your fucking shit out for us to laugh at? The fact that you are labelled brain damaged, you can't read or write, you wet your bed every single night, and you hide the fact that your father is a domestic servant. Or is it domestic slave?" All this, I interpreted from a few seconds of silent staring. My verbal attack had left me open to a verbal counterattack by the white boy, and on this verbal battleground, I perceived my personal secrets, embedded in Black poverty and disability as making me the weaker party in this battle. Not wanting to face the humiliation and embarrassment of a personal verbal attack, I began to silently plead for forgiveness, sympathy, and mercy. I knew that a physical fight, in the long run, did not do continual damage in the same manner that a verbal attack did. A verbal attack held power in your presence or in your absence and it could be remembered and used against you over a longer period of time. These violent truths had a way of making themselves anew over and over again, and I did not want to live with the shaming orature of my Black poverty and disability, as this would be the dominant orature that followed me around.

It seems, Baba, I did not want the white boy to do what I had done to him. With the power of making my personal information public, the white boy chose to respect my privacy. To let me know that he was not going to attack me, he softened his challenging stare and glanced downward as if to acknowledge his intent to call a truce. This led to the deflation of this heated situation and no one seemed too disappointed about missing the fight. It seems a greater lesson had been learned, and I have never forgotten that gracious act by a white settler boy. How is it, Baba, that I had become a part of the white settler system and a white boy was modelling Ubuntuness to me? How is it that I was learning from the actions of a white settler boy when I had closed myself off to hearing the teaching of our Black old ones?

In the structural hierarchy of white supremacy, we the colonized Ubuntu have learned that the humanity of the other is of little consequence to us until the other threatens to undermine our humanity (Fanon 1963). For the white settlers in Zimbabwe, it was the Black-led bush war that made Blackness visible beyond a useless visibility (Mugabe 1983). For me, it was the fear of having my personal information made public to the other boys in the orphanage by the targeted white boy that made him visible to me beyond a useless visibility. How did they get you, Baba, to play their game of white hierarchical masculine power? Was it through their religious intimidation and economic manipulation? In this neo-colonial global society, the humanity of the other is respected in the moment that the other threatens your humanity, which means the threat must be real, it must be an imminent threat geared for manifestation, and the harm must be calculable (hooks 2004). So my question to you, Baba, is how did you fight back? What was the threat you posed to them?

Baba, my need to be perceived as normal while embodying a Black body in a racist white political system made me lie about my peasantry Black status while also working hard to hide my disability. These secrets added to the already existing power difference that existed between the white settler colonial society prescription of normalcy and my self-perception. This is not to say that I did not know another standard of measurement, because I did. The Ubuntu standards have always been there for us, but you, Baba, encouraged me and demonstrated how to disregard our Ubuntu knowledge systems and, from early childhood, you trained me to know that the only standard that mattered was the white standard (Fanon [1952] 1967). Yet you were not consistent, because in certain critical situations you would revere traditional Ubuntu knowledge. How did you hold such tensions together?

The first time I remember being proud of my Blackness was when I saw Comrade Robert Mugabe as the prime minister of the new Zimbabwe. To me he was living evidence of heroic responsible Black power in action. He was the Black knight in shining armour and I wanted to be him. I loved Comrade Robert Mugabe because he showed a love for his Blackness without fear of whiteness (Meredith 1979). White folks were beside themselves with fear, hatred, and respect for Comrade Robert Mugabe because he led Black men and women who showed a lack of fear and reverence toward the colonial struc- tures of white supremacy. As much as I idolized Comrade Robert Mugabe, I knew from being labelled brain damaged that I could never reach his status or the level of education that he had acquired, which most whites in Zimbabwe openly acknowledge surpassed their own. Hence, Comrade Robert Mugabe became an anomaly I could not obtain, just like whiteness (Coates 2015; hooks 2002). Also, I was happy to be Black during the nights when Father Little (the warden of the orphanage) would sexually abuse the blond, blue-eyed boys. We were so conditioned to experiences of abuse that we simply accepted it. The abusers had brought us to the point where we did not question the abuse and we were happy when the abuse did not target us. Yet, in this hell, I still believed I was in a better place than you were, Baba.

Regardless of my disability, I knew I would never end up like you, Baba. Meaning, I would never be a domestic neo-slave for white people, because my sporting skills had opened doors that were not available to an orphanage child, especially a Black one. For starters, I was given a rugby scholarship to Prince Edward High School, one of the most prestigious schools in Zimbabwe. The Lions Club sent me on an Outward Bound course while other members offered to adopt me and still others were willing to give me good employ- ment with a respectable paycheque. While my rugby skills also gave me the opportunity to travel overseas, my visibility as a Black person in Zimbabwean sport was interesting, because it was both threatening and acceptable to the white settler society in Zimbabwe. My Blackness was threatening because it represented Blackness taking over everything dear to whiteness (hooks 2000). Yet, paradoxically, it was acceptable because I participated within their guidelines, thus conforming to whiteness (Fanon 1963). However, at the time, it seemed to me that my sporting reputation had moved me from depriva- tion to the freedom to make choices. The problem was that I had accepted whiteness and, therefore, I was not concerned with its cultural limitations as I contemplated my new entrance into the power of whiteness. At that time, the best and easiest offer to me came from the first female warden, Dianne.[4] After having known me for some time, she proposed a marriage with offers of luxuries that came with being white. I would have taken up Dianne's offer if I had not felt ashamed by the prospect of marrying a white woman I did not love, was old enough to be my mother, and was as manipulative as a hungry praying mantis. Under these circumstances, I kept all my options open by not committing myself to anything until I was sure that I could live with the decision I made.

As I made these choices to start a new life, you, Baba, were being kicked out of the very extreme margins of white settler society. You were old and most of the white settlers who had been your source of employment had left the country (Meredith 1979). The new Black elites had no need for you. From there on, you were homeless and penniless. The bushes were your home again, but this time you were alone as I was charting my way toward Outward Bound. I had told myself that I did not want to be a sexual slave to an older white woman, be a Black pet to a racist white family, or be defined through sports. I had told myself that I wanted to define myself through a meaningful career and the only way, at that time, I could perceive myself achieving that goal was by going to work for Outward Bound Zimbabwe. My employment with Outward Bound Zimbabwe, which was experiential learning, led to me to the opportunity of working for Outward Bound South Africa and later to the chance of immigrating to Canada with the help of my first wife, who was white and who connected me to Outward Bound Canada.

After separating from my first wife, I left the Outward Bound Canadian community because I felt I had lost their trust, especially as a number of them knew that I had a lover in South Africa. As my first wife was deeply embedded in the Canadian Outward Bound community, it made sense for me to leave that community. I was ready to also move on to another chapter of my life; the question was, would it be here in Canada or would it be in South Africa, where the Outward Bound School had offered me a senior position with no time limit on it? This meant that Outward Bound South Africa was telling me that I could call them anytime and say, "I want to come home and start that job." They wanted me after knowing about my shady defunct relationship. They wanted me while fully understanding all my strengths and limitations. In that moment, I knew that the ancestors had delivered me from the suffering. Fearing nothing, I called Immigration Canada and spoke to an agent. I informed him that my marriage to a Canadian woman had ended and I asked him if I would need to return to Zimbabwe. The agent was taken aback by my inquiry; he told me that he would have to check with his superiors, as he had never received such a call. After consulting with his supervisor, he asked, "Have you ever been on welfare?" To which I responded, "Never." He then asked if I had a job and I responded that I did. He then told me that I was the kind of person that they wanted in Canada and that I should enjoy my life in Canada without any worry. At that moment, I realized I could start afresh anywhere in the world, without exploiting anyone. Just like that, the ancestors had delivered me from deliberately and intentionally starting exploitative relationships. Through my rugby skills and the rugby network, I was able to be connected to job postings with the Vancouver School Board. I applied to a position as an alternative program worker within the Vancouver School Board and, to my amazement, my learning disability was as much an asset as my Outward Bound and sporting experience.

Baba, in my new life, you were a distant memory, I did not know of your struggling and suffering and, even if I did, I would not have cared. I was enjoying my life in Vancouver. I lived in a bachelor apartment on Fraser Street just above mid-Main. I was friends with a lot of the nightclub bouncers around the lower mainland. I had VIP status at most nightclubs and if I did not know the bouncers at a nightclub, I would just ask them to let me in. This worked for the most part because I was the only Black guy around, so it was never a problem for them to let me in. Working on call for the Vancouver School Board was perfect for me because they gave me steady work without any commitment beyond my work hours, and when my work was done I was free to play rugby and party hard. That is, until I started to work at Brock Elementary School in Vancouver. How those Indigenous and culturally diverse children got me to love them is a mystery. I do not know if it was the fact that I was working in special education and, therefore, I could identify with their at-risk status. I tried to keep them interested in school through sports, after-school programs, camping trips, intervention, and prevention programs that focused on drugs, sexual abuse, and youth violence. As these children and their families shared their oratures with me, I too shared my oratures with them. Our context was different, but our oratures had some shared common meanings and, from this base of shared meaning, I was able to let some of those children see that they had the power to help each other change their own lives. As I supported, challenged, and sometimes pushed them toward change, they did the same for me. Those children inspired me to take all kinds of literacy programs so that I could go to college. While working in my office, I remember one of them saying: "You could help a lot more kids if you were a teacher." And I responded to this advice by saying: "I can't make school work for me." And another one of the students said: "We can't make school work either, but you are not giving up on us, so we won't give up on you." In that moment, those children became my old ones and I responded to their challenging counsel by saying: "If you guys can work at it, then I too can try working at it." So the students I was serving became my mentors. This is the power of love and it inspired me to believe I could make a difference. Love gave me belief in myself (hooks 2004; Okri 1997). Using this inspiration, I went to see a white sister who was a great educator and planner. She helped me create my first self-directed education process map. As soon as I started this education route, I knew that regardless of the barriers in front of me, I would be determined to continue.

Baba, as afraid as I was about starting school again, I was even more afraid of letting those children down because I felt accountable and responsible for their counsel. Therefore, I worked hard at acquiring some basic literacy skills, but I would not have achieved this goal without the help of my adopted family members. I have Black brothers and sisters; Indigenous brothers and sisters; a Korean aunty; a white uncle; a Black father; two Black mothers; and an Indigenous mother. I wish I could think of another word that conveys how blessed I feel. My children and my wife make my cup overflow. I am aware that I am using Christian metaphors here, but fuck, what can I say? Relations with my in-laws are good, and even though there are still challenges, progress is being made every day. All these family members have played a role in my educational success. I see all these people that love me as the embodiment of my ancestors. I exist because they exist. This is Ubuntu.

The literacy programs that I took prepared me to start taking a night counselling certificate program at Vancouver Community College and, for the first time in my life, I started getting good academic grades. As soon as I completed the counselling certificate program, I was given a promotion to the position of youth and family worker at Brock Elementary School, which meant I could offer counselling to families and to students. Having tasted academic success born of very hard work, I was confident that I could take a university transferable certificate program in social services at Langara College. As this was an intensive full-time program, I had to leave my job and become a full-time student. This was hard to do, as I was walking away from a safe job to start living on student loans and disability-access funding. With a lot of community support, I transferred to the University of Victoria where I did a degree in child and youth care. After having worked hard to get to the university, I started to believe that I had the academic skills to relax a little more. I started to party a little more than I could handle and because of this my grades went down, which resulted in me having to explain my low grade in one of my courses to the program coordinator.

Remembering all the support and hard work that it had taken to get me to the university, I felt ashamed of how I was letting down so many people. I could not help but realize that I was squandering an opportunity that so many in Zimbabwe would have cherished. At this point it was clear to me that I was disrespecting the people who had supported me to be where I was and I was disrespecting myself by throwing away this good opportunity for no good reason. After that self-talk, I refocused on the hard work before me and, in no time, I was doing my MA in Indigenous Governance. I was working hard on the writing and editing of my papers, editing each one eight to twelve times before I felt it was good enough, and at other times, just hanging in there until something shifted and I got it right. These were just typical days at the office for me. Once I understood my academic process, I was confident that I could do my PhD, and achieving that goal became my driving force. In August of 2008, while doing my doctorate at OISE, University of Toronto, I journeyed to you with my young family. In the next Millet Granary, I introduce the oratures that came from my journey to you and you taking us to our ancestral family home.

In this Ubuntu orature, how has accountability and responsibility been represented?

How does this Ubuntu orature represent decolonial love?

How is this Ubuntu orature creating possibilities beyond colonial pain, isolation, abandonment, and hate?

The Journey to You and Our Journey Home

Methodological questions that guided my writing of this Millet Granary:

1. *How do I centre decolonizing actions in my life and in my scholarship?*
2. *How do we centre Indigenous love as liberating actions?*
3. *How do I ground relational respectful curiosity and open dialogue?*

Sanibonani Baba, a few years into our married life, I started having intense dreams about your death and it is then that I knew I needed to conclude my affairs with you. Mandeep understood right away how important this trip was for me. So she started helping me make our plans for going to Africa. When Mandeep's sister, my sister-in-law, Sandy (not her real name) heard that we were going to Africa, she made it clear that if we were going home to Africa then she was coming. Fearing that such a move would not endear me to my in-laws, I tried to dissuade Sandy from going by telling her of the hardships we would be encountering on this trip, but she was set on coming. Renée, my adopted Black sister, heard about our trip and told us she wanted to come too. I immediately agreed, as I saw this as a great opportunity for her to connect with the mother continent and our people. South Africa is also an important place for me, as you taught me that this geographical space is our natal home as Ngoni. Our journey to you started in our ancestral natal homelands and loosely followed the Ngoni migration routes. As we travelled north, I had a chance to "introduce" my new young Ubuntu families to a changing Southern Africa. Here are the journal notes from these experiences.

Figure 10. Waiting to get Baba travel documents at the Malawian Embassy in Harare, Zimbabwe.

Johannesburg

Sanibonani Baba, I am not going to bore you with the Johannesburg airport details for they are like any other airport details. I am not going to bore you with details that I do not care to remember. I am going to give you fragments of remembering that have been burned into my memory bank. Each memory is an orature among oratures. Yet this particular memory stands out and speaks to me in this particular time. It is possible that, at another time, another orature from this experience may stand out, but for now, here are the oratures that I want to share.

A medium-sized African man in his early fifties comes up to us and asks in a South African accent, "Waiting for Diamond Digger Lodge?" In an unrehearsed reply, in unison some of us say, "Yes" and others say, "Right." The man says, "Let's get your stuff and go. By the way, I am Madiba."

"Madiba is your name?" I question.

The man: "Yes, like Nelson Mandela."

As we start to talk about his name, he begins to lead us to the vehicle. As we near the vehicle, Madiba switches into his tour guide/operator role and says in his official voice, "Welcome to South Africa, is this your first visit?"

I say, pointing to the others: "For them, yes but not for me."

Madiba: "Where are you from?"

Me: "I was born in Zimbabwe."

Madiba: "Mugabe, that old man is too much. So you are my brother. What about them?"

Sandy says: "We are from Canada."

And Renée adds: "But, my parents are from Grenada."

As if not to be outdone, Mandeep adds: "Our parents are from India [meaning her and Sandy]."

For the rest of the drive, we talk easily with Madiba, who shifts from being informal in one conversation to being very formal in the next conversation. I wonder if it is always like this for him or if it is especially different today. I wonder how he views his brother travelling with three women, two Indian women and one Black woman. Does he wonder which one of these three is with me or has he generously considered me a polygamist?

Baba, as I go to register at the hotel, I notice that all the domestic workers are Black and all the administration staff are white. As they see us, all the Black staff very politely greet us with the exception of the white man, who is painting in front of the area where we have left our bags. His body language makes it very clear that he does not have to be polite to us. A white female tourist walks by and the white painter greets her with a smile. Aware that we have noticed him greeting her, he turns toward his work with a sour-faced expression, which communicates to me: "There is no smile or anything for you here, darky." As I walk towards the registration office, I see a Black sister working while tears run down her face, and from within the registration office I know from the accent, tone, and the information I can hear that the managing white staff are complaining about how every week a close relative in her family dies. I correctly assume that they are talking about the Black sister, who is the one who is crying. How have they missed the global news about AIDS devastating Black communities in Southern Africa? Has AIDS developed a racist ranking system or is it easier to make it a Black problem so we can distance each other from our relational bonds? In this situation, the first thought that comes to me is that I am still in a colour-conscious South Africa where white is at the top, all other colours are positioned in the middle, and Black is positioned at the bottom again. Even as we are told that we have taken control of our Black nations, we still feel and see white colonial power. I guess Desmond Tutu's (1994) *The Rainbow People of God* is still on a colour-ranking system.

Cape Town

Sanibonani Baba, we are in Cape Town, your favourite city. The cab driver, who is a white male, says: "Watch out for these buggers, they can steal you blind." He is talking about a young Black man who is looking tired and hungry. Here, Black masculinities are being positioned as a threat to white capitalistic interests and being Black and poor marks a man as a threat (hooks 2004).

The cab driver then adds: "You can find accommodation that suits your needs within this one block, just make sure that the rest of you stay with the bags while one of you looks for a place."

The Black brother from the street says: "Don't worry, brother, I'll take care of you. I know all the hotels around here. I will take you to a cheap, very good place. Don't worry, brother, I've got you covered. In less than twenty minutes, I will have you resting in your own place. But brother, I need something. I have not slept in two days. I'm hungry and tired. I do not need much, just a little. Can you help?"

I say to my brother from the street: "I'll see what we can do. But first help me. Just to be clear, I am not promising you anything. Are we clear about that?" My colonial capitalistic power and my fear of our Black masculinities make me forget our Ubuntu ethics of relational care. Instead of taking care of this brother's need for food first, I make him work for me. This is capitalistic power, which makes us put relational love aside while centring our colonial power and fear (hooks 2002; Okri 1997).

Brother from the street says: "Yes, brother, I understand. Whatever you can, give me. I will take it. It is all up to you."

"OK," I say to the street brother, but his statement sits heavily with me because I know the distance from his reality to my reality, from my perspective, lacks a good explanation because this shit just does not add up or make sense. In the face of such realities, I find myself firmly believing that my ancestors are directing and guiding me on my path forward. Even as I fuck up, I still feel loved and protected by the ancestors. Why am I being given all these experiences? What am I to learn from my ancestors, and then what am I to do with all this learning?

I do not know why I am tipping this cab driver, because I am sure he is a racist. I have not yet quite figured out the currency exchange rate and I give the cab driver a tip of about eight rand. I can tell from the smile on his face that I have tipped much higher than he was expecting.

Even as he tries to express his gratitude, the colonial reality between us emerges when he says: "Keep an eye on these Blacks. Sorry, I mean blocks."

With a hint of sarcasm, I say to the cab driver: "Don't worry; I think my brother will take care of us."

As the cab driver gets back into his vehicle, he mumbles: "Your problem," before driving away.

Brother from the street says to me: "Brother, come, everything is very close here. You don't have to go very far."

Mandeep says: "Go ahead, Babe, and we will watch the baggage."

Brother from the street says: "Let us start with this place across the road. All kinds of people like it and it is also called Ubuntu. I will wait for you here."

I ask: "Why?"

Brother from the street replies by saying: "If they see me with you on the security camera, they won't open the door for you. I am a street man. They do not like us. Better you go alone."

The man at reception says they are all booked up for the week and I am sad because this place has a great feel to it and the guests sitting around are indeed a reflection of the South African rainbow nation and, as a result, everyone wants to be here. Hence, there are no rooms left. Brother from the street takes me to three other places, which will not open their security gate and inform me through their intercom system that they have no rooms available. I wonder if there is no room because I am a Black African man (Coates 2015). I am starting to get frustrated when my brother from the street says: "Try this place; it is very good but is a little more expensive than the other places I have shown you." He leads me to a Daddy Long Legs Independent Travellers Hotel and I ring the security bell. I know the receptionist on the other side can see me. So I am surprised when I hear a very pleasant-sounding woman say: "Please come in, sir, you will find me at reception if you walk up the stairs." As I am walking up the stairs, I tell myself that this pleasant-sounding woman must be a Black woman but, when I arrive at the reception desk, I see a striking woman who is white, tall, slim, and brunette. She says: "Can I offer you a drink before I attend to your other needs?" I decline the offer of a drink and am shocked by her great service. This is a country of contradictions. One minute you are being despised and, in the next, you are being treated like a king. My experience with white people in South Africa taught me that the spirit of Ubuntu among white people is still a hit-and-miss affair. This being said, the hotel crew from Daddy Long Legs took such good care of us that we all became good friends and still keep in contact via Facebook's social network.

Sanibonani Baba, as these are journal entries, I am only giving you the facts that stand out for me, which means dates and times become compressed or flattened in order to engage with the experience or facts. Case in point, the rest of the orature of the brother from the street has no time indicators to convey the passage of time, because we met when we did and it was never planned. We never knew when we would meet our brother, but when we did meet we tried to take care of each other. Our brother was generous with his information while making sure we were safe. For example, the girls were out one night on the streets and a group of guys were making it hard for them to get back to the hotel by blocking their path. Being well known on the street, our brother gently intervened by making it clear that these were his sisters and the harassment stopped right away. For our part, we tried to give our brother from the street as much as we could, but sadly, after that encounter we saw our brother only one other time. To this day, I still hope that his luck changed and that he found that job he was looking for. I want to be hopeful about the fact that our brother was nowhere to be found on the last few days before we left Cape Town. I also wonder if he was able to stay and survive the economically induced xenophobia against Black migrants by Black South Africans. We never got to say goodbye to him and I still find this sad because I would have liked to have known him a little better. Who was he, what was his totem, and who was waiting for him back home?

To Durban on the Shosholoza Meyl

Sanibonani Baba, the train should have left fifteen minutes ago, but we have not started loading yet. I am a little anxious, because I am not sure if we are on the right platform. I have been assured that we are on the right platform, but I have seen many people coming and going and we are still here. When we came here to buy our train tickets, I remember the Congolese man who cut my hair yesterday warning me that this is the place where thieves make their fortunes. He told me not to allow anyone to take any of our bags out of our sight. When we left the hotel, the staff warned us about the high levels of robbery that take place in the train station. After checking in for the train, the desk clerk warned us to watch our baggage. She informed us to only get directions and assistance from official customer representatives who wore uniforms and were situated strategically throughout the train station. Again, Black masculinities have been positioned as the threat, but on the question of why, we all remain quiet. The answer to this question would require revolutionary change, but at this moment we only wanted change that benefited us.

After such cautioning, Baba, I see myself scrutinizing every young Black man who comes to stand near us. Though my colonial lens, I see the distance between myself and, what I perceive as, the other young and poor Black males. As I stand there, I become the Black colonizer fearing his own Ubuntu reflective masculinities (Fanon 1963). Fearing my own reflection, I notice two Black male youth pushing the biggest load of luggage I have ever seen. I wonder where the luggage owners are. Whoever they are, they seemed to be breaking all the warning instructions we have been given about caring for our luggage. From the direction that the young men have come from, an old coloured (of mixed race) grandfather, out of breath from trying to keep up, yells: "That is the right place, you can off load." The old grandfather inquires with the official if the young men can help get the luggage on the train and the official informs him that it would not be possible, but offers to get some attendants to load the luggage onto the train.

Grandfather turns to the direction that he has come from and about nine coloured elderly grandmothers are descending upon him in the most jovial manner. They are laughing, giggling, and joking with each other. These grandmothers' behaviour has a girlish mischief, which seems to contradict their elderly status. As I watch them, I see the inner child within each of the women, an inner child who has been oppressed by the many years of adult responsibility. Their joy and carefree behaviour is as fresh as morning dew on a blade of grass. Their smiles and jovialness are beginning to infect my overly alert and anxious behaviour. They are all talking at the same time and, when they notice this phenomenon, they begin to laugh at each other. I am quietly laughing at this drama that they are creating when I notice that my companions are also doing the same. Some of the women notice us laughing at them and they wave, smile, or say hello and then return to engaging each other in loud, friendly banter.

Baba, you will not believe that their mere presence has changed everything. These old ones have taken the fear away and replaced it with love. I have no anxiety or worry about losing anything. These old ones are helping me see all the other smiles on all the other people. Across from me on the furthest platform, I see a young man holding a newspaper. He is pretending to read it. Two other well-dressed young men approach him with two large bags and one of them whispers something in his ear. Slowly he closes his paper up and scans the area before getting up. For a brief moment, our eyes meet and he smiles at me and I cannot help but smile back. I turn to see if anyone else in our group has seen him, but the girls are engaged with watching the antics of the Gogos (grandmothers). When I look back again, the young men have vanished. I say nothing to anyone, but wonder if I had witnessed a robbery. Yet no one seems to be complaining about missing bags. Could it be that the young men were bootleggers selling stuff illegally on the train station premises? Whatever the case was, Baba, I am no longer scared of our Black masculinities, thanks to the jovial manner of those great Gogos and that grandfather. Regardless of the racist fear tactics used in South Africa, and regardless of the poverty and oppression that create violence, even in these situations a smile can win you over or it can distract you from your own anxieites.

As White People Come Home, Black People Leave

Sanibonani Baba, we see racism. We feel racism. Yet I force my family to keep silent until the pain is too much, then we fight amongst each other (Kuokkanen 2015). This, indeed, is a peculiar experience. Colonial history makes it possible. I am told it is over, but my experience and my feelings communicate otherwise. I am in my friend's home, en route to Swaziland. He lives in a beautiful neighbourhood with his beautiful white family. Like him, his neighbours are white. As we were driving up to his house, an armed security truck passed us on patrol and, as we were parking the car, a police truck slowed down to check us out. It is just before 5:00 p.m. and we are observing a Black exodus.

Mandeep says: "Why are all the Black people leaving?"

I say: "Because they are the domestic workers."

Renée questions: "Is it okay for us to be here?"

Sandy does not say a word but I can see that she is very uncomfortable. I tell everyone that it will be okay, because this is a very good friend. Our gracious hosts welcome us into their home. I am trying to get my family to relax in a colour-conscious South Africa, but it is not working. The next day, a Black house cleaner arrives and, on seeing visitors, makes a request for a uniform and we are all shocked into silence. For the first time, Sandy makes her discomfort known by enquiring about when we are leaving. I tell everyone that we will be leaving in three days. I tell everyone that our hosts are doing everything they can to make us comfortable so we should suck it up (hooks 2004). We spend the day at the beach and in the evening, we hang out on the river shore drinking and eating. The conversation is very formal and polite. My friend and I reminisce about our youthful experiences, but even there, Baba, I see the race lines (Mathabane 1986). I am now aware that my friend's memories are of a different Zimbabwe than mine. A colour-conscious South Africa reminds me that what we appreciated of our friendship was limited to small moments of shared humanity, but the white racism was always there (Fanon 1963). I guess if you experience racism all the time, you have to ignore it sometimes to give yourself some relief. Is this how we have survived, Baba?

On the Friday, two nights before we leave, our hosts want us to meet their friends at a costume party. Renée and Sandy make it clear that they cannot handle any more of this white-gated community and have no desire to meet any white racists. I think to myself that they are being a little melodramatic, but agree that they should stay back if they are not up to it. Mandeep does not want to go, but she feels obliged as my wife to come. I try to tell her that she does not need to go to the party, but she will not put this burden down, so we go together. The first thing we notice as soon as we get to the party is that there is no other visible race except for whiteness. Most people are speaking between English and Afrikaans. We are introduced to a few of our hosts' friends and it is painfully clear that we do not belong here. One of the guests comes up to us and says: "So how did you guys get into this party? You couldn't have gate crashed, or are you the servers?" This is meant to be a joke, but it seems only funny to them. We meet the host of the party and she introduces us to her parents.

The father settles down to speak to us as his wife and daughter leave. He starts by posing the following question: "So how do you like South Africa?"

I say: "It is a beautiful country."

And he says: "But crime is destroying it." I take his statement to mean Black people are destroying the country. I am always uncomfortable when white people make such statements because for the most part their statements are connected to Black masculinities within the context of poverty, crime, and anti-Black racism (Coates 2015).

To this, I say: "How would you know when you live in a fortified white community?"

To my challenging point, the father chooses not to respond and instead switches the subject to a topic garnering international attention: Indigenous African land repatriation. Forcefully he states: "So you agree with the government, that I should sell 40 percent of my farm to these Indigenous people?"

I say: "If you accept the fact that the land was stolen from the people and many of them were killed so you could possess this land in the first place, then this is a small price to pay." If there was any illusion of polite debate, it is now being disregarded and our true positions are being exposed without any relational respect. The binaries of Black and white are being reinforced deeply again. To temper our hostilities, our hosts intervene by making the excuse that they would like to introduce us to some other people. As we are all walking away, my old white friend says: "It looked like you needed some saving." To this point I say nothing. What could I possibly say to a white man who is comfortable in this environment? Can I ever reach him in any real meaningful way? He's as close to the centre of compulsory able-bodied white supremacy in Southern Africa as a white man can be (Kuokkanen 2015). I do not know if I have the energy to centre this relationship in my life, and I am not sure if the positives of maintaining this relationship justify the damage that it causes to my family and to our spirits.

Yet I have put my wife and my family in this racist situation. Our host and his wife offer to drive us back to their house right away. As they are offering their farewells to their friends, Mandeep and I wait for them in isolation. I look at Mandeep and I question myself: "How have I got my family into this racial nightmare? Where is the rainbow of love in this wealthy white haven of South Africa?" After spending three nights in my friend's white haven in our Black Africa, I felt grateful for having the resources to have the freedom to leave. As much as I may hate how these white racist communities exploit our people's labour, we in Southern Africa have not come up with better employment solutions or investments that target our masses of people who are always at the bottom of colonial capitalistic accumulation (Mugabe 1983). We need to create new economies that are not based on exploitation, colonial capitalistic accumulation, or the destruction of our environments (Kuokkanen 2015). You, Baba, were like many of our brothers and sisters who enter these unwelcoming white racist communities on a daily basis in order to keep their families alive. You understand the value of choice that has been denied to our brothers and sisters. Let us, as Africans, invest in our own communities so that we can give our own people the choice to work in environments where their dignity and self-respect are honoured in relational ways.

Swaziland

Sanibonani Baba, we are at the border crossing for Swaziland from South Africa. The customs officer gives us a broad smile and says to us: "Welcome to Swaziland." As he looks at my passport, he says: "Brother, you look Swazi and you have a Swazi name, so how did you end up being born in Zimbabwe?" I chuckle and say: "This is why I have come here. I am hoping I can use my name to help me connect with my ancestral roots." The customs officer shakes my hand and says: "Welcome home, brother. If you go to the parking area, I will take my break now so I can give you directions to your people." To my own research about the area, the people and traditions, the customs officer adds detailed maps and directions. I thank the customs officer and, as I start to drive toward our ancestral home, my sister Renée says: "This is a real homecoming."

Mandeep says: "I didn't like the racial tension in South Africa; it made it impossible to relax." We are all in agreement about feeling more relaxed in Swaziland. They tell us that apartheid is over in South Africa, but it did not feel like it for us. I am aware that we have power because through our education and resources we have been able to remove ourselves, unlike so many of our brothers and sisters still suffering from the colonial legacy of South Africa. Our responsibility is to continue to vocalize and mobilize against the racialized violence that persists within Southern Africa (Coates 2015; Mandela 1995).

We arrive at a guesthouse in Manzini and our host is very excited to hear about my efforts to connect with my ancestral home and people. She gives us more detailed directions to Mdzimba, the ancestral home of many Maseko Ngoni. Being here in Swaziland feels so liberating. For the first time, no one is asking me where I am from. I feel genetically connected to everyone around me. As we are driving into the Mdzimba Mountains, I see what I have only known through my academic master's research. The area of the Mdzimba (also known as Mdimba) Mountains was inhabited by the Mnesi (Mnisi) and Mncina[1] mafuko (clan systems) who were known for large stone-built umuzis (villages) that dotted the landscape.[2] The name Mucina connects me to Swaziland, using shared meaning/symbols that identify me as belonging to these communities.

Halfway up the mountain drive we stop to ask for directions, but there is no one around to ask. We do not want to intrude on a family homestead by entering their property to get directions. We want to go to the nearest old one's home so we can formally introduce ourselves in a traditional and respectful manner. While we wait for a vehicle or a pedestrian to go by so we can ask directions, I become aware that I am in no rush. I am relaxed and I say out loud: "I can feel that I belong here." Following my senses, I remove my shoes and let my feet connect with the soil. I feel grounded for the first time. I only wish you were here, Baba, to experience this wonderful moment with us. I rub my hands and feet into the soil and say a prayer to our ancestors for both you and me. After some time, a truck comes by and I wave to the driver to stop. After exchanging some pleasant greetings, I convey my mission and the driver of the truck directs us back to the base of the mountain, as the inhabitants of that area are all Masinas. At the base of the mountain, I ask for directions to an old one in the area and the directions I am given lead me to the door of old one David Masina. Upon hearing my condensed orature, old one Masina invites me to come into his house and sit down so I can give them the whole orature. I share with him all the oratures that you had given me, Baba, as well as the research I had conducted as part of my education. At this point, I ask old one Masina if the others can come out of the car and stretch their legs. He agrees to this, but insists that they not interrupt our important conversation.

When old one Masina is satisfied that he has all the details that he requires from me, he welcomes me home and then he shares with me oratures about how our people migrated from the area to as far up as Tanzania. He tells me that, in his lifetime, he has never seen a child of these lost ancestral relatives return home. He tells me that there is a greater reason beyond our understanding for me to end up at his doorstep, but he also tells me that he is unwilling to share his ancestral family knowledge until our family bonds have grown stronger. As I am introducing old one Masina to the rest of my family, his worker points out that we all look so alike she finds it unsettling. Old one Masina's daughter responds by saying that I am the brother she has been missing in the family.

Old one Masina asks if we can have some photos taken of us together before we leave. When I was back in Canada, I kept in contact with the Masina family through letters, but now I do it through Facebook. Since going to Malawi and meeting my paternal family, I have learned that the trajectory of my name is fraught with contradictions and complexities beyond my understanding. I am told that the Mucina name is reflective of how you, Baba, had disassociated yourself from your family. Yet in your teachings to me, you always insisted that I start my homecoming visit by going to the Mucina family, who you refer to as our maternal family. Knowing this knowledge has made me realize that names can communicate who we are, who we want to be, and, at times, who we are running from. Such revelations have not hindered the connections that I have developed in the ancestral homeland. I am also open to the fact that I may learn more about my connection to the Mucina name from the Mucina family in Lizulu. I know the connections that I have made to the land and the people in Mdzimba will bring me back to Swaziland, my ancestral home.

At this point of the journey, Renée, my adopted sister, leaves us and returns to Canada, and the rest of us continue on to Botswana using public transportation.

Botswana to Zimbabwe

Baba, we have been informed by our friends that there is no food in Zimbabwe and if we can find it then it will be too expensive. So they make us buy absolutely everything beforehand and we end up with two very large grocery bags. We go to the local bus station to find the buses going to Zimbabwe.

We see a luxury bus going to Zimbabwe, but I am informed that all the bus seats have already been sold out and the same bus will not be back for another two days. I do not want to wait for another two days as I am feeling a sense of urgency about getting to you. Thinking it would be a good experience for Mandeep and Sandy to get acquainted with the local African transportation system, I buy our tickets to leave that evening at six o'clock.

We spend the rest of the afternoon rushing around getting last-minute packing done and buying food for the road. The bus conductor had informed me to make sure that we had our bags there for check-in an hour before departure as space was at a premium on buses going to Zimbabwe. At five o'clock sharp we arrive with our baggage, but the bus looks overloaded already. The conductor, seeing our concern, informs us that there is lots of space and somehow he manages to secure our bags to the carrier located on top of the bus. The load of stuff on the carrier has doubled the height of the bus. Flabbergasted by the ingenuity and audacity of overloading a bus to such ridiculous proportions makes us want evidence of this phenomenon. As we are taking photos, I hear the locals expressing dissatisfaction at the fact that Zimbabweans buying so much is driving up the cost of commodities. The local businessman taking a break outside his store responds by saying: "I love Zimbabweans. They are honest, hard-working, and settle their debts. I will take a Zimbabwean over you lot any day." I laugh at this exchange and think nothing of it.

The bus conductor has anticipated our inexperience in travelling on local buses and so has kindly reserved us a bench seat for three in the middle of the bus. However, it is impossible to get to our seats, because all the floor space has been taken up. To get to our seats we have to stand on people's luggage. I am aware that fire regulations in this situation do not apply, so we make ourselves as comfortable as possible. Six o'clock rolls around and the bus is still being loaded. At eight o'clock, we still have not moved and I ask the bus conductor when we are leaving. He replies by saying: "Very soon, my friend, don't worry." The family behind us communicates to me in Shona that this means we are now officially on African time. At ten o'clock the bus starts to move, but the conductor informs us that we are going to a gas station to fill up with diesel. This, too, takes over another hour. When our bus starts to leave the gas station, some locals in their cars begin yelling: "Zimbabweans go back home." Such open hostilities make me wonder if it is that easy to forget that it was not that long ago when folks from Botswana made these similar kinds of trips to Zimbabwe. Did Zimbabweans treat these folks in the same manner? Have we learned so well how to be capitalist accumulators that we have forgotten how to share as relatives?

A Botswanan customs officer yells to everyone else: "The queue starts behind this gentleman," and everyone rushes over to queue behind me. Everyone wants to be processed as quickly as possible so he/she can continue the journey home. A few people with very large loads are disgruntled with how badly they are being treated and refuse to move. On seeing this open challenge, one of the officers starts using violent tactics. He throws people's belongings onto the road, which forces people to rush over to rescue their possessions. At the same time, there is a woman who seems to be unwilling to be intimidated or she may just be overly exhausted and cannot move. Either way, the customs officer approaches her with great violent haste, but she cannot see him as he is in her blind spot. He violently slaps her across the face and the woman doubles over in pain, but no one moves to help her. Somehow, the woman manages to get herself closer to us.

Sandy, who is standing next to me, says: "I can't believe that man has just hit that woman." As she is saying these words, we both realize that Mandeep is standing in the area where the woman was attacked. The officer is maliciously heading toward Mandeep and the realization of what is happening freezes us. The officer raises his hand in a motion to slap Mandeep hard on her back. When somehow he becomes aware that she is not African, he turns his slap into a forceful pat on the back. He says: "Madame, you'll have to move to where the others are. Do you understand?" I sigh in relief and the man behind me puts his hand on my shoulder and says in Shona: "Do not worry, they can still see her humanity but, for some reason, they cannot see our humanity even though this Black skin binds us as family." The actual processing by customs takes less than five minutes per person and I cannot understand why we went through hours of unnecessary suffering. I can only speculate that absolute power corrupts when it is being applied to the poor and vulnerable because the chances of consequential action by the poor and vulnerable are greatly diminished when they are focused on trying to survive (Coates 2015; Fanon 1963).

Zimbabwe to Malawi

The Zimbabwean customs official informs us that we each need a visa for sixty dollars U.S. and, jokingly, informs us that all this could have been avoided if Canada had not imposed a visa requirement on Zimbabweans. The easygoing nature of the Zimbabwean customs official is relaxing everyone, but some of our bus passengers are trying to take advantage of this. Those who had bought large flat-screen TVs, refrigerators, car parts, bicycles, and other non-essential goods must pay duty. The problem is, the owners of these goods are making it difficult to trace their whereabouts and this is wasting our time. The bus driver threatens that we should leave these unclaimed goods and drive away, but his bus conductor informs him that all will be resolved in good time. So we wait and quietly complain.

At three o'clock we start loading the bus again, but our bus conductor slips on some spilt cooking oil on top of the bus and he cannot continue doing his great job of loading the carrier. His two assistants take over, but everyone can see they are not doing as good a job as he was doing. Sure enough, after driving for about an hour, things begin to fall off the top of the bus. At a police roadblock, the Zimbabwe police help secure things onto the carrier once again. Around six o'clock, one of the back tires explodes because of the rubbing of the bus frame against the tires. There is no spare tire on the bus, because it had been removed to make more space for goods. Luckily, the tire explosion takes place near the town of Gweru where it is scheduled to stop. So very slowly, the bus inches its way along to the nearest gas station, but all efforts to locate a spare tire prove to be futile. So we wait for the bus's emergency response team to deliver us a spare tire. At this point, we have been on the bus for more than thirty-four hours.

To distract ourselves from our ongoing bus problems, we exchange our foreign currency for the local currency and socialize with the friendly staff at a local bar. The local cuisine is perfect for easing our hunger and the sharing of local beer with community members helps pass the time. Five hours go by before a spare tire is fitted onto the bus and, by this point, all the passengers have become quite familiar with one another. Political issues like feminism, power, equality, and sexism are thoroughly debated and various forms of Christianity are discussed but, in my opinion, traditional Ubuntu spirituality is not included in the conversation (Memmi 1965). The discussions are held in both English and Shona. When the conversation turns into Shona, I translate it for Mandeep and Sandy. The closer we get to Harare, the more humorous the oratures are. When we arrive in Harare, the tension of the nightmare bus ride seems to dissipate for all of us, but it's as if the gods want to keep us in check because, just after the first stop in Harare, the bus's axle falls apart. For the first time, people express dangerously violent outrage. The bus crew works as swiftly as possible to ensure the bus makes it to the final bus stop of Mbare, using a makeshift pin to hold the axle together. An unbelievable forty-two hours later, we unload from the bus and we promise each other that we will not put ourselves through such an ordeal again. But we do. The only difference is that we do it to get to your home, Baba.

Innocent, a Zimbabwean friend we had met in South Africa, picks us up at the bus station. He takes us to the apartment that Kevin (our other friend) has allowed us to use. At the apartment, we meet two other young men who are also staying there, Oliver from the Democratic Republic of the Congo, and Joe, the younger cousin of Innocent. Joe works for a company as a computer technician and, therefore, we see very little of him. Oliver, on the other hand, is trying to make his fortune in Zimbabwe like most of our friends in the illegal diamond trade business. All are good people doing shady businesses in order to survive. The oldest of this group of men is a man we dub as Uncle Munya. It is Uncle Munya and his business associates who take us in an open pickup truck to the township of Mbare where we eat the best barbecue I have ever had in my life. As we enjoy meat and sadza (thick cornmeal porridge) and drink beer, I become aware that many people have an illegal trading business as their main business or side job.

If these men and women failed at their jobs, we would not be enjoying such a wonderful barbecue. But little did I know that you, Baba, could not enjoy such luxuries. Unbeknown to me, five minutes' walk from where we are enjoying our barbecue, my Maiguru's (maternal aunt's) family members are trying to sell vegetables in order to survive. They are so poor that if the police raid them and take away their vegetables, they will struggle to replace them and maybe even go without food. Whereas the butcher store, which operates the barbecue that we are enjoying, is the meeting place for high-end illegal traders and it is situated right next to the police station. As good as the barbecue is, I cannot fully enjoy it, because about sixty metres away from us there are kids feeding on our leftover bones that have been thrown into a rubbish heap. These beggars and food scavengers are kept at bay intermittently by other children who are hired to do so. The colonial act of divide and conquer, which was applied to us using racial markers, has now been modified and is being applied along class lines (Fanon 1963). The envious stares of the poor confirm that we have made it out or that we are the inheritors of our families' breakthrough into the new Black wealth (Coates 2015). Yet, I still remember how I used to forage for food in garbage heaps just like the kids I am watching. I was one of them and now I am sitting on the other side. I want to identify with their struggle, I want to help, but I do not want to be in their position because I have not forgotten my memories of hardships or those I have heard from other street kids or other kids in the orphanages. Among each other, we have shared oratures about how

Figure 11. Relying on memory from nineteen years ago, I found Maiguru's home in the township of Mbare. This was no small feat because I had only been to her home twice before and, arguably, Mbare is the largest township in Zimbabwe.

we each came to forage for food in garbage heaps and at other times we have shared dreams of better futures. It is from those shared moments of humanity that I am inspired to write and act.

The next day, I take Mandeep and Sandy to see St. Joseph's House for Boys, the orphanage where I was raised as a ward of the state. The place looks rundown. There is mould on the walls, windows are broken, electrical wires are exposed, and there is no running water in the bathrooms. I see some of the boys who are still in the orphanage from five years earlier when I did some outreach work through my child and youth care degree program with funding from Langara College. The aim of that trip had been to offer the staff residential care training so that they were able to provide better care for the children, as most of the staff had little formal training in residential child care. As part of that trip, I did workshops for the boys using my own experience as a foundation for engaging questions and fears about leaving the orphanage. I talked about the actions that I took that allowed me to be successful beyond the orphanage while also honestly reflecting on actions that limited my successes. Besides giving professional and personal advice, I also came with money that was used to purchase food.

So you can see how the boys in the orphanage are surprised to learn that I have come empty-handed. As I am leaving, I hear one of the boys say: "Where is the money and computers?" I pretend I do not hear the comment, because if I answer it truthfully I would have to say: "I am sorry, but I am on a very limited personal budget and this trip is about connecting with my family." Thinking these words seems harsh to me and I know I could never say them aloud to any of the boys. Yet I feel a sense of shame for having done nothing to help the boys, and because of my feelings of shame, I choose to disengage through my active silence.

I wish now that I had been brave and engaged truthfully about my limitations and failures toward them. Especially as I was reminded by the fact that to achieve my goal of finding you, Baba, I needed the help of Baba Colin (the orphanage cook). The fact that I could not find you without the help of Baba Colin, who had also helped me track you down in 2003, reminded me that I was connected to the orphanage and it to me, the orphanage and its people are my family and will always be family (Okri 1997). Baba Colin had learned that you were not staying with the young family who had been caring for you when I left you. After a day of searching, Baba Colin found an address for where you were staying, but when we arrived there no one could tell us where you had gone, so we tried to track you down. As we were searching for you, we heard many oratures about your poverty and homelessness. Most people talked about how they had played a role in preventing your death from starvation. The one consistent orature that I kept hearing was about how you and four other old men were living in the bushes. Three of the old men had been found dead and another was missing, presumed dead by most people. You, Baba, were the only one who was reported to be in relatively good health. On hearing these reports, I felt guilty for not having taken better care of you as your firstborn son.

That night, I led our family into a discussion about how we could care for you. Our total savings at that moment were around five thousand dollars and we also had an emergency fund of about two thousand dollars. This to me meant that we could only afford to get property and still have enough money to build a very small house for you in the townships or rural communities. The problem was you would not have your family or community around you. In the midst of my planning, Mandeep questioned: "Do we know if this is what Baba wants?" Not wanting to impose anything on you, we decided to suspend all these questions until we met you the next day. In preparation of our meeting, while still in Canada, I had bought you a whole suitcase full of clothes and other essential items. In Botswana, Mandeep had taken charge of buying you a large bag of groceries. As we had no transport, we were dependent on our friends. Innocent's cousin, Joe, borrowed a family member's car that he used to help us get to you.

When we found you, I was just thankful that you were still alive. Looking at you, I was taken aback by how emaciated you were. I remember you telling us that you were having stomach problems, which affected what foods you were able to digest. As you were speaking, I kept asking myself: "How have I let this happen to you, my own Baba? How will I explain this to our ancestors?" Oh! Baba, I felt great shame and you only made my shame even greater when you started to share the little we had given you. How is it that with so little to your name, Baba, you were so generous? I see now that your generosity was not limited to familial blood or kith and kin. You were the love that was Ubuntu and this is why you were never a stranger in unfamiliar places (Okri 1997).

Baba, your Ubuntu practice is hard to follow and I still have a lot to learn. As we were talking, I watched you make a pile of things you wanted to give to my brothers and another pile of food that you wanted to share with your community. As you were making your sharing piles, you also gave me your oratures about your struggles, your farming activities, planned future business adventures, and familial hopes. After hearing some of your oratures, I felt that they had a common theme of finding final settlement and so I asked you if you wanted to take us home to our family community of Lizulu. Thoughtfully, you informed us that you were ready to go home, but you were afraid that everyone you knew was dead and no one would know you. You were also afraid that you would not fit in with the community after being away for so long. Your family had been fragmented for so long that you even suggested that we could go alone while you stayed in Zimbabwe. I assured you that we would not leave you in an environment in which you did not feel safe or happy. With this promise from us, you hesitantly and cautiously agreed to take us home to Lizulu. At the age of thirty-five years old, I was so excited to be going home with my Baba. I was a little kid again in your care and, at the same time, I was an adult who was caring for you. It seemed we were completing our fragmented and colonially battered Ubuntu circle.

My excitement about going home to Lizulu began to infect you too and you suggested we leave right away. I reminded you that we needed travel visas for us and you would need an emergency travel document. To this suggestion, you laughed. "Who will stop me from travelling on our soil? These are all my people, my lands, and I have worked the soil from here to home. I know all the languages and the names of all the places," you told me confidently. Philosophically and politically I agreed with your position, but we were running out of time and could not change our travel plans because we were short of funds and had school commitments back in Toronto. Wanting you to get us home for the first time with as little problem as possible, I told you that we were going to the Malawian Embassy and getting you a travel document. I remember what you said in response to my authoritative direction, and the weight and responsibility of what you said is still haunting me. You placed your right hand on my shoulder as if you were transferring the burden of family responsibility over to me and then simply said: "Baba, the sun is rising to your authority. I support this and will not get in your way." Until now, I have not shared with anyone the heaviness of these words you gave me.

On our way to the Malawian Embassy, you behaved like a little child who had new toys. You wanted to stop and show us off to your community of friends and I behaved like a strict parent. I kept telling you: "Sorry, we need to leave. Sorry, we do not have time to meet other people because we are late and we need to go now if we are to get your emergency travel document before the embassy closes for the day." We arrived at the embassy during lunchtime, so we had to wait for an hour before they reopened again. However, the security man informed us that the embassy on that day closed at 3:00 p.m. and there was a long line of people ahead of us, so he speculated that we might have to come back again. I told the security man that I did not want to wait another day because for the first time in my thirty-five-year-old life I was going home. The security man asked why this was so and you gave him our family orature about our fragmentation. When the other embassy workers heard our orature, they made it clear that we would get your emergency travel document that day. The security man offered his professional photography services for your identification photo. This service he offered for a fee, in U.S. dollars.

Early the next morning, we caught the bus going to Malawi at the Mbare bus stop. I noticed that you were not engaging in conversation with any of us, so I engaged you in light conversation until we neared Nyamapanda, which was just before the border with Mozambique. Nyamapanda was also the home of Lee and Simba, my half-brothers. If the bus ran this route more than once a week, I would have suggested we stop and see them, but we were running out of time and, to ease my conscience, I asked you when you last saw my brothers. I was expecting you to tell me that you last saw them about a month ago, but you said: "In 2005, Lee came to see me for some money because he needed shoes, but his younger brother, Simba, will not talk to me because he feels I have abandoned him, which makes him very angry. How do I explain to him that I cannot present myself to his mother's family when I have nothing to offer them? I am the hunger created by a lack of food in abundance and I am poverty beyond the comfort of measure. I am silent because I cannot find the words that stop my suffering" (Baba, personal communication, 13 August 2008). Your truth creates uncomfortable silence. I want to offer you some comfort, but blame keeps making its way toward my lips, so I too keep silent, because this is what I can offer as support without judgement. I am sorry I did not break the silence of our suffering when you were offering me the opportunity then. I hope it is not too late to start following your lead of breaking the oppressive silence that acts to fragment our family further. Baba, I have reconnected with Simba through Facebook and I am arranging for Simba and his family to meet all the other paternal family members in Malawi.

The Malawi we took you to, Baba, was not the Malawi you left. The city of Blantye impressed you so much that you told us that you were willing to live there if things did not work out at home in Lizulu. You were so proud of this new Malawi that had blossomed while you were away, and entertainingly you said: "I will stay here and die in my own country among my own people." We spent two nights and two days in Blantye before going to Zomba where a friend lent me his car for our usage. As we were driving to Lizulu, you started to get sick. You complained of abdomen pain and reported that your stomach felt sour. I had to stop the car a few times so you could throw up or so we could prevent you from throwing up. Travelling at a much slower speed, we got into Lizulu around 3:00 p.m. As soon as we arrived in Lizulu, we presented ourselves to the chief, who informed us that our family lands and properties were in Mozambique and we would need a letter of clearance from the police, which the chief assured us would take less than five minutes. The more important task was to find a family member who could take us home. Within half an hour, the chief's staff had found one of your nephews, Fixon.

Fixon informed us that most of your family members had passed on from this life to the world of the ancestors. I could not help but watch the facial expressions you made as you heard about the death of each family member that you inquired about. Fixon told you that there were extended family members who knew you and wanted to see you. As it was getting late, we made plans to go to our village early in the morning the next day. Just before we left for our motel, you asked Fixon very reluctantly, as if you did not want to hear the answer: "What of my sister, Janet?" On hearing this question, Fixon flashed a huge smile while telling you that your sister was doing very well for herself in Lilongwe, the capital city of Malawi. She had built her own house in the capital city, had two living children, Moses and Regina, and from her other children who were in the living dead realm, she had many grandchildren. Your eyes reddened with tears as you told us that you wanted to go to your sister right away and you made it clear that you had no interest in meeting any other family members.

At this point, we would have left if it were not for the wise counsel of the chief and the persistence of Fixon. I remember the two of them managed to make the point that you needed to take us to our home village, so that our ancestors could connect with us. To this point you retorted by saying that our ancestors were always with me and, therefore, I did not need to go to a village full of the offspring of those who had caused you so much pain. The chief wisely told you that your retort was good while adding that if you took us to our home village you would be showing respect for our ancestors. The chief also added that your father had ensured that you had walked on the soil that held the remains of our ancestors, as a way of making sure you were connected to our lands and people (Wane 2009). The chief then asked: "Will you deny your son this connection?" Under such pressure, you agreed to go to our home village the next day.

About forty family members were at the home village to welcome us home and they kept apologizing that they did not have time to inform other family members that were in schools or working in other parts of the country. I could not believe so many people were related to me. I felt wonderful belonging to them and they to me. I am not sure if you felt the same connection that I felt to all these family members. I have learned from past experiences that you sometimes use your smiles and sweet words shields to hide your realities. I therefore wanted to know how you felt about being welcomed by some family members whose parents may have had a hand in your leaving.

However, I must tell you that it felt good to see you show pride in me. I remember hearing you say: "This is my son and his family; they live in Canada and want to ensure I am taken care of before they go back to university in Canada. When they are done school they will help me start a bottle store here in Lizulu, but for now, I will live near my sister so we can age peacefully and die surrounded by family." By the time we left, almost every adult family member knew your plans and you showed a level of strength and pride that I had not seen in you. Even if we could not achieve everything you wanted, it was good to see you feel energized about your dream. Somehow, from that moment, your joy was mine and your problems were mine.

Fixon offered to take us to Dadakazi Janet in Lilongwe. I was a little frustrated with Fixon's directions because he was directing us by memory and could not give us reference points to help map our trip. His way of doing things required us to trust him while our Western academic training required us to depend on evidential data. With no other choice, I was forced to trust and depend on Fixon totally. I was uncomfortable at being in this position of total dependence. My discomfort kept me questioning and challenging his directions, which started to make him nervous and this led to directional errors. When I realized what I was doing, I apologized to Fixon and let him lead us, even if this wasn't easy to do. Needless to say, Fixon got us to Dadakazi Janet as soon as I got out of his way by suspending my judgement about his navigational methods. What is now interesting is that I only know directions to Dadakazi Janet's home through memory and not the conventional Western way of using the local street names. The lesson here for me is that if we want the outcome of a specific knowledge, we must honour its rightful process (Wane 2009; p'Bitek 1984).

On arrival at Dadakazi Janet's, the neighbours informed us that she had gone to church. So we went nearby to her son and daughter's home, but her son (Moses) was away on business and her daughter (Regina) was also at church with her. Luckily, a niece informed us that she would send a message to Dadakazi Janet and cousin Regina to inform them that they had visitors at home. Regina and nephew Joseph were the first people to come back from church. After exchanging a formal greeting, Fixon informed Regina as to who you were. On hearing that you were Dadakazi's brother, Regina started laughing so hard I thought she would start crying. While still laughing hard she got up, went and gave you a big hug and then told us that she had seen many things but she never believed or dreamed that she would see us. Regina informed us that Dadakazi had named one of her children after your memory, but unfortunately, the child had died. Looking at me, Regina informed me that Dadakazi had had a hard life but even at her lowest point she never stopped wondering about her brother, Peter Dee (Baba). As Regina was talking, more family members were coming in. In all this excitement, I remember Regina hugging me while telling me that we were family. Within a few minutes, we were all talking over each other in a spirit of familial love. By the time Dadakazi Janet arrived, the room was full of family and communal laughter (Okri 1997).

As soon as Dadakazi walked into the room, we all went quiet, but the excitement in our hearts kept dancing. Dadakazi was about to ask who the visitors were when she locked eyes with you, Baba. As she stared into your eyes, she seemed to lose her voice. Regina then asked: "Who is that?" And Dadakazi,

Figure 12. My cousin Regina and my Dadakazi Janet. This photo was taken a few days after Baba and his sister reunited following sixty-eight years of not having any form of communication with each other.

after a moment of disbelief, said: "This is my brother who has been lost in some foreign lands. I have wondered for many years if he was dead; yet I could not explain why I felt him. I have missed you, my king. My heart is full of love and pain at the same time and I have no words to share. Now let me meet my family." Lovingly, Dadakazi welcomed us home with hugs, but as soon as she was done, she raced over to you and locked her arm around your arm. Looking at me, she said with deep, slow, emotional excitement: "Baba, thank you for bringing my brother back to me." I was speechless and after some time, you, Baba, broke the silence by saying: "We should also thank my daughter-in-law, because I believe she is the one who pushed your son to come find me." Dadakazi gives Mandeep a quietly spoken thank you before she focused back on you again, Baba. The two of you were inseparable from that moment on.

As news of your arrival spread, Dadakazi's friends began coming to witness this extraordinary happening. If Dadakazi was sugar through her words, then her friends were her salt, because they lamented you for abandoning her in this lonely world. Dadakazi's friends conveyed to you how much she had lost and, on top of that, how much she had worried over you. In all these discussions, you remained silent and at times, when things got heated beyond my comfort,

I would defend you by reminding people that you were now here and the important thing was for us to start building our family so it could be whole. I told the family and Dadakazi about how you were living in Zimbabwe and asked them if you could stay with them while we tried to find you a place near Dadakazi, so that you would not be separated from your sister again. As we were looking for a place for you, Regina called us to a family meeting. At this meeting, she informed us that if we made you and Dadakazi live apart we would embarrass ourselves before the community, as people would ask why we were keeping two old relatives apart who had found each other in old age after being separated a long time ago by colonial and familial fragmentation. Regina then informed us that the family wanted Dadakazi and you to live in her house while we used the money we would have spent on getting a new piece of property to build a new home on Dadakazi's property.

On hearing the family's decision to keep Dadakazi and you together, I felt comforted and relieved about your safety. The little savings that we had we handed over to the family to start building our new family home. All this happened in late August of 2008. Since being back in Canada, we call home to Malawi when needed and we try to send some money to help our family financially. In early June of 2009, you got news from Zimbabwe that Lee, my brother, had died in a road accident. In August of 2009, Khumalo, your grandson, was born and, three months later, on 6 December 2009, you left this living world for the world of the living dead ancestors. Cousin Regina, on 5 June 2010, also left this world to be with you among our ancestors. Baba, take care of Lee and Regina, and please guide Dadakazi toward some peace, because she has dealt with too much loss for one person. We are trying to support her as best we can from here in Canada. In reference to your death, Baba, I am not sad in any way because you are with our ancestors and I know that you died in your family home among your loving family members. You have left me the thread to continue connecting our family beyond fragmentation. In June 2011, I graduated with a doctorate of philosophy in education and your granddaughter Nandi was born on 8 December 2011. In June of 2017, we took your grandkids back home so that they would know all their relations. Like all families, we too have our challenges and disagreements, but we are trying to keep our family together as best as we can. Baba, I have said many things, but now I clap my hands as a way of welcoming and honouring your spirit. I am now listening, so please inscribe your spiritual wisdom on this blank page.

Respectfully, your son,
Dr. Devi Dee Mucina Komba

For Baba's voice

In this Millet Granary I have shared my perceptions and experiences of being in relation with my Baba. I have tried to theorize these perceptions and experiences using critical Ubuntu theories, but, more importantly, I have focused on re-membering (bringing our family together again). Now that we are connected by this orature, where do you end and where do I begin? Could the sacred cycle of breath connect us as one, Ubuntu? The next Millet Granary is a letter to Nandi and Khumalo about how their mother and I came together to start building our family.

How are these oratures decolonizing Indigenous masculinities?

In what ways are our Indigenous oratures engaging feminism?

What is the main point that you take away from this Ubuntu orature?

Figure 13. The day we got married, surrounded by all our friends.

Creating Our Family

Methodological questions that guided my writing of this Millet Granary:

1. *What was the process that allowed me to intimately and vulnerably offer love?*
2. *How do I do decolonizing Ubuntu actions with my own family?*
3. *How do I centre love in the face of adversity and fear?*

Sanibonani Nandi and Khumalo,

I know you will want to know how an African (me) and a Sikh South Asian Indian (your mother) met and started a family, but to tell you that orature, I must tell you the orature about how I came to Canada, because that orature connects to how our family orature comes to be. While I was working for Outward Bound Zimbabwe (a wilderness experiential educational program), I wanted more of a Western lifestyle than was available in Zimbabwe. So when I first started to date Liz (not her real name), an amazingly smart and adventurous white settler girl from Canada, I thought I had hit the jackpot, because I wanted to live my life in as adventurous and carefree a way as she seemed to be living her life. She seemed to give love freely and, in a very colonially calculated manner, I took everything she offered and demanded more through the whispered promise of those charming words "I love you."

I loved Liz as much as anyone could love a stranger. I was connected more intimately to the seduction of white supremacy and knew its ways more than I knew Liz. I think I wanted her colonial white life more than I wanted her (Fanon 1963). This is not to say that I did not care about her, because I did. I just did not know how to see her as a human instead of as a stepping stone, because I had learned in the context of compulsory white supremacy that my maleness still held masculine power in the global heteropatriarchy of compulsory white supremacy (hooks 2004). I loved Liz with the intent of insuring that I got the lion's share of material and emotional benefits. She gave, and I took everything she had to offer (Coates 2015). Above all, she believed in me and in my abilities and would not allow me to be overshadowed by my disabilities. As she was getting ready to go back home to Canada, we began to talk about our future together. I did not want to let her go and so I asked her to stay in Zimbabwe for a little longer, but it was not possible. She then suggested that I come to Canada, as there were better career and educational opportunities for me, especially for helping me expand beyond the limitations of my learning disabilities. Thus to better transcend the limitations of colonial white supremacy in Zimbabwe, I was unwittingly signing up to be a settler on Indigenous lands in Canada. Of the Indigenous struggle here in Canada, I had not been informed, but I should be honest and say that knowing of the Indigenous struggle would probably not have stopped me from coming here to Canada, because at that point in my life I wanted the exploitative power of white supremacy (Hill Collins and Bilge 2016; Kuokkanen 2015). As I write these words, I cannot help but wonder what was motivating Liz to be in our relationship. What did she really want with an African stranger? What was her game? What did she want?

Coming to Canada seemed like a great plan and Liz began to help me apply for a job with the Western Canadian Outward Bound School. The school was delighted to have me come over and they began to assist me in getting a work visa. As we were completing the paperwork, we went to the Canadian Embassy in Harare to make sure that we were doing the paperwork correctly, and that is when we learned that the whole process would be much faster if we applied under the Family Reunification Program of the immigration process. We were informed that if we were married in Zimbabwe before we submitted our immigration papers, I would be given landed immigrant status without any conditions. So right away, we began planning to get married, and that is when we learned that Zimbabwe does not have an equivalent of a fast Las Vegas wedding deal. We tried everything to get married in Zimbabwe, but we failed and, as a practical joke, someone directed us to the political headquarters of ZANU–PF to seek information about getting a marriage certificate. Our youthful naivety led us to accept these directions without critically questioning the relevance and connection of a political party to marriage certificates. The reserve police guarding the building laughed at our ignorance and asked us to reflect on what connection there was between the political party of ZANU-PF and our desire for a marriage certificate. Another reserve police officer asked us to determine if we were terrorists and, finding us harmless, told us to get lost. Having failed at securing a fast marriage certificate, we submitted my immigration papers to the Canadian Embassy in Harare under the Family Reunification Program with the understanding that Liz and her family would sponsor me over to Canada and, within ninety days of landing in Canada, I would marry Liz.

As Liz left for Canada, I felt confident with our plan, which would see me leave Zimbabwe for Canada. While waiting for my immigration papers, which were coming from South Africa, I took advantage of the chance to visit the fast-changing South Africa. When I contacted the South African Outward Bound School, which at that point was in the Amathole Mountains of the Eastern Cape, about my coming to South Africa while I waited for Canadian immigration papers, they happily offered me a job because I had worked with some of their top visiting instructors in Zimbabwe. Having two International Outward Bound institutions offer me jobs made me feel more confident, and the only family I wanted to share my good fortune with was the other boys from the orphanage, because I knew they would understand how much my life was about to change. As I said goodbye to the other boys from the orphanage, we knew I was escaping the physical death that came with extreme poverty. I was escaping the extreme emotional isolation that came from colonially created structures, which made us as Ubuntu abandon each other, while exercising ruthless colonial predatory behaviours, which again alienated us from our Ubuntu cultural selves (Okri 1997). In our colonially created misery, the other boys in the orphanage and I saw our survival as being intimately connected with our ability to orientate ourselves to white supremacy, and what better way was there to do this than by leaving Africa (Fanon 1963)? Through Liz, I was gaining a white familial support system. At my farewell party, I was told by the orphanage staff and the other orphanage boys that I was a good role model because I was leaving the orphanage in a much better state than when I had come into it. My best friend in the orphanage, Juan, who committed suicide some years later in South Africa, told me that my amazing luck had got me this far and as usual it was now up to me to fuck it up.

I felt like a new man leaving Zimbabwe. The future looked bright and I was optimistically open to whatever the future had to offer. I was leaving the suffering legacy of our Indigenous Black mothers and fathers behind. Even though I understood that, I was on the margin of whiteness and its governing structures. I was happy to be admitted to those margins of whiteness. Just like in the orphanage, I knew that if I aligned myself with the right white people, I could exploit them to get more colonial power (Fanon 1963). I feared that not having colonial power made me more vulnerable to its violence, which I had experienced enough times as a faceless victim beyond the margins of being a person than is acknowledged by compulsory white supremacy. I wanted to matter beyond being a commodity, while understanding my limitations as a hated Black body (Fanon 1963). I therefore was ready to do anything in order not to be vulnerable to the fear of colonial destruction. To keep the fear at bay, I signed up to be a colonial destroyer and taker of the power of compulsory white supremacy (Okri 1997). In a way I was telling the African world to fuck it, to let someone else suffer the full force of colonial destruction, I would take what I could get at the margins of compulsory white supremacy (Coates 2015; hooks 2004).

Now, I should also tell you that just before I left for South Africa, I searched for my Baba and found him. But you should know that the telling of my journey to my Baba was my way of communicating to him that, despite his failing as a parent, I was succeeding. The pain of family fragmentation and isolation is still there and I am still working on understanding the colonial forces that shaped my Baba's and Amai's actions within colonially dominated Indigenous spaces. The colonial realities, which led to my Baba losing his first family before his union with my Amai, are the same colonial realities that led to our family's fragmentation, the imposition of capitalist accumulation as our gods, our participation in our own dispossession, and our willingness to participate in the imposition of white supremacy as the only viable governance structure (Césaire 1972). Yet I clearly remember that before I left for South Africa, I targeted Baba as the main cause of my suffering, with Amai coming a close second. I never reserved any of this rage and anger for white supremacy and its governing colonial governance structures (Fanon 1963). Was confronting white supremacy too much of a mammoth task at that time? If I was hiding from the true enemy, then it seemed Baba was immune to my humiliating and vengeful behaviour because, instead of being embarrassed, he saw my appearing before him as an opportunity to right some of his mistakes. At the time I did not understand that he was asking me to re-member (bring our family together again). Mesmerized by colonial acceptance to the margins and not understanding the Indigenous task that my Baba was trying to place before me, I did not understand what Baba meant when he said, "With you as my blade we can rebuild what I failed to do." Yet instead of orienting myself toward Baba's words and developing a dialogue with him, I chose to ignore him while further silencing him by giving him all the Zimbabwean money I could withdraw from my account. I had access to Canadian dollars through Liz and to South African rands through my new job with Outward Bound South Africa, so giving away my Zimbabwean money meant nothing to me, but I knew that this was a lot of money for my father. Hence, I left Zimbabwe feeling good about myself.

I arrived in South Africa on 30 December 1993, and joined the excitement of Baba Nelson Mandela leading South Africa into its first free elections. Within the first two days of being in South Africa, I made friends beyond the Outward Bound community and I was invited to a New Year's Eve party at the Hogsback Village Hotel. There I met Beth (not her real name), a white, fiery South African blond woman, who practised law with Indigenous African clients, most of whom were too poor to afford her services. She had been given an African name, which she used, and from the moment we met, it was as if we were old friends. The partying was so good it went on for a few days and a small group of us from the party grew very close. We began to spend a lot of time together and I started to get relationally intimate with Beth. As Beth was my friend, first and foremost, we were quite intimately connected to each other's oratures before the sex started (hooks 2004). My network of friends in South Africa supported my efforts to access resources, without imposing their help and support on me. The loving support of my friends and professional peers in South Africa gave me the confidence to believe that I, an African Indigenous man with a learning disability, could navigate my biggest fear and challenge of being successful within the global colonial education system. Giving and receiving reciprocal relational care made me feel optimistically confident about my future (Archibald/Q'um Q'um Xiiem 2008).

Imaginatively, for the first time in my life, I began to think about living beyond survival. Yet the fantasies of my imaginative thinking could not overpower the colonial reality of fear that ruled most of my everyday acts (Fanon 1963). If I had been an honourable man, who was not ruled by fear at that time, I would have ended my relationship with Liz. Instead, I kept my relationship with Beth a secret from Liz while making Beth aware of my relationship with Liz. At this point, I would like to apologize to Liz and Beth for taking advantage of their love and for using them for my own ends. This was selfish accumulative greed on my part, but in some ways, I was exercising what white patriarchy had taught me to do, which was to exploit anyone and everyone in my pursuit of colonial capitalistic power (hooks 2004). It is possible that I am just making excuses for my indiscretions in order to make myself feel better, but here is the truth. I live with the pain of knowing that I have hurt two caring individuals and that pain I cannot escape. Even as I make these statements, I see that my feelings are colonized because I am silent about the Black love that was offered to me. Why was I able to see white love and recognize it? Why did I have to make a conscious effort to remember the numerous times I was given reciprocal Black love (Memmi 1965; Fanon 1963)? Why did I not allow myself to see Black love?

The answer is simple: I did not see it as holding power within the matrix of white supremacy (hooks 2004). To all those that tried to offer me intimate love beyond whiteness, I am sorry for not knowing or even trying to be open to love. As the good imitator of white supremacy that I was, I would have taken from you in the exploitive accumulative manner of capitalistic white supremacy (hooks 2004), just like I did to white women. I am giving you all these oratures, Nandi and Khumalo, because I am realizing that Indigenous decolonizing cannot be limited to my political actions, it must be a total process, which is inclusive of my intimate personal life (Hill Collins and Bilge 2016; Kuokkanen 2015). This kind of decolonizing action requires continual work in the context of toxic colonial masculinities, but I am motivated in the continual work of decolonizing my Indigenous masculinities because I have experienced reciprocal Ubuntu love. I do not want you, Khumalo and Nandi, to be motivated in your intimate relationships by the white supremacy goal of colonial exploitative accumulation, I want you to love powerfully and vulnerably, I want you to be Ubuntu. I believe this is the best gift I can give you.

While I was visiting South Africa, my Canadian immigration papers arrived, but I was not ready to go because I knew I was going to miss my friends very dearly. My South African friends were evidence to me that I could stand on my own two feet; that I could build caring relationships beyond the orphanage; and that I could enter into intimate, supportive, and caring relationships built on equality (Mandela 1995). I am not saying I practised what I knew at that moment in South Africa, I am just saying that I knew I could do it. Up to this point, most of my past friendships had been based on what I could gain from the people I made friends with, and I had never totally trusted other people. I had come to believe that people would let you down when you needed them and, if they could use you, they would. I understood that this was the way of the colonial dog-eat-dog world (hooks 2004). It was therefore my aim to do the eating up of others before I was eaten up. I justified all my colonial behaviours as acts of survival in a mean and hateful world, but this was the act of suppressing the whole truth in order to justify a specific reality that suited my needs. The loving evidence that challenged my colonial reality I feared and would not take seriously, and marked it down to exceptional moments in an otherwise well-established exploitive colonial context (hooks 2004).

Leaving our geographical territories and our relations for other people's territories is a common familial response to colonial pressures in my family. Collectively, my Baba and my Amai have been fragmented seven times from families that they started because of colonial impositions, and this knowledge only references the oratures that I know. There are seven fragmented Indigenous families that are biologically connected to me. They exist, but we know little to nothing about each other. How can we not see that the personal is very political? That it imprints a memory that shapes our actions, regardless of our knowing it or not knowing it? As I write, I am seeing that I am a continuation of Baba and Amai. Are their successes and their challenges mine because did I not leave one colonial dream for another? In the wake of my movements, are there not many who have been hurt just like in the wake of Baba's and Amai's movements? Yet I have pressed on without paying attention to other people's feelings, or to my own for that matter (Okri 1997).

I was feeling like a zombie when I arrived in Canada on 22 June 1994. Liz, my wife to be, met me at the Vancouver International Airport and the experience of South Africa was parked and hidden somewhere deep in my mind. I would be lying if I did not tell you that it was wonderful to see and be reunited with Liz. We had a few days to be together before we both had to work, so we camped out. When we got to the Outward Bound School, everyone made me feel at home. People began to prepare me for the culture shock I would experience, and what a shock it was. As we did our experiential education high up in the mountains, snow whiteout conditions were a frequent occurrence, even when there was no snow in the low-lying areas. In the middle of summer I had to be taught how to navigate in whiteout snow weather conditions. Preparing for my first Outward Bound course in Canada was made easy for me, as I was paired with a very experienced senior instructor. In our group, we had three girls and seven boys and all were between the ages of fourteen and eighteen. I was very scared of messing up something, as there was a lot to learn and I had never seen so many mountains where I could lose a group. However, the course got off to a great start, as we were all excited about the trip and we were all in good physical health. As we started out on our expedition, we walked through an old-growth forest and I was eaten alive by the mosquitoes. The bugs and mosquitoes were so bad that they gave me cold shivers and I tried everything the students told me to do to keep the mosquitoes off me, but nothing worked. This experience was so hard on me that I began to tell my co-worker and students that I was planning to leave the course and Canada at the midpoint, when we stopped to get our food resupplied. The bug situation was so bad I wanted to go back to South Africa or Zimbabwe, but my co-worker and the students showed me some techniques that helped to reduce the number of bug bites I got. I also discovered, to my relief, that above the tree line the mosquitoes were greatly reduced in number. In the end, I survived the trip and went on to run other courses. I think the mosquito incident had something to do with teaching me about how we can overcome great adversity when we have the right support system and access to useful education (Douglass 1989).

In August of my first year in Canada, Liz and I had to get married, as stated on my immigration papers. The marriage seemed imposed upon us, yet we had been well aware that this day would come. There was no feeling on my part that I was making a life-changing decision. It all felt like I was just complying with an established agreement with immigration, and there was also a sense of amusement about the fact that I was getting married. There was no planning put into the marriage; we just found a justice of the peace in the phone book and asked her to marry us. We literally ended instructing our respective Outward Bound courses, raced down to Shannon Falls in Squamish, and got married in a ten-minute ceremony with five Outward Bound work colleagues as witnesses to the whole process. To celebrate the marriage, we went to downtown Squamish for a Chinese dinner. We would not have had those five witnesses if the program director's wife had not asked us at breakfast what we were doing for our break before the start of the next courses, and that is when we shared with people that we were getting married. I do not even remember who it was we asked to be our two witnesses for the marriage ceremony. All I remember is that the director's wife rounded up as many of the staff as she could find on very short notice to come support us. When we were waiting in the parking lot for the justice of the peace to arrive, the director's wife noticed that Liz was dressed in her hiking shorts and sandals. So she ran to her car and found a dress that she had left in there that Liz used for the ceremony. Just when we thought we were ready for the ceremony, we realized that we did not have rings to give each other, but somehow they appeared too. I do not remember where the rings came from that we used to be married. The most memorable part of the whole ceremony was going to downtown Squamish for the Chinese food and the Dairy Queen ice cream cake. I wonder what kind of perspective Liz has on this whole process.

When the summer Outward Bound courses were over, I asked Liz if we could spend the winter in Vancouver because I wanted to take literacy classes so I could learn to read and write, and I also wanted to reconnect with the sport I loved playing, rugby. To facilitate our plans, an Outward Bound senior instructor offered to let us stay on his boat moored along the coast between Ladner and White Rock (two suburbs outside downtown Vancouver). Liz agreed to this arrangement, but made it clear that this was not her preference; she hated big cities and was doing this only to support my educational endeavours. I, on the other hand, loved Vancouver. I found it to be the perfect city because it offered quick access to the wilderness while also offering big-city life.

Through my Vancouver rugby networks I started to find better paying jobs, which meant I was settling into the Vancouver scene quite nicely, whereas Liz was not coping with the city life well. At the time, I found it strange that the same Liz, who in Africa had adapted to every situation, could not adapt to new situations here in Canada, where she was culturally at home. It may be possible that Liz was not choosing to adapt because as a cultural insider to colonial whiteness, she could exercise a certain level of autonomy, which I had no reference to. The point I am making is that Liz had the cultural capital in the colonial context to remove herself from unwanted or uncomfortable situations (hook 2004). I, on the other hand, had been colonially conditioned to feel fortunate to participate in colonial whiteness, so for the most part I spent little time contemplating the existential question of whether I should participate or not. For me, the more important question was, would I be viewed as competent to participate in colonial whiteness and, if I were viewed as competent, what could I do to improve my chances for admission to participate in colonial whiteness (hooks 2004)? As I write these words on these pages, I am becoming aware of the fundamental philosophical worldsenses that shaped our cultural difference. I think these differences between us were greater than our commonalities. I cannot speak for Liz because I do not know what motivated her to be invested in our relationship, but I know that I was motivated by gaining capitalistic accumulation more than doing the work required to nurture our friendship and relationship (Archibald/Q'um Q'um Xiiem 2008). Doing relational work requires emotional honesty and trust, two emotional qualities that I had locked away for fear of them opening me up to being vulnerable to colonial exploitation. As I was not invested in doing the hard work of honest relationship building, because I feared being vulnerable with another person,

I closed myself off to honest loving actions as a way of ensuring my security against what I viewed as the weakness of vulnerability in colonial contexts (hook 2004). This is why I spent more time away from Liz than I did with her.

A few months after we had been married, our relational breaking point materialized; it was October 1995. We had been invited to our rugby club's Halloween party. Everyone was having a great time dancing and drinking. At some point during the party, Liz disappeared and no one could find her. A whole group of us started searching for her, but no one could find her and I became quite worried. I was about to call the police when one of the rugby girls questioned if she had gone home, which I thought was unlike Liz, but possible, as she had the car keys. Seeing the car in the parking lot, I went over and wiped the frosted back windows. There in the back of the car was Liz wrapped up in a sleeping bag, trying to sleep. I could see her whole body shivering from the cold. Standing there, I knew I was being unfair to her as I realized that she was a person I respected but did not love, and I had never opened myself up to that reality. I had only allowed Liz into my life as my vehicle for my colonial desires (hooks 2004). I did not know who Liz was as a person below the surface. I did not know her childhood oratures; I did not know her friends beyond our work peers; I did not know her hopes or her fears; and yet she was my wife. The dirty colonial business of exploiting people was in that moment proving to be too much for me and, as I reflected on what I had done to Liz in order to be in Canada, I was filled with regretful emotions (hooks 2004). I was and am not proud of my actions: I had purposefully and intentionally taken actions to exploit Liz. To this day, I am still deeply ashamed of those exploitative actions that I took against her.

I also suspected that Liz did not know who I really was, but I did not know how to introduce myself to her. It was easier to question how she had allowed herself to be so easily fooled by me instead of questioning if she could handle living with the man I truly was. I opened the car and asked Liz why she was sleeping in the car? As she explained her actions, I knew our relationship was over. The next day I broke up with Liz and, over a period of time, we separated our lives from each other. After my breakup with Liz, I wanted and tried to form long-term relationships, but they never seemed to work. I seemed at the time to be comfortable with unworkable relationships because they protected me from being intimately vulnerable with other humans (hooks 2004). I think I feared being vulnerable with another person because I believed that my familial fragmentation was destined to be repeated in my relationships. I think this is why most of my relationships at that time lasted between a month and six months, while the longest two relationships I had each lasted for two years before I got scared and ran from the challenges of those relationships (hooks 2004). After I left Liz I worked at the Outward Bound School for two more seasons, but it was hard. Staff members at schools like Outward Bound are like family and, when they saw that Liz had been hurt, they rallied around her and I knew I was messing up the family spirit, so I left Outward Bound. Some rugby people helped me apply for a job with the Vancouver School Board. My first job was working at an alternative high school in the Vancouver East district as a substitute youth worker. The program was known as the Eastside Alternative and I dealt with youth who were on behaviour modification programs. Working with youth and children in challenging contexts was hard work, yet I found this work very fulfilling and rewarding.

After six months of working at Eastside, the worker I was substituting for returned and I went back to on-call until another long-term substituting position opened up at General Brock Elementary School for an alternative worker in an extended learning class. The teacher running this program was Deborah, a dynamic Indigenous educator. In all her educational work with students, Deborah always centred and demonstrated relational social justice. Her exemplary engagement with students made me a better educator and a better caring human being. Our partnership was so effective that Deborah advocated that I be hired as a full-time employee, and when the Ministry of Attorney General, Community Program Division was looking to hire a community project worker for the Vancouver region, the principal and Deborah had no hesitation in recommending me for the position. This meant I got to know the students in both the educational school setting as well as through the community recreational setting. It is through these Indigenous community engagements that I started to learn about Indigenous resistance to the governing colonial structures of capitalistic accumulation as supported by white supremacy in Canada (Kuokkanen 2015). As these Indigenous oratures intersected with my own oratures, I could not help but start to care about Indigenous peoples on this landmass of Turtle Island. My brothers and sisters, I am learning so much from you and it is my hope to set up cultural dialogue exchanges between our peoples. I believe we could learn so much from each other.

Through my work, I advocated for Indigenous children and supported struggling families, but mostly I played with children. While playing, I even surprised myself with the good advice I gave to other people and, at some point, I started to believe my own advice. It may be that after working and watching so many students face and overcome so many challenges in different environmental settings, I could not help but be inspired to face my own academic learning challenges. So I signed up to do a literacy program through the Low Back Society Program. The program helped me find ways to cope with my learning disability and, within a few weeks, I was ready to take my general education development test. Even though I barely passed some of those exams, I was thrilled, excited, and confident that I could make it through college. For the first time in my life, I was becoming intentional (Coates 2015). I was not just letting life happen to me. I was actively planning for my future rather than just letting it unfold is it would (Mandela 1995). However, I must tell you that each step that I took toward higher education was hard and scary. There were times I wanted to give up, but because I had relational supportive systems (children and youth from the school community, their families, and other educational colleagues) around me, I was able to keep going despite my fears. Therefore, I can say my educational path reflected how communal social interaction can support life learning (Mutwa 1969).

It is under these conditions that I signed up to do the counselling program at Vancouver Community College. For some unknown reason, I actually made a deal with the youth that I would give them updates and evidence of my progress if they would do the same about their educational progress. Reflecting back now, I can see that I was using the African Indigenous philosophy of Ubuntu to create a teaching pedagogy grounded in dialogue about how we mattered to each other. This meant that through our dialogical engagements, in each other's storied life space, we were mattering to each other. I can therefore say that this group of youth gave me a meaningful purpose for pursuing my education, because through them I learned to believe that my work could help youth develop meaningful relationships in and through education. The successful completion of my counselling certificate program led to my promotion to the position of school youth and family worker. The advice of the same youth I was counselling was paying off for me and I can truly say our relationships were reciprocal (Archibald/Q'um Q'um Xiiem 2008). I still doubted my ability to do a university program, so as a way of testing the waters, I decided to take a social service worker's certificate program at Langara College in Vancouver, which also gave me transferable university credits. Hence, as the cohort of youth I was working with transitioned to high school, I resigned from my position and became a full-time student. As afraid as I was, I was now 100 percent committed to my education and, after completing my social service worker's certificate program, I transferred to the University of Victoria.

It was when I was a student in the School of Child and Youth Care (SCYC) at the University of Victoria that I met your mother. I had seen your mother around the SCYC, and the very first moment I saw her I was attracted to her, but I kept my distance from her because I was dating someone else. As we were in different program years, I did not see her again for a long time. The next time I saw your mother was after I had just gone through a breakup. She invited me to her birthday party, but I did not go because I was not interested in pursuing a serious relationship after just ending one. After that incident, I did not see your mother again for about a month. The next time we met, we were in the same statistics class and I sat next to her. At some point in the class, our arms brushed against each other and I felt the energy of attraction. During a break in that class, I told a friend that I wanted to date your mother. The friend, who was also South Asian, tried to dissuade me from dating your mother because, as she put it, "dating Indian girls with a traditional Indian family is dating serious trouble." She even offered to set me up with her cousin, but I was only interested in your mother; as I conveyed earlier, I had started being intentional and was not happy with having life just happen to me. I had come to understand that to be intentional with the planning of one's future required a certain amount of capital power, which I was gaining as I climbed higher to each level of colonial education (Fanon 1963). These were the rewards within the colonial matrix of white supremacy, but the real test was how much I would use this privilege and power to recentre the resurgence of Ubuntu as an act of love beyond colonial capitalistic accumulation education.

At the end of class, I wanted to invite your mother out, but I did not know how to do it. So I just told her I would see her next week. At the next class, your mother sat with her friend, Auntie Bell and, because I was late for class, one of my friends had saved a seat for me so I sat with him. At the end of that class, Auntie Bell asked if a group of us wanted to go to the campus pub, and your mom and I both looked at each other to inquire if we were going. As we began to walk to the pub, your mom and I fell into step with each other. We started chitchatting while walking to the UVIC student pub. I remember asking your mother what book she was reading and she told me that she was reading *A Fine Balance* by Rohinton Mistry. Without too much prompting, she proceeded to give me a review of the book and a synopsis of how the book had influenced her life. At that moment I knew your mom was a complete package from my perspective. She was very intelligent, very attractive, and, most importantly, knew how to live in poverty and did not seem to fear extreme poverty. The seriousness with which she had engaged me in a discussion about her reading of this book told me that she was not a person who wanted to play dating games. This threw me off my own dating game, which I was enjoying. I knew at that moment that I needed to make up my mind about what I wanted, so in a very abrupt manner, I excused myself from your mother and left.

For the rest of that week I debated two questions with myself: Do I risk opening up myself to knowing your mother, knowing this would lead to me falling in love with her, or do I keep being single and uncommitted (hooks 2004)? I guess with the guidance of the ancestors I made up my mind that I would risk everything to be with her. At the next class, I sat again with my friends while your mother sat with Auntie Bell. Through class, I planned how I was going to make a move on your mother when class was done. With my plan in mind, and as soon as the class was done, I went over to your mother and Auntie Bell and started to talk to them with the intention of setting up a date with your mother, but as I was talking, I could sense that your mother was being standoffish and showing no interest in me. I did not know what she had found out about me, which undermined my confidence and made me forget my game plan. With all kinds of doubting thoughts racing through my mind, I found myself at a loss for words. I remember very awkwardly asking your mother and Auntie Bell what they did for fun and your mother saying with detached attitude, "Not much, we study." Realizing that your mother was shutting down all avenues of communication, I started trying to find an exit strategy, and then your Auntie Bell asked what I was doing that evening. I told her that I had no plans and she invited me to their place. Without losing a beat, Auntie Bell told your mother to drive with me so that I would not get lost.

To my delightful surprise, your mother agreed to this plan and, as we walked to my car, she started to talk more casually. Yet, in my brain, I was trying so hard to find a way to communicate to your mother that I was interested in her sexually, but I could not find the right words to communicate this wish in a discreet and respectful manner. As I started driving, I reached across the car's gearshift box and gently held your mother's hand, and she in return squeezed my hand and held it tightly. That is how your mother and I started dating. From that point onward, every day after school, I was at their place, and sometimes you mother would ask me to go to my home so she could hang out with your Auntie Bell. The first time your mother stayed at my place, she noticed that inside my address book there were a lot of loose pieces of paper with different girls' names and phone numbers. I can remember your mother saying to me, "If you only want fun then I am not that girl, and if you want a serous relationship with me then all these games must stop." My response to your mother that day was to take all the pieces of papers, rip them up, and throw them in the bin. I was ready to start a serous relationship and I was ready to love beyond my fears of abandonment (Coates 2015).

Within a few days of our dating, your mother and I started a ritual of taking walks in the early evening, and it was on these walks that your mother steadily laid out the full challenges that our relationship would face in reference to her family and her Sikh Indian community. I can remember on these walks your mother telling me that her Sikh Indian family would not welcome me and instead would actively try to end our relationship because I was Black and not part of the Sikh Indian community. Having faced this kind of racism before, I remember trying to convey to your mother that things like this had a way of working themselves out over time. I even gave her some examples of couples that had overcome these interracial challenges and I remember your mother saying, "My extended family and my parents will not get over the fact that you are Black, so if we are going to date you will need to understand the following rules:

- Our dating is risky and dangerous for me, so only pursue this relationship if you want a future with me.
- This relationship has to be kept secret until we are sure that we want to get married.
- If we get married, you need to be prepared that my family will disown me. It is going to be you and me and the family we start.
- And if any of the above realities do not work for you, then walk away from this relationship."

When your mother was done talking, I was so angry I could not speak because I was once again witnessing my Black Indigenous Ubuntu embodiment be a site for racial prejudice, expressions of fear, and outright expressions of anti-Black sentiments (Coates 2015). Now, I should tell you that if I had been given these rules at any other time in my life, I would have walked away from this peculiar situation, but not this time. A few days before, your mother and I were taking a walk while I was eating an orange. A small part of the orange flesh became stuck in my beard. When your mother saw the orange flesh stuck in my beard, without thinking, she took it out and ate it. That action signified to me uninhibited and unreserved love and, in that moment, I knew I had found the love of my life. So our shared love connected us, but the mixing of our Black and Brown embodiment created a racial and cultural threat for Mandeep's parents and some extended family members. As mad as I was about the racial prejudice that I was going to face from your mother's parents, I used the technique that our Black ancestors have used since olden times to survive. I reduced my boiling anger to a manageable simmer (Gates Jr. and Oliver 1999) and told your mother, "If you are ready to fight for this relationship, then I will fight for it too."

For the first few months of our dating, I was not able to take your mother out on a nice dinner date because I did not have much money over the summer months after paying for school. So we cooked for each other and did a lot of trail hiking around Victoria, BC. Then, just before the start of the fall school year, I got a notice from the government stating that I had been given a Millennium Grant as part of my student loan application. At the same time, I also learned that the government had approved my disability support funds and that our SCYC department had awarded me a scholarship. All this good news about money made me believe that the funds were already in my bank account. A few days later, I told your mother that I was taking her out for dinner the next night and I would come and pick her up at 6:00 p.m.

The next evening, I showed up looking good and your mother was looking good too (even though I keep describing your mother as looking good, which is true, she is an incredibly amazing scholar who inspires me every single day). I had made reservations at a top-end restaurant in downtown Victoria and, when we arrived, we did not have to wait to be seated at a table. As our order of drinks was coming, your mother questioned if we could afford eating at this restaurant. I told her not to worry, as I had this covered. The service we were given was top-notch and the food was delicious. As we were ready to leave, I asked for our bill and gave our server my VISA card. After about five minutes, our server returned and asked if I could come with her as she was having some problems and needed my help. When we were out of earshot, she informed me that my VISA had been declined and that she had tried it a number of times without any luck. She asked if I had another card and I told her we could use my bankcard, but it too was declined. At this point, she asked if I had a friend who could come and settle the bill so that it would not cause a problem on my date. It was at that moment that I knew that the only person I would feel comfortable asking for help in this kind of situation was your mother. With my head down, I walked over to your mother and asked if she would pay for our bill. She lovingly laughed at me and called me a jackass before taking care of it. The situational context of that debt can never be repaid and, to this day, I remain in your mother's debt.

Interestingly before your mother was 100 percent sure that I was committed to our relationship, she introduced me to your Masi Sandy (not real name of your auntie). I think your Masi Sandy did not know how to relate to a Black man who wore earrings, had a nose ring, and had dreadlocks. (Yes, I had dreadlocks back in the day, before I started going bald.) Her first instinct was to worry that I was a player and would take advantage of her sister. She was guarded during our initial meetings but became more open to getting to know me and soon I was her big brother. Your Masi Sandy and I hung out together and argued about everything from politics to religion, and she was your mother's strongest support system for dealing with her family. Outside of your mother, no family member has suffered more for supporting our relationship. At one point, I thought she too would be disowned by your mother's family for supporting our relationship. Here is what I remember about your Masi Sandy: in the face of her own fears and anxieties about the possibilities of her family breaking apart, she offered to remain a part of our new family. I thank your Masi Sandy for being a heroic baby sister because, as you will find out, she was tested and she supported relational love above all else.

By the time I met your mother, I was turning into a serious student, but I still had a well-known partying history, which in small-town white Victoria was not hard to achieve. In Victoria, Black folks are exotified by educated white liberals. In the first year of university, I had tried hard to be a good student, but I was always being dragged off to parties. At some point, I began to enjoy the parties more than I was enjoying school. Luckily for me, when the school year was done I saw that even the greatest party comes to an end and everyone goes back home. So during my first summer at the University of Victoria I found myself all alone and homeless. It is then that I started to understand the importance of gaining an education in order to understand the socio-political systems and structures in which we are embedded. This is when I started to question how I was resisting this kind of exploitive and oppressive political system in my life. Sadly, the evidence to my inquiry told me that I was a product of the colonial system (Fanon 1963). This is when I started to wonder how I could use my education to explore how I could learn to live a better-informed Ubuntu life (Mutwa 1986). The act of starting this kind of educational questioning led to the end of my party-focused days.

At times your mother felt that she was robbed of the "fun partying" me, but once I saw education as my path for decolonizing, I could not go back to hiding from my Ubuntu responsibility on colonial dance floors (Mucina 2007). The law library that your mother had introduced me to became my party space, professors and other Indigenous scholars became my comrades in learning more about decolonization. As your mother was a year ahead of me in the SCYC program, when she graduated, I still had a year to go. Our relationship was still a secret from her family, so I could not and did not go to her graduation ceremony.

Before your mother graduated, she made sure that she had a job offer as a social worker in Vancouver. This distanced her from her family and the Sikh Indian community of Victoria, which were starting to talk about our relationship. Around this time, your mother told her brother, your Mama (uncle) about our relationship and, according to your mother, your Mama told her that if their parents found out about our relationship, it would cause them major stress and seriously affect their already frail health. Your Mama then told your mother to keep our relationship a secret and to keep him out of this mess if she was going to tell their parents. Other family members in Vancouver started to find out too and it did not help when one of your mother's family members, who is a police officer, saw us walking from downtown Vancouver together. I tried to walk away from your mother so that it did not seem like we were together, but he asked your mother who her friend was and also made it clear that he was not interested in creating waves about our personal lives.

As more family members started to find out about our relationship, your mother started to worry about her parents finding out through another person, which would be more shameful for them. At this point, your mother began preparing to confront her parents and, each time she contemplated confronting them with the news of our relationship, the more it became clear to her that her family would not accept our relationship. Not being able to see an alternative to disownment by her family, your mother started to experience anxiety and depression. As if she did not have enough to worry about, your mother began to also worry about our physical safety, as we did not know the kinds of interventions her parents would take to prevent our relationship from continuing. As a precaution against physical danger, your mother informed her employers about our relational situation, and I informed some Vancouver police officers I knew through my previous work with the Vancouver School Board. As I was still at school in Victoria, we arranged for your mother to share a house with some close friends of ours in Vancouver. All this was unnecessary, but at that time, we did not know that such violence was beyond the context of her family. The news headlines were filled with stories of honour killings committed against young South Asian women, so we did not want to take any unnecessary risks with your mother's life (M.K. Mucina 2015).

Roundabout this same time, I started having intense dreams about my Baba and Amai and I could sense that major change was also happening for my own parents. I decided to do my educational work experience in the orphanage that

I grew up in. Going to do my practicum or internship at St. Joseph's House for Boys in Harare was a way for me to give back to the place and people who cared for me when no one else could. My way of giving back was by putting my child and youth care training into practice with the boys at the orphanage and, more importantly, by sharing my life experience beyond the orphanage. My aim was that by sharing my life experience with the boys, I could help prepare them for life beyond the orphanage. It was also my plan to find my Baba and Amai and begin the process of reconciling our fragmented family in whatever new relational configuration we could create collaboratively. I should also say I wanted my parents to see how much of a success I had become without their help. Half-truths are easier to sell than the completely complicated and contradictory truth. Hence, my fundraising efforts only communicated my desire to help the boys who were still in a situation that I had transcended and did not refer to my personal familial motivations. I secured the funding for that trip through the Langara College community and the University of Victoria's Child and Youth Care Program.

Just as I started to think about preparing to leave for Zimbabwe, I learned through the orphanage that my Amai had passed over to the ancestor world. As I did not know my mother very well, I was more saddened by the fact that I would not be able to engage with her in a physical manner in the building of our relationship than by the news of her passing away. Yet with the news of my Amai's passing away, my journey to Zimbabwe took on a new sense of urgency for me. There was so much I wanted to know about my family, and now one of the sources for that information was gone, and the other, I could sense, was nearing the end of his life. Therefore, I felt a sense of urgency to get as much information from Baba as I could. As to what happened on my trip to Zimbabwe, you can read that in my letter to Baba. All I can tell you at this moment is that while I was in Zimbabwe, your mother and I found ways to communicate frequently. There was not any element of my life that she was not aware of. On that trip, I was critically aware that your mother was my best friend, and I was also very aware that I missed her very much.

When I came back from that trip I took your mother to the Seasons in the Park Restaurant in Queen Elizabeth Park, Vancouver's mountain-top restaurant, and there, with a view overlooking the city, I proposed to her. I was so thrilled and overjoyed when your mother said yes to my proposal of marriage, because it meant that my best friend and I were going to navigate life and address the joys and challenges of building a family together. To support your mother with the decision to disclose our relationship to her family, we started going to counselling sessions, which revealed to us that the systemic support systems in Vancouver were not equipped for dealing with the issues that arose from interracial relationships among minorities. Our most effective support system was our friends and their parents. If it were not for them, our lives would have been much harder.

The plan that your mother had devised for disclosing our relationship to her family went along these lines. She would tell her father first as a way of ensuring that his authority as the head of the family was not undermined, and then after that she would tell her mother. Your mother had also decided not to tell her Bibi (her grandmother), who was in poor health, about our relationship; she was comfortable with her parents telling her Bibi when they saw fit. This part of the orature I cannot do justice to as I am only giving you the censored version that your mother shared with me. If you want to know what was said, I would encourage you to ask your mother. From what I remember and understand, when your mother told your Nanaa (maternal grandfather) about our relationship, he told her to end it immediately. He told her that no one would ever need to know about our relationship and that he would still be able to find a suitable Indian man to marry her. He also told her how in their culture marriage was more than two individuals getting together; it was two communities and two families joining together, and the two people marrying symbolized this communal joining. This is why marriages were carefully planned. A good marriage was meant to bring honour and not shame.

Her father told her that our union would bring shame to his good name and he was not going to let that happen (M.K. Mucina 2015). When your mother told him that she was not looking for his permission and that she was only seeking his blessing, he refused to give it and told her that he would give her a little more time to come to her senses before he related to her the consequences of the actions she was taking. He also told her that she was not to reveal the nature of our relationship to her mother, as this would kill her. From what I could gather from your mother, her father confided to other family members about this problem and they collectively harassed her in hope of scaring her into changing her mind. At this point, I had started my MA degree in Indigenous Governance at the University of Victoria and was commuting between Vancouver and Victoria.

When the time for reflection that had been imposed on your mother by her father had lapsed and your mother was unwilling to end our relationship, she was told to come home for a family conference. As she felt threatened and unsafe around her family, she asked your Masi Sandy to come with her as her support. Your mother's biggest worry was that her transgression and refusal to conform to her parents' wishes was going to be blamed on her mother and Bibi as evidence that they had failed to exercise good female parental authority over her (M.K. Mucina 2015). From that logic, your mother's decision to be in a relationship with an Indigenous African man was being viewed as not good behaviour by a good Sikh woman and daughter. In an effort to protect her mother and Bibi, who did not agree with her decision of being in a relationship with a Black man, she maintained very little contact with them. This was to ensure that your Nani (maternal grandmother) and Bibi were never implicated by your grandfather and the extended family for any decisions that your mother had made in reference to our relationship (M.K. Mucina 2015).

Your Nanaa, Nani, and Bibi all took turns trying to persuade your mother to change her mind and, when that failed, they tried to bribe her. When that failed, they threatened her with excommunication and isolation. Yet she would not give up her position, so they began to threaten bodily violence toward themselves and her, and this is when your mother had a mental breakdown. She reported to me that she ran from the house, because she knew that there was no happy outcome for anyone in her predicament. To have her lover and friend, she was losing her family and community. Your Masi Sandy found your mother wandering in the streets in a fog of mental confusion. She took your mother back to the house and helped her take her medication. Although your Nani and your Bibi did not change their position, they were moved by her suffering and offered as much support as they could under this situation. They also held onto the hope that your mother would change her position.

When your mother got back from the family conference, she informed me that her family wanted nothing to do with our relationship and were not open to meeting me. So we decided to move on with our lives without involving your mother's family. Yet to abate any possible violence directed toward your mother because of perceived family shame, we decided to move to Toronto. In Toronto, your mother was entering the Master of Social Work program at the University of Toronto. Before we left for Toronto, we wanted to get married with our friends and our support network in British Columbia. This is how we decided to have a secret wedding on Thetis Island before we left for Toronto. I can remember your mother making a conscious effort not to invite even the few family members who were supportive of our relationship to our wedding, because she did not want to create divisions within her family and embarrass her parents any further. So your Masi Sandy is the only family member who was a part of our wedding, the rest of the folks at our wedding were our close friends. Early in the day, before our wedding ceremony, your Mama called your mother and left a message that he was offended that she had not invited him as her only brother to her wedding. To let us know that they were aware of what was happening, just a few minutes before our wedding ceremony, your grandparents called your mother and berated her for arranging her wedding without informing them. Hence, both groups of family members, those who challenged our relationship and the few who openly supported our relationship, were united in their anger of not being a part of our wedding ceremony.

After our wedding ceremony, your mother was called to another family conference and your mother went to it thinking that her parents were now willing to reach some kind of new compromise. When your mother arrived at their home, her father told her that he and the family were willing to overlook all the transgressions that she had committed if she was willing to go to India right away and submit to an arranged marriage. Your mother rejected this idea and her father told her that she was no longer his daughter and that he would never speak to her again. For the longest time, over eleven years, her father would not speak to her or me. Your Nani, on the other hand, told your mother in secrecy that she was still her daughter and that she would find a way to keep in touch. Like us, she too felt that it would be wise for us to move away from British Columbia. Your Bibi, on the other hand, was worried about your mother moving away; she was old and she worried she was going to die while your mother was away and all she wanted was to die with her small family around her. Your Bibi therefore tried in vain to find a workable solution that would allow your mother to remain close to her.

Your mother had to go to Toronto by herself and stay with a friend of ours while she looked for a rental apartment for us to live in. I had to stay behind to prepare and present my MA thesis proposal to my committee before I left for Toronto. With your mother gone, I talked to your Masi Sandy two to three times a week. So it was not unusual when she called me at midmorning on a Friday; what was shocking was to hear that your Nanaa wanted to meet with me. I remember asking your Masi Sandy why your Nanaa wanted to meet me now after having made it so clear that he was not interested in meeting with me. Masi Sandy was more optimistic about this meeting, and she told me that she had been talking to her father about me and that she had explained to him that it was through my help that she had managed to become more successful at college. She was convinced that he was starting to see that it was possible that I was a good person beyond the racial stereotypes and prejudice that he held against me. On the other hand, I had experienced enough prejudice and racism to know that my character could not change systemic barriers. Yet I agreed to the meeting because I did not want to undermine any opportunity to create some change regardless of how little it was. I was trying so hard not to let past history undermine possible new realities that we could create (Okri 1997). But decolonization must be a two-way process. Decolonization is not about being fair, it is about creating change within me and then using my personal change to engage with others, inclusive of our enemies. But I digress, so let me return to the orature.

Of all the places that we could have met in the city of Vancouver, we ended up meeting at Queen Elizabeth Park, just below the restaurant where I had proposed to your mother. I am not sure what the ancestors were trying to communicate to me. Your Masi Sandy, not wanting to disclose my address, offered to drive me to and from the meeting. We all met at 3:00 p.m. Your Masi Sandy and I were the first to arrive and within ten minutes, your Nanaa and your great uncle arrived. Your Masi Sandy introduced me to your Nanaa and I went to shake his hand, but he refused this gesture. Yet your great uncle stepped forward, introduced himself, and shook my hand. Your great uncle then told me that your Nanaa had arranged this meeting because he wanted to say some things to me. At this point, I noticed the configuration of how we were standing. Your Nanaa and your great uncle were one team standing on the lower ground, and your Masi Sandy and I were another team standing on the higher ground. I therefore positioned myself in such a manner as to not be speaking to an old one from a position in which I was standing above him and then I told your Masi Sandy who was standing next to me like a bodyguard that it might be a good idea for her to take a walk while we talked. Your Masi Sandy rejected this idea in her usual uncompromising manner, which made it appear as if she was on my side against her father, a scenario I had been desperately trying to avoid. I told your Masi Sandy that she had done her part of bringing us together so we could have this conversation, but if we were going to be frank with each other then we would need to do it alone.

Your Nanaa also told your Masi Sandy that she needed to stay out of this conversation, as it did not concern her, while your great uncle assured your Masi Sandy that there was nothing to worry about, as our meeting was only about speaking frankly with each other and posed no physical danger to anyone. As soon as your Masi Sandy gave us what she viewed as some acceptable space to talk, your Nanaa asked me: Why are you breaking up my family? I responded to this by letting him know that I was not breaking up his family, but in actuality was adding to it. He in turn responded by saying that my efforts to add myself to his family were not wanted and would never be acceptable. He made it very clear that I would never be a part of his family and no passing of time would change his position. I asked him why he held such a position and he told me that we did not share the same cultural values, customs, or even a language. I acknowledged that the language was a cultural barrier for our families, but then pointed out that from my engagement with and reading of Sikhism there was room for us to bridge the joining of our families. At this point, your Nanaa started yelling for me to stop trying to educate him on Sikhism, as it was his culture and religion and there was nothing I could teach him about it. He told me that it would be best for me to keep my mouth shut on that subject, as reading or going to some community events did not make me understand his religion or his community.

He then proceeded to tell me that I was not wanted in his family, to which I responded by saying that I was not trying to marry him; I had married his daughter and it was with her that I was trying to start a family. To my challenge, he responded by saying, "Because you have no family, you are taking my family. You are breaking my family and because of you, my daughter will have no family." Empathizing with your Nanaa's feared loss, I told him that his daughter had made her own decision to be with me and if she was to change that decision I would not stop her, as I understood how much she loved her family and how much they meant to her. Your Nanaa then said to me, "If you know all this, why are you walking over the cliff with her?" And if your Nanaa had left me with that statement alone it is very possible, out of love and care for your mother, that I may have considered walking away from our relationship as a way of lessening the pain I was causing so many people. But your Nanaa made the mistake of belittling your mother by saying to me, "If she can walk away from her family, who have known her all her life, what makes you think she won't walk away from you, whom she has only known for a very few years?"

Your Nanaa's words made me realize that he was a man who had been shaped by a racist world. His sexism was his fear of losing patriarchal power in a world still dominated by men regardless of the intersection of cultures (hooks 2004). His experience of colonial violence had taught him to only see and validate the humanity of his own family within the context of Sikh cultural identity. His fear of the outside world, I speculate, cannot be separated from his family's violent experience during the partition of India and Pakistan. I imagined that everything that did not embody the idealized representation of Sikh cultural identity could be perceived as a threat, especially in Canada where he experienced a great deal of racism (M.K. Mucina 2015). Using this logic, I could see how he saw my Black embodiment as a threat to his social status within his own community. But there was more to it than just social status within communal settings. There was also the question of racial hierarchy, where my Blackness was perceived as threatening to destroy their light Brownness. In the racial hierarchy of white supremacy, Brownness has been viewed as being better than Blackness and globally, in colonized spaces, many Brown bodies have bought into this belief (Fanon 1963). Hence, all the empathy that I was beginning to feel for this man turned to hostility and I remember saying to your Nanaa, "I have chosen to walk the path of life with your daughter and, if we are making a mistake, she and I will have to deal with that mistake together."

Your Nanaa then asked me if I had done or given your mother something to alter her thinking. I laughed at this proposition of insinuating that I was using witchcraft, because this is something that someone from my community would have insinuated. Your great uncle then intervened and informed me to take this questioning seriously, as it was important for your Nanaa to know that his daughter was making her own decisions without undue influence of any form from me. I did not know how to prove my innocence against using witchcraft and the only response I could give was to say, "Since I'm here with you, why don't you get someone to call your daughter and that way you can be assured that I am not using undue influence to control her, and if you can convince her to leave me then I will walk away right now and never speak with her again." To this suggestion, your Nanaa offered no response and, instead, turned to your great uncle and informed him that he was done. Without another word, he turned and began to walk toward the car. Your great uncle thanked me for agreeing to the meeting, shook my hand, and wished me luck. Your Masi Sandy tried to go give your Nanaa a hug goodbye but he rebuffed her efforts and my heart was filled with the deepest sadness. As your Masi Sandy drove me home, I apologized for fragmenting her relationship with her father and I remember her telling me that it was her father who was letting a distorted form of honour cloud his judgement (M.K. Mucina 2015).

Not too long after that encounter with your Nanaa, I left to join your mother in Toronto. At first, your Nani would contact your mother in secrecy whenever she could. Then your Bibi with the help of your Nani started contacting your mother too. Khumalo and Nandi, do you see how the women from your mother's family embody decolonizing actions? Do you see how they take actions beyond fear? Do you see how they centre love above all else? Do you see how they understand that decolonization is a two-way process that starts with us? But even men within your family have this capacity to centre decolonization actions. Take your Mama for example; I had excluded him from our lives because I perceived him as holding the same position as that of his father. I therefore never directly engaged him or gave us an opportunity to get to know each other. I had made an effort to get to know your Masi Sandy, but the fear of rejection more than the fear of physical violence had inhibited me from reaching out to your Mama (Hill Collins and Bilge 2016) in the same way that I had reached out to your Masi Sandy. This is not to say that your Mama had expressed any desire to get to know me, but it is an acknowledgement that I had not reached out to him directly. The lesson that I have learned here is that you cannot decolonize effectively from a position of fear (hooks 2004). When your Mama got married to your Mami, it was the women that insisted your mother be a part of the wedding preparations and ceremony. It was through the work of your Nani, Bibi, Masi Sandy, and Mami that your mother and her brother (your Mama) started to rebuild their relationship (Green 2017; Kuokkanen 2015; M.K. Mucina 2015; hooks 2004). This is love guiding decolonization (hooks 2004). Your mother was so happy that her siblings were rebuilding their relationships even as your mother's relationship with her father deteriorated.

While in Toronto, to help supplement our funds from our student loans, I started to work full time for East Metro Youth Services as a youth worker, while working late at night on my master's thesis. When I completed my master's, I started working on my PhD and your mother began to practise social work again while she was deciding on her PhD research program. After having completed my PhD coursework, I decided to go back home to Southern Africa with your mother. On hearing that we were going to Africa, your Masi Sandy informed us that she was coming with us. Not wanting to damage the budding relationship between her and your mother, your Nani, and Bibi, I tried to dissuade your Masi Sandy from coming to Africa, but I failed. No surprise there. This is the same trip to Africa that your Auntie Renée, my adopted sister, came on. It was also her first trip to Africa. After visiting South Africa, Swaziland, and Botswana, we went to Zimbabwe, and your mother and your Masi Sandy became great sources of support for me as I struggled to find and connect with my Baba's and my Amai's families.

Within a year of getting back from Africa, Khumalo, you were born in Toronto. You were three weeks earlier than the due date, so a backup midwife delivered you at the Women's College Hospital in Toronto, as our midwife was away. Your Masi Sandy, who was visiting us at that time, also helped the midwife deliver you.

After your Masi Sandy went back home, Auntie Renée and her family were our major support systems. A year after you were born, Khumalo, your Nani came by herself to visit us, which was no easy task for her, as she was going against her husband's wishes. These women join an illustrious list of Indigenous women from around the globe who keep me balanced through love and who inspire me to give love even when I want to give hate (M.K. Mucina 2015; hooks 2004; Mutwa 1986). This is not to say that men have not given me love, it is only to say that from my personal experience, I have experienced more consistent love and humanity from Indigenous women. A friend has argued that the consistency I experience between a woman and myself is the balancing between the masculine and feminine. At the centre of my friend's argument is the belief that a healthy human being embodies both the masculine and feminine, which is to say they are Ubuntu. It is my aim to work at centring my masculinity with my femininity so that my decolonizing actions are guided by love.

By the time you were born, Nandi, relational connections started to change somewhat. Nandi, I should let you know that you were born at home. You were coming so fast that our home-birthing plan was greatly challenged. I can remember sprinting with your brother in a jogging stroller toward the daycare when another parent going to the same daycare offered to take your brother there. As I sprinted through the apartment door along with the backup midwife, who had been held up by student housing security at the main entrance, the main midwife informed me that you were ready to come into the world. I held your mother's hand and watched you come into the world. As soon as you did, you were surrounded by love. We have cared for both you and your brother using the advice we received from Nani, Grandma Mildred from Zimbabwe, Grandma Wendy, and Grandpa Carlos from Grenada. I am so hesitant to name all the uncles and aunts that have cared for you because I know I will overlook someone, but I want to highlight those who are close to us and have helped you both understand the dynamism of your Blackness without making you conform to whiteness. All of the talk about Black Power, decolonizing, social justice, and antiracism that was done with Uncle Imara, Auntie Tanya, and Auntie Renée was to ensure you never felt insignificant in a sea of whiteness and white supremacy ideologies. You have always been surrounded by loving protective Black people as a way of ensuring that you understand your Blackness and love yourselves beyond colonially constructed notions of Blackness.

Before your Bibi passed away, she requested that I come and meet her in the family home. This meant that your Nanaa had to tolerate me in his home on a few occasions over the visits that we made to British Columbia before we moved back, which we did in 2016 because I had started working at the University of Victoria in the Indigenous Governance program. By 2017, your mother had also gotten a job with the University of Victoria in the School of Child and Youth Care. Yes, this is the same school where we started dating as students. I was/am excited to be able to centre my teaching and research on Indigenous scholarship, while rebuilding old and new friendships. We have also developed strong familial relationships with your Mama and Mami, and it is wonderful to see you both developing strong connections with your cousins and other family members. Your Nani and I have built a respectful relationship, but your Nanaa still struggles with our relationship. The funny thing is that I notice that there are times when he lets his guard down and actually enjoys engaging with us, but then he remembers that we are the enemy family and he shuts down. I wonder if seeing other interracial marriages within his extended family and the larger Sikh community has eased his fears about having his good name shamed in the community. I think you can both speak about your experience of having a grandfather who does not actively engage with you but just passively responds. I wish I could change that for you but I cannot, so your Amai and I prepare you every day with Ubuntu teachings of social justice and love so that your spirit is not worn down by offering unlimited love and only being given back reserved, slow limited love. I wish biological ties were not so important to identity because, like me, you are surrounded by so many loving community grandparents (Wane 2000).

Personally, I would never advise you to continue giving love when your actions are not reciprocated. You do not ride a broken bicycle that does not work, you try to fix it and, if you cannot fix it, you contemplate its future. Can it be used as a decorative ornament or be recycled? Now, I know your grandfather is not a bicycle, but I hope he does not wait too long and loses this opportunity to build a strong and meaningful relationship with you both, because you are wonderful kids. So much has changed and yet the historical remnants of the past still shape our current life.

I wish I could stop the racism in the world from touching you. I wish I could assure you of love and acceptance from within your family, but I cannot assure you of any of these things. All I can give you are the tools to face a contradictory world. A world so beautiful, yet so deeply ravaged by human violence and poverty. A world controlled by the colonial capitalistic accumulation structures of white supremacy, yet Indigenous knowledge about our relational connectivity is on the path of resurgence. We are of nature and nature is we. All elements are connected, we are one, but to understand this intimate connection we must have free will, which is the power to exercise individuation. Yet we can also use individuation to isolate ourselves from the whole. This is the contradiction that we live in and must live through. If we orient ourselves toward love, which is to say Ubuntu, a humanistic path inclusive of all elements begins to emerge. It is my hope that my oratures remind you that individuation motivated by fear, greed, and hatred stunts growth, while relational love for all elements honours all so that we all grow to be better beings.

Khumalo and Nandi, I want to conclude this Millet Granary by connecting everything that I have taught you to your current context as diasporic Indigenous Black Ubuntu. You both have been to Southern Africa and I know we will continue to develop these communal and familial connections. We have also started to immerse you in the Ubuntu spiritual ways while offering you Ubuntu rituals and ceremonies so that you are both grounded as loving peaceful warriors. In a dreamtime communication with the ancestors, I was directed by the ancestors to offer all the Ubuntu teachings, rituals, and ceremonies to our diasporic Indigenous Black Ubuntu. I am happy to share the fragments that I have and to learn from your fragments of Indigenous Black Ubuntu knowledge.

So I question you, Nandi and Khumalo, where do I end and where do you begin? Could the sacred cycle of breath connect us as one, Ubuntu?

Respectfully, your Baba,
Dr. Devi Dee Mucina Komba

I have shared with you the colonial actions that I took to be here in Canada; I have shared with you the Ubuntu actions that I have taken with your mother to start building our family. It is now time to synthesize the kinds of deeds that nurture your Ubuntu regeneration beyond colonialism while conveying our social connections to all elements. The next Millet Granary engages social individual actions of Ubuntu regeneration beyond colonialism.

Khumalo and Nandi, what have you learned about making courageous change?

What have you learned about fear and what have you learned about love?

How does this Ubuntu orature represent decolonizing actions with our families?

What do you think of the women's actions and men's actions in this Ubuntu orature?

Regenerating Everyday Ubuntu Actions

Methodological questions that guided my writing of this Millet Granary:

1. *What individual and social actions can we take to regenerate relational Ubuntu ways?*

2. *What guidance does Ubuntu offer for relational peace?*

3. *Does Indigenous Ubuntu power present a threat to other ways of being in the world?*

Sanibonani Nandi and Khumalo, living an informed regenerated Ubuntu life must be our goal, and our effort to live this informed Ubuntu life becomes our resistance to colonialism. Our planned, intentional Ubuntu social actions of liberation beyond colonialism affirm our power and identity and reflect our resilience in the face of colonialism (Biko 1996). Our social relational actions of regeneration beyond white supremacy and its colonial governance structures are based on our Ubuntu responsibility to our familial bonds. Our Ubuntu political philosophy of social actions are informed and motivated by Ubuntu love, which in its enactment is also resistance against our own oppression without oppressing other people (Mandela 1995; Mutwa 1969). Ubuntu love also means we stand against the oppression of other people in our decolonization process, because we understand the interconnectedness of all relationships in our territories and in the world at large. This means we will endeavour to approach our politics, our healing medicines, our economic interactions, and our spirituality from a relational, holistic, caring Ubuntu position (Okri 1997; p'Bitek 1984). This being said, there are some simultaneous collective actions that we need to maintain as we work to fulfil our own social actions of self-liberation. These collective Ubuntu actions of resurgence are grounded in a commitment to dialogue that leads to regeneration, critical honest actions of restitution, and open transparent education (Kuokkanen 2015; Tengan 2008).

However, we cannot wait for restitution, because waiting will weaken our Ubuntu spirit, while on the other hand, we cannot start reconciliation without truly contemplating the place of restitution. This results in reconciliation without serious engagement in meaningful restitution with Indigenous peoples. To illustrate my point, I would like to give two examples: one from the Zimbabwean context and the other from the South African context, which I hope communicate something to the white settler colonial governments of Australia, New Zealand, and Canada, and to the Indigenous peoples of these territories and nations resisting colonial governance. Reconciliation is never enough because it disturbs the status quo but does not change the fundamental relationship of governing power. It is a good first step in the right direction, but it is far from addressing the inequities that Indigenous peoples have suffered and, fundamentally, it does not make the wrong actions of the past and present right again, as shown in the Zimbabwe and South Africa example.

When the white settler government of then Rhodesia offered the Zimbabwean people an empty promise of reconciliation as a way of hanging onto power in the mid to late 1970s, the Zimbabwean people were left with no other choice but armed resistance. Comrade Robert Mugabe (1983), in *Our War of Liberation: Speeches, Articles, Interviews, 1976–1979,* conveys that in the false empty promises of colonial reconciliation, war was the only tool of liberation. In his own words he reflects on the ruling party's actions:

> From its very inception, ZANU was unequivocal in its approach to the liberation struggle. It purposefully chose war as a means of achieving liberation. It must always be borne in mind that a system sustained by violence can only be overthrown by violence. War can only be defeated by war. So, because the essence of settler power was force, ZANU decided to adopt the very method of force to defeat it and create a just system based on people's power, whose main anchor and guarantee shall remain a popular force. Accordingly, if ZANU at its birth was to become a truly revolutionary movement, it had to forge an instrument of force, sharp and devastating to the enemy. This sharp instrument was ZANLA, whose structure only materialised some years later. Today, ZANLA stands as a

mammoth liberation army, dreaded by the enemy but revered and adored by the people as the vanguard of their liberation struggle. (60)

With the support of our Black communities as well as international support for the Chimurenga (the armed struggle) efforts, who would have dared question the war leadership of Comrade Robert Mugabe? The people's war actions were grounded in collective self-defence against colonial forces and the desire of the Black Indigenous collective to exercise the right of self-determination. From my context, such anti-colonial actions are justified.

The problem of war as an intervention arises when Comrade Robert Mugabe (1983) reaffirms the party's 1976 principles in Geneva. What is in question is the following section from principle (b), which reads: "Our army remains the bulwark of our political power. If the vote is the product of the gun, then the gun which has created it must continue to protect and secure it. Guns and votes are inseparable partners" (100). Yet when the same Black Indigenous people chose to exercise their votes in opposition to the party's wishes, we all know too well what happened. Old Indigenous feuds between the Ndebele and Shona Ubuntu became the main justification of violence in Matabeleland, a province of Zimbabwe. The guns were then turned on the Indigenous peoples that they were meant to protect. The historical evidence of what happened is recorded as scars on the bodies of the people, it is recorded in the minds of the people, and it is recorded in the soil that holds mass graves that are still being found. It is projected that, between 1982 and 1987, thousands of mostly Ndebele people were killed in what was called Operation Gukurahundi.[1] Zimbabwe's vice president, John Nkomo, who was at the time of speaking these words the ZANU-PF national chairman and the Speaker of Parliament, told the Integrated Regional Information Networks that no one was ever trying to deny the existence of Gukurahundi. Nkomo relayed the following message: "Even President Mugabe has acknowledged Gukurahundi as a time of madness, which must never be repeated, so that means government is in a position to redress what happened" (*Irin News* 2007). We cannot enact genocide and then claim that our social actions were guided by a time of madness. Violence is only justified as self-defence when deadly action is directed at individuals or collectives. Indigenous political domination or survival within capitalistic colonial governance does not in any way constitute self-defence.

The other point is that failure to enact restitution as an important meaningful role of reconciliation only perpetuates the resistance against colonial settler governance. This is exemplified by the violent seizures of land in Zimbabwe. Yes, the governing party in Zimbabwe exploited the Indigenous people's genuine grievance about the need for land restitution, but we should never lose sight of the Indigenous people's genuine grievance about having access to their lands and sacred ceremonial shrines (Tengan 2008). This is what I have learned from the Zimbabwean context.

Interestingly enough, the two themes I have highlighted here are equally affirmed in the South African context as reported in the *Mail and Guardian* in a 7 February 1997 article, "The Parable of the Bicycle." This parable was told by Father Mxolisi Mpambani during a panel discussion on reconciliation at the University of Cape Town (UCT), organized by the Truth and Reconciliation Commission and the UCT's Department of African Studies. In reference to what reconciliation is without restitution, Father Mxolisi Mpambani helps us see who benefits from reconciliation and who loses: "There was Tom and there was John. Tom lived opposite John. One day, Tom stole John's bicycle and every day John saw Tom cycling to school on his bicycle. A year later, Tom walked up to John. He stretched out his hand. 'Let's reconcile and put the past behind us.' John looked at Tom's hand. 'And what about the bicycle?' 'No,' said Tom, 'I'm not talking about the bicycle. I'm talking about reconciliation.'" The point being made here by Father Mxolisi Mpambani is that white settler society has never taken seriously the importance of restitution as a precondition for reconciliation toward the Indigenous peoples of the world. Yet in Haiti's overthrow of the colonial settler society of France, whose elite were the slave masters, France demanded reparations and the preposterous demands were supported by the colonial capitalistic global community, which threatened Haiti with economic isolation (Franklin and Moss Jr. 2000). The racist attitude of white settler society cannot be overstated here.

What is evident in all of these examples is that social justice is never placated with tokenisms and self-serving actions of reconciliation, regardless of whether it is a colonially mimicking Black government or a white settler government. The need for social justice and meaningful restitution never leaves the minds of the people. This is reflected in Zimbabwe and South Africa where the land question is at the centre of Indigenous peoples' fights. Are Canada, New Zealand, and Australia not watching? Will they not learn and set an example for the other colonizing governments of the world?

Nandi and Khumalo, I have highlighted what I see as the limitations of reconciliation and I see those limitations as being reflected in the report of the Truth and Reconciliation Commission of Canada (2015), but I do not want to continue to dwell here on those limitations and lose focus on the strengths and inspirational aspects of the Commission's work. I think the greatest strength of the Commission's report is that it allows you to hear directly from the Indigenous peoples and nations that have lived through genocidal actions and policies; that have been dispossessed of territories; and that continue to experience exploitative attacks against their bodies and territories (Truth and Reconciliation Commission of Canada 2015). This report gives a truthful accounting of the impacts of capitalistic accumulation as structured by the white settler colonial government of Canada. The "Calls to Action" section of the report offers concrete actions that the colonial government must take in order to address the inequities that exist against Indigenous peoples and nations of Turtle Island. For example, the specific calls to action that speak to Canada's Indigenous child welfare programs outline how the government can address the detrimental effects of these programs on Indigenous children, families, communities, and nations. This is important information for both of you to know so that you do not continue to perpetuate the colonization of the Indigenous peoples of Turtle Island by not knowing the history and legacy of colonization within Canada.

The Truth and Reconciliation report (2015) highlights the importance of education in creating change, and I could not be more firmly in agreement with the report. Educational social justice inspired by relational responsibility and critical truths must guide your education. As an immigrant to Canada, it did not take me long to understand and see the inequities that Indigenous peoples experienced within the colonial governance structures. As a new immigrant, I was not told about Canada's nation-to-nation relationships with Indigenous nations. I was not told about existing treaties; contested treaties; failed treaties; unseated territories; or about Indigenous nations fighting against further encroachment onto their territories. I was welcomed because I spoke one of Canada's official languages and, of course, these are colonial languages (English and French).

There was no acknowledgement of Indigenous governance structures or the diversity of Indigenous nations, languages, and customs. There was no acknowledgement that I needed permission to be on these Indigenous territories. Canadian white settler colonial governance instilled in me mental amnesia because its members had convinced me that this was their land and only their rules applied. I had forgotten about my Indigenous Ubuntu etiquettes that should have informed me as a visitor and as an Indigenous immigrant to other Indigenous people's territories. However, when I arrived on Turtle Island, I never even attempted to exercise those protocols because I saw Canada as belonging to the white settler colonial society. White Canadian friends affirmed this colonial position by teaching me about the colonial European history of Canada as the real history of Canada. A white friend once told me that everyone was welcome to Canada and that individuals could practise their own ways, as long as their actions did not undermine the fact that Canada was a Christian European country. Of course, when I challenged that statement, that former friend tried to academically justify her position and tried to convince me that I misunderstood the essence of her position. So I want to give both of you, Nandi and Khomalo, some navigational advice that I have adopted as my relations with Indigenous peoples and nations have strengthened within the Canadian colonial context.

The first lesson that I have learned and remember as an Indigenous person is that I am an uninvited visitor on the ancestral lands, waters, and territories of other Indigenous peoples. I therefore make every effort to exercise relational responsibility and accountability as I live, work, and play as an uninvited guest of the Songhees, Esquimalt, and WSÁNEĆ peoples whose historical relationships with the lands and waters continue to this day. The second lesson is seeking permission to live in the territories of other Indigenous peoples. This we did as a family, through the support of the Indigenous community at the University of Victoria. This means we seek to obey the Indigenous laws and customs of the Songhees, Esquimalt, and WSÁNEĆ nations. The third lesson I have learned is that to live responsibly, while exercising respectful curiosity, requires strong relational ties. This means your mother and I have actively taken our family to Indigenous community events within the Songhees, Esquimalt, and WSÁNEĆ nations as a way of developing strong local Indigenous friendships and relationships, that help us understand our responsibility to the territories and the local Indigenous nations. Your mother and I actively keep expanding these activities so that we get an accurate understanding of our responsibilities across Turtle Island. Our current and most ambitious goal is to start learning one of the Indigenous languages of the territory where we live, work, and play.

This is an ambitious goal that we may not fully realize, because there a limited number of fluent language speakers who want to give us their precious time that could be better used by Indigenous families from these territories. To live with Indigenous peoples on their territories without making some effort to speak with them in their own language is considered among the Ngoni to be a sign of disregard for them and their customs (Mutwa 1969). I remember, once when I was young, I asked my Baba why he spoke so many Ubuntu languages and he replied, "How will I build good relationships if I do not even make an effort to know the languages of our neighbours?" Indeed, to know only our own issues, our own struggles, and our own languages is to be self-centred, which limits our relational learning. This is why we have taken you to an equal number of Black Lives Matter and Idle No More events. We want you to understand that all Indigenous struggles against white supremacy and its governance structures of exploitive colonial capitalism are connected without situating them as the same. Our inability to understand this keeps us complicit in each other's oppression, while colonialism and its languages present themselves as the most sensible path toward any viable future worth pursuing (Kuokkanen 2015).

Nandi and Khumalo, as diasporic Indigenous Ubuntu living on the territories of the Songhees, Esquimalt, and WSÁNEĆ nations, I have come to realize that, regardless of how we came to the territories of other Indigenous people, it is how we seek to live with the Indigenous people of those lands and waters that communicates our Indigenousness. Indigenous Ubuntu ways guide us as Ubuntu to seek and understand the relational web of life that connects all relational elements. This we call Ubuntu, or I could say "love." Love for me is respectfully honouring our survival relational need of each other in the web of life. These sacred relational ties we the Indigenous peoples of Southern Africa express as Ubuntu spirituality (D.D. Mucina 2015; Mutwa 1969). This means that Ubuntu spirituality is simply the expression of important sacred relationships. Ubuntu spirituality expresses this by stating, "We exist because you exist" (D.D. Mucina 2015; Mutwa 1969). I believe the misuse and exploitation of Indigenous spirituality in colonial capitalistic accumulation has led great Indigenous Black scholars like Frantz Fanon to become confused about the role of relational Ubuntu spirituality in Indigenous governance. In *The Wretched of the Earth*, Fanon (1963) states: "Culture has never the translucidity of custom; it abhors all simplification. In its essence it is opposed to custom, for custom is always the deterioration of culture. The desire to attach oneself to tradition or bring back abandoned traditions to life again does not only mean going against the current of history but also opposing one's own people. When a people undertakes an armed struggle or even a political struggle against a relentless colonialism, the significance of tradition changes" (224).

Fanon's (1963) point on African spirituality is that it has become meaningless and the idea of nurturing it for him is preposterous and foreign.

Yet Fanon cannot see or define the function of African spirituality in ways that are outside the colonial relationships. It is interesting to note that Fanon does not investigate African spirituality in any meaningful African way and instead dismisses African spirituality as superstition, open for exploitability by men and women who want power. For Fanon, spirituality is no less a tool of colonialism than Christianity to which he advocates that "we must put the DDT which destroys parasites, the bearers of disease, on the same level as the Christian religion which wages war on embryonic heresies and instincts, and an evil yet unborn" (42). Fanon sees spirituality as justification of religious customs, which have their power source in faith. Please take note of how Fanon links spirituality to religion and religion to custom. To Fanon, spirituality becomes another open door for what he calls "colonialism, which had been shaken to its very foundation at the birth of African Unity, recovers its balance and tries now to break that will to unity by using all the movement's weaknesses. Colonialism will set African peoples moving by revealing to them the existence of spiritual rivalries" (160). The great Fanon, with these words, has positioned our spirituality against our Ubuntu unity of governance, and he will not even acknowledge the existence of spirituality outside a colonial relationship. To any challenge we may offer, Fanon has concluded: "No, there is no question of the return to nature. It is simply a very concrete question of not dragging men towards mutilation, not imposing upon the brain rhythms which very quickly obliterate it and wreck it" (314), whereas Njoki Wane (2009), Molefi Kete Asante (1996), and Vusa'mazulu Credo Mutwa (1969) all state that we cannot confront compulsory white supremacy without the renewing power of Indigenous spirituality. The point I am making is that Fanon (1963) has missed the centrality of spirituality for Ubuntu. I believe our Indigenous Ubuntu history, from olden times to the present, clearly communicates that we are spiritual beings. Our multiple forms of religions are our efforts to express our spirituality. We can corrupt our religious institutions, but we cannot corrupt our spirituality, because it is the energy flux in all things. This is who we are and we cannot run away from it any more than a tiger can remove its stripes. Yes, in the name of spirituality, we can abuse each other, but we can also use our Ubuntu spirituality to honour our diverse ways of gaining renewal in our specific communal context. Even when Baba and I did not agree on religion, he always seemed to know that my Ubuntu spirituality would guide me in a good way. Meaning, my spirit is my guiding inner voice that at times protects me through what people call the sensing ability, or what we call an instinctual "feeling."

My spirit is also at work when I hear my inner relational voice questioning the merits and consequences of my actions for the dignity, respect, and pride of other people. In addition, I would hold that following my inner relational voice is taking relational spiritual actions, which is an act of resistance against colonialism. Ubuntu social actions of regeneration are rooted in each other. This means that, as an Ubuntu person, each time you take any of the following everyday actions, you are living Ubuntu social individual actions of regeneration beyond colonialism and creating Ubuntu spiritual change. Your social actions become demonstrative changes that can inspire the rest of us and, if you share these Ubuntu experiences, you are adding to our collective knowledge production. Remember, all these social actions come with responsibility for intent and impact. All the Ubuntu social actions of regeneration beyond colonialism that I outline here are reflective of my actions as determined by my context, relations, and cultural values. You may need to change some things and add other things:

- Do not impose your Ubuntu social actions of regeneration on anyone else. Do these actions because they are good for you, and any other reason beyond this loses the caring actions of love.
- Love yourself, love your Blackness, love your Indigenousness, love your spiritual ancestors, and love humanity while being weary of the abusers and the usurpers.
- Take responsibility for all actions you take or offer.
- Honour our ancestors—we exist because they exist.
- Give thanks for all of our relations because all elements are part of the energy flux that makes up life.
- Learn the ways we honour the spirit of the land and the spirit of the waters.
- Develop your knowledge production by first developing your mental awareness through authentic Ubuntu education.
- Use our oratures as medicines for fighting hate, pain, abandonment, isolation, gender violence, and fragmentation.
- Use our oratures to teach because they allow us to build collective confidence and allow for honest, critical engagement from a respectfully curious position. This is the expression of love, which is the basis for researching our truths in our shared humanity.
- Fight colonially imposed fragmentation by choosing to create relational engagement.
- Protect your families because the Ubuntu family is the foundation of our Indigenous institutions; break the family and we struggle to find our voices.

- Invest in our own communities as a way of developing self-reliance, so that we give our people the choice to work in environments where their dignity and self-respect are honoured.

- Be aware of how you are actively moving the centre of discourse from colonial structures to Ubuntu structures so that you can share these social actions of Ubuntu resurgence and regeneration beyond colonialism.

- Use and revive our languages as a way of fostering specific knowledges and environmental stewardship practices.

- Be open to change, it is the only constant in our changing world.

Here are some questions that should guide your actions:

1. Do my actions honour the spirit of Ubuntu love?

2. What are the consequences of my actions for our people?

3. Can I keep using my actions to sustain our total liberation?

4. Can I guarantee my actions do not oppress other people?

A close reading of Ubuntu social actions of liberation makes it clear that at the centre of these actions is the revitalization of relational care starting with the social self in a manner that is not self-indulgent so that we connect to all elements in our web of life. Ubuntu emphasizes that the wholeness of our Ubuntu kinship ties, which extends to our ancestors in the afterworld through the spiritual realm, also connects us to the present and to the spiritual future. As we Ngoni say, "I exist because my ancestors existed and the future will exist because I exist." The solutions of Ubuntu social actions of regeneration beyond colonialism are both immediate and sustainable over the long term because they are motivated by love for self, family, community, and all our relational bonds. Nandi and Khumalo, I hope I have given you an adequate blueprint to start your Ubuntu learning. Now that we are connected by this orature, where do you end and where do I begin? Could the sacred cycle of breath connect us as one, Ubuntu?

Respectfully, your Baba,

Dr. Devi Dee Mucina Komba

In this Millet Granary, I have synthesized the Ubuntu social actions of Ubuntu regeneration beyond colonial white supremacy that were spread out throughout this academic work. In the next and final Millet Granary, I would like to end in the same way we began this intellectual journey. I want to conclude the teachings I have given you with a final orature that I have created for you.

Do you now see that Ubuntu is relational love?

What Ubuntu relational actions will be challenging for you and why is this so?

Who will benefit most from your relational Ubuntu actions?

What is your biggest challenge to applying the guiding actions of relational Ubuntu?

Umuntu Ungumuntu Ngubuntu

I tell stories not to play on your sympathy, but to suggest how stories can control our lives. . . . Stories are wondrous things. And they are dangerous [things too]. . . . For once the story is told, it cannot be called back. . . . [A] story told one way could cure, that the same story told another way could injure. . . . "They aren't just entertainment / Don't be fooled / They are all we have, you see / All we have to fight off / Illness and death. You don't have anything / If you don't have the stories."

—Thomas King, *The Truth About Stories*

It is only fitting that I end this work with an orature that starts with "Paivapo" (many, many granaries ago), there was a time when human beings and animals could telepathically communicate. During this period of history, when human beings wanted meat, they went into the forest and asked for an animal that was ready to go to the spirit world to present itself and, before killing the animal, the human being would explain his/her actions and then thanked the animal for offering itself.

It was after performing such a ritual that a hunter was returning home with an old eland antelope. As he neared home, he heard his family crying. He dropped the eland and ran to investigate the problem. As soon as the hunter's wife saw him, she explained that the elephant, which they had welcomed into their home, was now violently asserting ownership of their home. At this point, the hunter inquired if his wife had tried to explain to the elephant that this was their home, which, out of Ubuntu hospitality and generosity, they had shared with the elephant. How could the elephant have forgotten that it was the pelting rain that had driven him to seek shelter for his delicate trunk from the human family? Had he not assured them that when the rain was over he would leave and had they not agreed to accommodate only his trunk in their small home? Yet he had gradually tricked them into believing that his head also needed protection from the elements and, once his head was in, his body just simply followed. This is how hospitality had become dispossession. But this betrayal by the elephant felt temporary, as the elephant had always assured the human family that he understood that they held title to their home. However, the current report that the hunter was getting from his wife now made it clear that the elephant was claiming both ownership and title of their home. The hunter's wife informed him that when she had tried to kick out the elephant, he had aggressively and menacingly asserted that possession was nine-tenths of the law. The elephant had also informed her that, since he had possession, he was going to use any means at his disposal to protect his property.

Afraid of antagonizing the elephant into a violent reaction, the hunter circumvented his old homestead, on his way to organizing a meeting about the problem elephant. After gathering us together, he clears his throat and says: "For as long as I have lived I have never seen animals behaving in the strange manner that elephants are doing. It started with them destroying our fields, but we all agreed that this was bound to happen because we shared space. Now an elephant has taken over my home and he is unwilling to listen to common sense. On top of this, the elephant is threatening any human being that comes near my home. My question to you is this: Do we believe this is an exceptional elephant or do we believe that this is the start of a planned attack by elephants against us?"

Someone yells: "Look, we all saw this coming; these elephants have been taking over everything. If we do not do something now, we will soon all be out of our homes; my suggestion is that we attack the elephants first and rid ourselves of the problem!"

Someone else yells: "I think we need to think about the consequence of our actions for our future and for our relational interconnectedness with all beings."

Someone else yells: "The problem is that we do not understand elephant logic. If we want to resolve this problem, then we must learn elephant logic. Once we understand elephant logic, then we can use it to reason with the elephants."

Someone else yells: "In the past when our ancestors had problems with our other relatives they just moved. Why do we not move?"

Someone else yells: "I do not want to use elephant logic because I do not want to behave like an elephant, but I also do not want to move onto the territory of our other relatives. This means for me, I will only fight when I have to protect my home and family."

Someone else yells: "We need action and less talk."

Someone else yells: "Hey, reader, what actions do you have to recommend for resolving this problem? Speak now or forever hold your peace."

Someone else yells: "Can we trust this unknown reader with such an important matter?"

An old one speaking confidently but quietly, says: "Reader, speak your thoughts; after all, what is put into action here will affect all of us. Do you see our greater responsibility?"

In this work, I have advanced that sharing personal memories and oratures will produce a foundation for educational Indigenous engagement with honouring our diverse knowledge productions. Ubuntuness teaches me that my Indigenous Black ancestors are guiding my way. Working from an African-centred approach ensures that I start from my personal Ubuntu knowledge and work toward our collective Ubuntu knowledges.

I have located my voice as a way of highlighting my responsibility to the people who taught me this contextual knowledge that I share with you. Using Ubuntu epistemology, I have tried to show you how we are a continuation of our ancestors' legacy or, put another way, we are a reflection of their existence. Our well-being is their well-being. We know ourselves because we exist and we exist because they exist. This way of thinking has its roots in the most important guiding philosophical principle of Ubuntu: "Umuntu ungumuntu ngubuntu," which very loosely and very poorly translated means, a person is a person among other persons or an element is an element through its relationship with other elements and there is a sense that humanity is bound up as one. The realm of the spiritual and the realm of the living become one through the teachings of Ubuntu (D.D. Mucina 2013).

Most importantly, I have shared these oratures with you in the hope that they will guide you as well as they have guided me. Oratures are our ways of trying to find common meaning from our unique experiences and this confirms our interrelatedness. There are so many oratures that could be told, but I have chosen to tell you these oratures. I hope the way I have told you these oratures has also exposed my intentions to honour our Ubuntu knowledge production. Yet my oratures (now your oratures) can never be the whole truth because I am giving them to you (King 2003) through my experiences, which are different from those of Baba and Amai. So I wonder if the commonalities of our experiences are enough to give you a whole truth. By telling you this orature, I have given it to you. It was my orature until the telling. What you hold in your memory of this orature is yours. I wonder, from your social location, what have you made different? What have you removed? What have you kept as the constant theme that binds us to each other and to our ancestors?

Time has come and gone. That which I knew is no longer the same. It has changed, but some fragmented influence of that experience is here as memory. This social phenomenon of remembering is important for learning, as it stores all kinds of experiences. Remembering is further enhanced in its effectiveness by the fact that it is a social phenomenon that engages experience, imagination, and motivation. To me, the drum in the right hands is like a logbook of messages that communicates oratures of love, the arrival of a new life, the exit of an old life, union, war, and so many other messages. The caves are our libraries. They are full of pictographs, hieroglyphics, and petroglyphs, which communicate to us about the past, the present, and the future.

These Ubuntu teaching oratures are ours regardless of where you are on the globe; hear them and they will connect you back home to Africa. Yet do not fear to regenerate this knowledge because you are Kwaca (the freedom spirit of dawn, the renewed beginning of the Ubuntu spirit). Respectfully remember that this experience of Ubuntuness does not have precedence over other experiences. In fact, I have tried to express that the experience of Ubuntuness can show the commonalities of beings without undermining the diversity within the world. In the case of our African ancestors, their social communal self-recognition was what they termed Ubuntu, and they identified this knowledge that they acquired and have given to us as Ubuntu epistemology. In the orature, I expressed this by stating that the memory we have of ourselves is what we the descendants of the old Ubuntu ethnic groups call Ubuntu knowledge, which is the expression of our Blackness as experienced by our ancestors and now us. I told you that I write and remember my Ubuntu history as a way of awakening my total self. Yet, I know that our Ubuntu past history resides in all of us and we acquire more of it through sharing reflective oratures of our memories as they connect us to each other and to our ancestral selves. In our honouring ceremonies of our ancestors, we formalize the remembering of our ancestral knowledge as the blueprint for regenerating the present using our past knowledge and experiences.

I have gone through the colonial education system and now, more than ever, I see the value of Ubuntu for the development of a strong, diverse Indigenous

Blackness. This being said, I must also acknowledge that I am not the same as when I went in. I have survived the colonial system, but I have changed too. I question a little more, I speak a little less, I listen a little harder, and I wonder a little more. But the most important thing that I do is that I talk a little more to our ancestors and I thank them a little more for our lives. Malidoma Patrice Somâe (1994), in *Of Water and the Spirit*, reminds us that if some of us had to forget the spiritual past as a way to survive, then some of us will have to remember the spiritual past as a way to survive too. All these oratures and many others are necessary for creating our whole identity as Ubuntu. Our oratures are our healing gifts to one another. We need these oratures as we need medicine. Oratures are the medicines of our spirits and our souls because we are oratures among other oratures.

Relatives from the maternal family, I come in thanks and honour because without you there would be no me. Relatives from the paternal family, I hope you will keep welcoming us all home. I hope our being away has not left a void that we cannot fill with love. May you help us feel whole again. May you help us connect with the old and may you make room for the new family members that we bring to you. Now that we are linked by this orature, where do I end and where do you begin? Could the sacred spiritual cycle of breath connect the past, the present, and the future into one, Ubuntu?

Khumalo and Nandi, I have taught you all the Ubuntu oratures that I know; it is now your turn to add to these oratures, as I am done. The future awaits your oratures.

Respectfully, your Baba,
Dr. Devi Dee Mucina Komba

Notes

Acknowledgements

1   Black personhood (Ubuntu) is shaped by the philosophical realities and spiritualities of being connected to all global relations and energies.

Introduction

1   Please note, where you see individual I mean the social individual because the Ubuntu individual is collectively given meaning.

2   The Yoruba feminist scholar Oyèrónké Oyěwùmí (2001) finds the Eurocentric term of worldview unacceptable when speaking about Indigenous African knowledge production because it privileges only one sense of knowing when Indigenous cultures centre multiple ways of sensing and knowing the world. To address this shortcoming, she has termed the multiple Indigenous ways of knowing the world as worldsense.

3   "Nguni, whose name means 'people who have no land.' The Nguni was formed out of myriads of different tribes, and even today their language contains hundreds of words, which were taken over from these [other Ubuntu] tribes" (Mutwa 1969, 47–8).

4   Instead of chapters I use Millet Granaries that reflect the sustaining nature of these Indigenous knowledges.

Millet Granary 1: Kwakukhona as a Methodology

1   The idea of writing letters as a strategy for engaging the larger communal politics and their political impacts on familial life first came to me through my engagement with Black feminism in Dr. Wane's class. More precisely, African feminism gave me another vantage point for speaking a little more critically about how my African male context shaped how I told Amai's (mother) orature. African feminism helped me hear the oratures of African women in ways that challenged how I projected my oratures as the truth of understanding on the context of my Amai without critiquing my patriarchal position. As I could not speak for my Amai, I felt that the only way I could speak truthfully and hold so many tensions was by personally and directly

speaking to her. This was my first letter in my dissertation and it worked so well that I decided to go back and write letters in each chapter. Being introduced to the work of Shawn Wilson (2008), *Research Is Ceremony: Indigenous Research Methods*, was for me very affirming as this scholarly work confirmed that we could centre our educational oratures in ways that were endemic to our meaning-making structures. And, in case I was challenged, I was ready to say, "Shawn Wilson did it already."

2   Some songs may also require dramatized performance as a way of making a point or entertaining the audience.

3   The concluding structure of this story is informed by the structure used by Timothy Wangusa (1989) in *Upon This Mountain*.

4   McRuer (2006) in *Crip theory: Cultural signs of queerness and disability*, talks about "Compulsory Able-Bodiedness," which made me think of how Blackness is viewed from a "compulsory approximation to Whiteness."

Millet Granary 2: Ubuntu Philosophies Emerge from Relational Living Theories

1   The word "bushmen" is a derogative word that was, once again, invented by the white man. Our brothers and sisters that they call bushmen are known as San (called the BaTwa by Bantu) and Khoi-Khoi, while the BaMbuti and Ik, just to name a few other Indigenous peoples, were reduced to the label of pygmy.

Millet Granary 3: Passing Ubuntu Knowledge to the Future

1   With our many shades of Blackness, we self-define as Blackness to honour the power and challenges of experiencing the world from our Black social location. Blackness to me embodies the diversity of shades that constitute Blackness as a social construction or in other contexts the perceived lack of Blackness.

2   Spirit in the Ubuntu worldview is the energy flux in all things. It is the energy that creates the building blocks of all things and it connects all matter to the living energy source of Unkulunkulu (The Great Deviser or The Great Spirit).

3   Just for ease of communication, from here on I will refer to "white supremacist capitalist patriarchy" just as white supremacy.

Millet Granary 4: Ubuntu Oratures and Relational Accountability

1   In *My People, My Africa*, Mutwa (1969, 47) tells us that Nguni means "people who have no land." He tells us that the Nguni were formed from different tribes, and even today their language contains hundreds of words, which were taken over from those other Ubuntu tribes.

2   I did not know this was my Great Grandmother's name. I only knew that she died before Baba left his family.

3   Komba is a Swahili word for galago, and Isinkwe or Nhlathini Umntwana is the equivalent in Zulu.

4   A Shona and Swahili word meaning disaster, terrible occurrence, great tragedy, or mass killing. The term "Maafa" communicates and reflects the suffering of Africans and African descendent peoples through slavery, imperialism, colonialism, invasion, oppression, dehumanization, and exploitation. For more, see http://en.wikipedia.org/wiki/Maafa.

Millet Granary 5: A Letter Across Many Borders to Amai

1   It was through reading *Stigmata: Escaping Texts* by Hélène Cixous (1998) that I understood the profound connection that existed between my Amai and me.

Millet Granary 6: Finding Baba, Finding Our Fragmented Family

1   When an Ubuntu Baba calls his own son "Baba," he is giving his son the highest form of respect.

2   Worm was a nickname that the man had been given by his employers because they could not pronounce his African name.

3   Referencing the TV miniseries based on Alex Haley's 1976 novel, which portrayed the journey of an Africa Indigenous family's will to survive the commodification of Black bodies through American slavery.

4   I have spoken about Dianne at length in my letter to Amai.

Millet Granary 7: The Journey to You and Our Journey Home

1   Mncina has also been presented as Masina, Macina, and Mucina. The latter is how I depict my name.

2   Matsebula reported that between the Black Mbuluzi and Komati Rivers is where many Mucina lived.

Millet Granary 8: Creating Our Family

1   Mutwa (1964, 383) informs us that this Ubuntu text and pictograph conveys the importance of education to the Ubuntu.

Millet Granary 9: Regenerating Everyday Ubuntu Actions

1   Gukurahundi is a Shona word that conveys the washing away of the chaff by the early rains.

Bibliography

Achebe, C. 1988. *Hopes and Impediments: Selected Essays, 1965–1987*. London: Heinemann Educational.

Adichie, C.N. 2009, July. *TEDGlobal: The Danger of a Single Story*. http://www.ted.com/talks/chimamanda_adichie_the_danger_of_a_single_story.html.

Ahmed, S. 2006. *Queer Phenomenology: Orientations, Objects, Others*. Durham, NC: Duke University Press.

Archibald, J. / Q'um Q'um Xiiem. 2008. *Indigenous Storywork: Educating the Heart, Mind, Body, and Spirit*. Vancouver: UBC Press.

Asante, M.K. 1996. *Afrocentricity: The Theory of Social Change*. Rev. and expanded ed. Chicago: African American Images.

Ashforth, A. 2005. *Witchcraft, Violence, and Democracy in South Africa*. Chicago: University of Chicago Press.

Bâ, M. 2012. *So Long a Letter*. Longville, IL: Waveland Press.

Baldwin, S.S. 2000. *What the Body Remembers*. Toronto: Vintage Canada.

Basso, K.H. 1996. *Wisdom Sits in Places: Landscape and Language Among the Western Apache*. 1st ed. Albuquerque: University of New Mexico Press.

Biko, S. 1996. *I Write What I Like: A Selection of His Writings*. Edited by A. Stubbs. London: Bowerdean Publishing.

Boaduo, A.N., and D. Gumbi. 2010. "Classification: Colonial Attempts to Fracture Africa's Identity and Contribution to Humanity." *The Journal of Pan African Studies* 3, no. 9 (June–July): 43–9.

Boucher (Chisale), C. 2012. *When Animals Sing and Spirits Dance: Gule Wamkulu: The Great Dance of the Chewa People of Malawi*. Mtakataka: Kungoni Centre of Culture and Art.

Brown, L. 2008. "Cut Black Dropout Rate to 15%, Schools Told." *The Star, Digital Access*, 18 June. https://www.thestar.com/life/parent/2008/06/18/cut_black_dropout_rate_to_15_schools_told.html.

Burnham, O. 2000. *African Wisdom.* London: Piatkus.

Canonici, N.N. 1996. *Zulu Oral Traditions.* Durban: University of Natal.

Cartwright, S.A. 1851. "Diseases and Peculiarities of the Negro Race." *De Bow's Review of Southern and Western States: A Monthly Industrial Literary Journal.* http://www.pbs.org/wgbh/aia/part4/4h3106t.html.

Césaire, A. 1972. *Discourse on Colonialism.* New York: Monthly Review Press.

Cixous, H. 1998. *Stigmata: Escaping Texts.* London: Routledge.

Coates, T-N. 2015. *Between the World and Me.* New York: Spiegel and Grau.

Collins, R.O. 1968. *Problems in African History.* Englewood Cliffs, NJ: Prentice-Hall.

Cook, C., and J.D. Lindau. 2000. *Aboriginal Rights and Self-Government: The Canadian and Mexican Experience in North American Perspective.* Montreal: McGill-Queen's University Press.

Corntassel, J., T. Alfred, N. Goodyear–Ka'ōpua, N.K. Silva, H. Aikau, and D. Mucina, eds. 2018. *Everyday Acts of Resurgence: People, Places, Practices.* Olympia, WA: Daykeeper Press.

Coughlan, S. 2006. "All You Need is Ubuntu." *BBC News Magazine,* 28 September. http://news.bbc.co.uk/2/hi/uk_news/magazine/5388182.stm.

Crenshaw, K. 1991. "Mapping the Margins: Intersectionality, Identity, and Violence Against Women of Color." *Stanford Law Review* 43, no. 6 (July): 1241–1300.

Crowe, R. 2004. "Crafting Tales of Trauma: Will This Winged Monster Fly?" In *Provoked by Art: Theorizing Arts-Informed Research,* Volume 2 of Arts-Informed Inquiry Series, edited by A.L. Cole, L. Neilsen, J.G. Knowles, C. Luciani, and the Centre for Arts-informed Research, 123–33. Halifax, NS: Backalong Books.

Crush, J., B. Williams, E. Gouws, and M. Lurie. 2005. "Spaces of Vulnerability: Migration and HIV/AIDS in South Africa." *Development Southern Africa* 22, no. 3 (June): 293–318.

D'Aguiar, F. 1994. *The Longest Memory: A Novel.* London: Chatto and Windus.

Dangarembga, T. 1988. *Nervous Conditions.* Harare: Zimbabwe Publishing House.

Deutsch, K.W. 1969. *Nationalism and Its Alternatives.* New York: Knopf.

Diamond, J. M. 1997. *Guns, Germs, and Steel: The Fates of Human Societies.* 1st ed. New York: W.W. Norton.

Dimitrow, R. 2010. *Strategic Silence: Public Relations and Indirect Communication.* New York: Routledge.

Diop, C.A. 1974. *The African Origin of Civilization: Myth or Reality.* 1st ed. New York: L. Hill.

Douglass, F. 1989. *Narrative of the Life of Frederick Douglass, an American Slave.* New York: Anchor Books.

Emecheta, B. 1979. *The Joys of Motherhood: A Novel.* 1st ed. New York: G. Braziller.

Eze, E.C., ed. 1997. *Race and the Enlightenment: A Reader.* Boston, MA: Blackwell Publishers.

Fanon, F. (1952) 1967. *Black Skin, White Mask.* Translated by Charles Lam Markmann. New York: Grove Press.

——. 1963. *The Wretched of the Earth.* New York: Grove Press.

Farrington, B. 1966. *The Philosophy of Francis Bacon: An Essay on Its Development from 1603 to 1609 with New Translations of Fundamental Texts.* Chicago: University of Chicago Press.

Franklin, J.H., and A.A. Moss Jr. 2000. *From Slavery to Freedom: A History of African Americans.* 8th ed. New York: McGraw-Hill.

Goss, L., and C. Goss. 1995. *Jump Up and Say! A Collection of Black Storytelling.* New York: Simon and Schuster.

Green, J. 2017. *Making Space for Indigenous Feminism.* 2nd ed. Halifax, NS: Fernwood Publishing.

Guinness Publishing. 2017. *Guinness World Records 2018.* Stamford, CT: Guinness Media.

Hall, S. 1997. *Representation: Cultural Representations and Signifying Practices.* Thousand Oaks, CA: Sage Publications.

Harvey, D. 2005. *The New Imperialism.* New York: Oxford University Press.

Henry, P. 2006. "Africana Phenomenology: Its Philosophical Implications." *Worlds and Knowledges Otherwise* (Fall): 1–22. https://globalstudies.trinity.duke.edu/sites/ globalstudies.trinity.duke.edu/files/file-attachments/v1d3_PHenry.pdf.

Hill Collins, P. 2002. *Black Feminist Thought: Knowledge, Consciousness, and the Politics of Empowerment.* New York: Routledge.

Hill Collins, P., and S. Bilge. 2016. *Intersectionality.* Cambridge: Polity Press.

hooks, b. 2000. *Feminist Theory: From Margin to Center.* Cambridge, MA: South End Press.

———. 2004. *We Real Cool: Black Men and Masculinity.* New York: Routledge.

Imbo, S.O. 2002. *Oral Traditions as Philosophy: Okot p'Bitek's Legacy for African Philosophy.* Lanham, MD: Rowman and Littlefield.

Irin News. 2007. "Calls for Justice 20 Years after Massacre." 16 January. http://www. irinnews.org/news/2007/01/16/calls-justice-20-years-after-massacre.

Kenyatta, J. 1962. *Facing Mount Kenya: The Tribal Life of Gikuyu.* New York: Penguin Books.

King, T. 2003. *The Truth About Stories: A Native Narrative.* Toronto: House of Anansi Press.

Kishindo, P.J. 2002. "Flogging a Dead Cow: The Revival of Malawian Chingoni." *Nordic Journal of African Studies* 11, no. 2: 206–23.

Kuokkanen, R. 2015. "Gendered Violence and Politics in Indigenous Communities: The Cases of Aboriginal People in Canada and the Sámi in Scandinavia." *International Feminist Journal of Politics* 17, no. 2: 271–88.

Locke, J., R.H. Horwitz, D. Clay, and J.S. Clay. 1990. *Questions Concerning the Law of Nature.* Ithaca, NY: Cornell University Press.

Mail and Guardian. 1997. "The Parable of the Bicycle." 7 February. https://mg.co.za/ article/1997-02-07-the-parable-of-the-bicycle.

Malcolm X. 1967. *Malcolm X on Afro-American History.* 1st ed. New York: Merit Publishers.

Mandela, N. 1995. *Long Walk to Freedom: The Autobiography of Nelson Mandela.* Boston: Little, Brown.

Massey, D. 1978. "A Case of Colonial Collaboration: The Hut Tax and Migrant Labour." *Botswana Notes and Records* 10, 95–8. http://www.jstor.org/stable/40979541.

Masubelele, M.R. 2008. "The Role of Bible Translation in the Development of Written Zulu: A Corpus-Based Study." PhD diss., University of South Africa, Pretoria.

Mathabane, M. 1986. *Kaffir Boy: The True Story of a Black Youth's Coming of Age in Apartheid South Africa*. New York: Macmillan.

McRuer, R. 2006. *Crip Theory: Cultural Signs of Queerness and Disability*. New York: New York University Press.

Memmi, A. 1965. *The Colonizer and the Colonized*. New York: Orion Press.

Meredith, M. 1979. *The Past Is another Country: Rhodesia 1890–1979*. London: A. Deutsch.

Michalko, R. 2002. *The Difference that Disability Makes*. Philadelphia: Temple University Press.

Michalko, R., and T. Titchkosky. 2001. "Putting Disability in Its Place: It's Not a Joking Matter." In *Embodied Rhetorics: Disability in Language and Culture*, edited by J.C. Wilson and C. Lewiecki-Wilson, 200–28. Carbondale: Southern Illinois University Press.

Morris, D.R. 1965. *The Washing of the Spears: A History of the Rise of the Zulu Nation under Shaka and Its Fall in the Zulu War of 1879*. New York: Simon and Schuster.

Mucina, D.D. 2006. "Revitalizing Memory in Honour of Maseko Ngoni's Indigenous Bantu Governance." MA thesis, University of Victoria, Canada.

———. 2007. "Emergence from Colonialism: Memories and Stories of Bantu Life." In *Notes from Canada's Young Activists: A Generation Stands Up for Change*, edited by S. Cullis-Suzuki, 171–181. Vancouver: Greystone Books.

———. 2011. "Story as Research Methodology." *AlterNative: An International Journal of Indigenous Peoples* 7, no. 1 (May): 1–14.

———. 2013. "Ubuntu Orality as a Living Philosophy." *The Journal of Pan African Studies* 6, no. 4 (September): 18–35.

———. 2015. "How to Respond When Disability is the Problem." *Relational Child and Youth Care Practice*, Volume 28, Issue 4, 91–99.

Mucina, M.K. 2015. "Transgressing Boundaries of Izzat: Voices of Second Generation Punjabi Women Surviving and Transgressing Boundaries of 'Honour' Related Violence in Canada." PhD diss., University of Toronto.

Mugabe, R. 1983. *Our War of Liberation: Speeches, Articles, Interviews, 1976–1979*. Gweru, Zimbabwe: Mambo Press.

Murdock, G.P. 1959. *Africa: Its Peoples and Their Culture History*. New York: McGraw-Hill.

Mutwa, C.V. 1964. *Indaba, My Children*. Johannesburg: Blue Crane Books.

———. 1969. *My People, My Africa*. 1st American ed. New York: John Day Co.

———. 1986. *Let Not My Country Die*. South Africa, Pretoria: United Publishers International.

Mvula, E.T., and M.N. Chikumbutso. 2008. "Izibongo." *New Dynasty, Special Coronation Edition*, 9–10. Blantyre: Dzuka Publishing Company Limited.

Okihiro, G.Y. 1996. "Oral History and the Writing of Ethnic History." In *Oral History: An Interdisciplinary Anthology*, edited by D. Dunaway, D. King, K. Willa, American Association for State and Local History, and Oral History Association, 199–214. Walnut Creek, CA: AltaMira Press.

Okri, B. 1997. *A Way of Being Free*. London: Phoenix House.

Ong, W.J. 2002. *Orality and Literacy: The Technologizing of the Word*. New York: Routledge.

Oyěwùmí, O. 2001. "The Translation of Cultures: Engendering Yorùbá Language, Orature, and World-Sense." In *Women, Gender, Religion: A Reader*, edited by E.A. Castelli with the assistance of R.C. Rodman, 76–97. New York: Palgrave Macmillan.

p'Bitek, O. 1984. *Song of Lawino and Song of Ocol*. London: Heinemann.

Reagan, C.E., and D. Stewart. 1978. *The Philosophy of Paul Ricoeur: An Anthology of His Work*. New York: Beacon Press.

Ricard, A. 2007. "Africa and Writing." In *African Literature: An Anthology of Criticism and Theory*, edited by T. Olaniyan and A. Quayson, 7–15. Malden, MA: Blackwell.

Richter, L., and R. Morrell. 2006. *BABA: Men and Fatherhood in South Africa*. Cape Town: HSRC Press.

Salmón, E. 2012. *Eating the Landscape: American Indian Stories of Food, Identity, and Resilience*. Tucson: University of Arizona Press.

Sandoval, C. 2000. *Methodology of the Oppressed*. Volume 18 of The Theory out of Bounds. Minneapolis: University of Minnesota Press.

Shakespeare, W., W.J. Craig, and E. Dowden. 1912. *The Tragedies of Shakespeare* (The Text of the Oxford Ed. Prepared by W.J. Craig; with introductory studies of the several plays by Edward Dowden, and a full glossary). London: Oxford University Press.

Somâe, M.P. 1994. *Of Water and the Spirit: Ritual, Magic, and Initiation in the Life of an African Shaman*. New York: Putnam.

Tengan, T.P.K. 2008. *Native Men Remade: Gender and Nation in Contemporary Hawai'i*. Durham, NC: Duke University Press.

Titchkosky, T. 2007. *Reading and Writing Disability Differently: The Textured Life of Embodiment*. Toronto: University of Toronto Press.

Truth and Reconciliation Commission of Canada. 2015. *Honouring the Truth, Reconciling for the Future: Summary of the Final Report of the Truth and Reconciliation Commission of Canada*. Winnipeg, MB: Truth and Reconciliation Commission of Canada.

Tutu, D. 1994. *The Rainbow People of God: The Making of a Peaceful Revolution*. New York: Doubleday.

Vassanji, M.G. 2003. *The In-Between World of Vikram Lall*. Toronto: Doubleday Canada.

Vera, Y. 1992. *Why Don't You Carve Other Animals*. Toronto: TSAR.

Walcott, R. 1997. *Black Like Who? Writing Black Canada*. Toronto: Insomniac Press.

Wane, N.N. 2000. "Reflections on the Mutuality of Mothering: Women, Children, and Other-mothering." *Journal of the Association for Research on Mothering* 2, no. 2: 105–116.

———. 2009. "Indigenous Education and Cultural Resistance: A Decolonizing Project." *Curriculum Inquiry* 39, no. 1: 159–78.

Wangusa, T. 1989. *Upon This Mountain: African Writers Series.* Oxford: Heinemann International.

White, M. 2007. *Maps of Narrative Practice.* 1st ed. New York: W.W. Norton.

Wilson, S. 2008. *Research Is Ceremony: Indigenous Research Methods.* Halifax, NS: Fernwood Publishing.

World Health Organization (WHO). 2014. "The Men's Health Gap: Men Must Be Included in the Global Health Equity Agenda." *Bulletin of the World Health Organization* 92, no. 8 (March): 545–620. http://www.who.int/bulletin/volumes/92/8/13-132795/en/.

Index